Early Childhood Research and Ed
An Inter-theoretical Fo

Volume 4

Series Editors

Joseph Agbenyega, Peninsula Campus, Monash University Peninsula Campus, Frankston, Australia

Marie Hammer, Faculty of Education, Peninsula Campus, Monash University, Frankston, VIC, Australia

Nikolai Veresov, Faculty of Education, Monash University, Frankston, Australia

This series addresses inter-disciplinary critical components in early childhood education such as: Relationships: Movements/Transitions; Community and contexts; Leadership; Ethics are driven by a range of theories.

It brings depth and breadth to the application of different theories to these components both in the research and its practical applications in early childhood education. In-depth discussion of theoretical lenses and their application to research and practice provides insights into the complexities and dynamics of Early Childhood education and practice.

This series is designed to explore the application of a range of theories to open up and analyse sets of data. Each volume will explore multiple age periods of early childhood and will interrogate common data sets. The notion of theoretical coherence as a methodological principle will underpin the approach across each of the volumes.

Nikolay Veraksa · Ingrid Pramling Samuelsson
Editors

Piaget and Vygotsky in XXI century

Discourse in early childhood education

 Springer

Editors
Nikolay Veraksa
Lomonosov Moscow State University
Moscow, Russia

Psychological Institute, Russian Academy
of Education
Moscow, Russia

Ingrid Pramling Samuelsson
Department of Education, Communication
and Learning
University of Gothenburg
Göteborg, Sweden

ISSN 2946-6091   ISSN 2946-6105 (electronic)
Early Childhood Research and Education: An Inter-theoretical Focus
ISBN 978-3-031-05749-6   ISBN 978-3-031-05747-2 (eBook)
https://doi.org/10.1007/978-3-031-05747-2

This Springer imprint is published by the registered company Springer Nature Switzerland AG
The registered company address is: Gewerbestrasse 11, 6330 Cham, Switzerland

Contents

1   **Introduction** 1
Nikolay Veraksa and Ingrid Pramling Samuelsson

2   **Vygotsky's Theory: Culture as a Prerequisite for Education** 7
Nikolay Veraksa

3   **Learning and Development in a Designed World** 27
Roger Säljö and Åsa Mäkitalo

4   **Dialectical Thinking** 41
Nikolay Veraksa and Michael Basseches

5   **Social Representations of Play: Piaget, Vygotskij and Beyond** 65
Bert van Oers

6   **Children's Perspectives Informing Theories and Nordic
Preschool Practice** 87
Camilla Björklund and Ingrid Pramling Samuelsson

7   **Preschool Children's Pretend Play Viewed from a Vygotskyan
and a Piagetian Perspective** 109
Polly Björk-Willén

8   **Piaget and Vygotsky: Powerful Inspirators for Today's
Students in Early Education and Developmental Psychology** 129
Elly Singer

9   **Constructivism and Social Constructivism in the Study
of Relationship Between Early Childhood Education Quality
and Executive Function at 5–6 years Old** 145
Anastasia Belolutskaya, Darya Bukhalenkova,
Evgeniy Krasheninnikov-Khait, Igor Shiyan, Olga Shiyan,
and Aleksander Veraksa

**10 Piaget and Vygotsky's Play Theories: The Profile
     of Twenty-First-Century Evidence** 165
     Nikolay Veraksa, Yeshe Colliver, and Vera Sukhikh

**11 Vygotsky and Piaget as Twenty-First-Century Critics of Early
     Childhood Education Philosophizing** 191
     Niklas Pramling

Editors and Contributors

About the Editors

Prof. Nikolay Veraksa is a specialist in preschool education, works at Faculty of Psychology, Lomonosov Moscow State University, Moscow City University and Psychological Institute of the Russian Academy of Education, Head of UNESCO Chair in Early Childhood Care and Development, Honorary Doctor of the University of Gothenburg. He is a co-author of the most popular educational program in Russia for children in preschool "From Birth to School" as well as a program in English "Key to Learning." His main interests are development of child thinking and personality.

Ingrid Pramling Samuelsson is Professor in Early Childhood Education at Gothenburg She also holds an UNESCO Chair, since 2008 in ECE and Sustainable Development. She has been World President for World Organization for Early Childhood Education (OMEP) between 2008 and 2014. Her main research area is young children's learning and how teachers can provide the best opportunities for this in communication and interaction, in play as well as other activities in preschool. She has numerous publications and developed a preschool pedagogy labeled Development Pedagogy, based on many empirical studies. She is Honorary Doctor at Abo University in Finland. She has also been a board member in Swedish UNICEF, and during later years engaged in research, development, and publications about ECE and ESD, and started an Network in Sweden for developing practice based in research.

Contributors

Michael Basseches Suffolk University, Boston, MA, USA

Anastasia Belolutskaya Moscow City University, Moscow, Russia

Polly Björk-Willén Linköping University, Linköping, Sweden

Camilla Björklund University of Gothenburg, Gothenburg, Sweden

Darya Bukhalenkova Lomonosov Moscow State University, Moscow, Russia

Yeshe Colliver School of Education, Macquarie University, Sydney, Australia

Evgeniy Krasheninnikov-Khait Moscow City University, Moscow, Russia

Åsa Mäkitalo Department of Education, Communication and Learning, University of Gothenburg, Gothenburg, Sweden

Niklas Pramling University of Gothenburg, Gothenburg, Sweden

Ingrid Pramling Samuelsson University of Gothenburg, Gothenburg, Sweden

Igor Shiyan Moscow City University, Moscow, Russia

Olga Shiyan Moscow City University, Moscow, Russia

Elly Singer Utrecht University (retired), Utrecht, The Netherlands

Vera Sukhikh Faculty of Psychology, Lomonosov Moscow State University, Moscow, Russia

Roger Säljö Department of Education, Communication and Learning, University of Gothenburg, Gothenburg, Sweden

Bert van Oers Section of Educational Sciences, and LEARN! Research Institute, Vrije Universiteit Amsterdam, Amsterdam, The Netherlands

Aleksander Veraksa Lomonosov Moscow State University, Moscow, Russia

Nikolay Veraksa Faculty of Psychology, Lomonosov Moscow State University, Moscow, Russian Federation;
Psychological Institute, Russian Academy of Education, Moscow, Russia

Chapter 1
Introduction

Nikolay Veraksa⬤ and Ingrid Pramling Samuelsson

Abstract The book is devoted to modern interpretations of the ideas of Lev Vygotsky (Vygotsky, L. S. [1981]. The instrumental method in psychology. In J. V. Wertsch (Ed.), The concept of activity in Soviet psychology [pp. 134–143]. Armonk, NY: M. E. Sharpe.;) and Jean Piaget (1968). These authors had a powerful influence on education. Their discourses complemented each other: whereas Vygotsky developed his theory in the direction from society (culture) to the individual child, Piaget's movement was the opposite: from individual child to society. This resulted in two important results of the application of theories: the development of children's consciousness in Vygotsky and the egocentrism of culture as a form of cognition of reality in Piaget. As more than 120 years from birth of Vygotsky and Piaget passed, their theories, which represented Eastern and Western views, were implemented in different cultural and educational settings. The book will give comprehensive analyses of Vygotsky's and Piaget's theories implementation in modern early childhood education.

The book is devoted to modern interpretations of the ideas of Lev Vygotsky (1981) and Jean Piaget (1968). These authors had a powerful influence on education. Their discourses complemented each other: whereas Vygotsky developed his theory in the direction from society (culture) to the individual child, Piaget's movement was the opposite: from individual child to society. This resulted in two important results of the application of theories: the development of children's consciousness in Vygotsky and the egocentrism of culture as a form of cognition of reality in Piaget. As more

---

N. Veraksa (✉)
Faculty of Psychology, Lomonosov Moscow State University, Moscow, Russia
e-mail: neveraksa@gmail.com

I. Pramling Samuelsson
University of Gothenburg, Gothenburg, Sweden
e-mail: Ingrid.Pramling@ped.gu.se

N. Veraksa
Psychological Institute, Russian Academy of Education, Moscow, Russia

than 120 years from birth of Vygotsky and Piaget passed, their theories, which represented Eastern and Western views, were implemented in different cultural and educational settings. The book will give comprehensive analyses of Vygotsky's and Piaget's theories implementation in modern early childhood education.

These two approaches confront modern world with the need to analyze the problem of childhood: Is childhood a period of cultural exploration or is it a special form of relationship in which both the egocentrism and consciousness of the child, and the egocentrism and consciousness of culture are represented?

The book will address Piaget and Vygotsky as founders of modern issues in education. The book will analyze the problem of the relationship between the natural and the cultural in the context of Vygotsky and Jean Piaget theories. It should be noted that in parallel with the discussion of natural and cultural issues in children's development and education, which are asked by interpreters of cultural-historical theory, it is equally important to consider the problem of egocentric and objective. The cultural belongs to the characteristic of education organized by adults, and the natural comes from the child. Current trends show that there is a definite attempt and even the task of working with the natural in child development. But maybe it is time to take the slogan "Learning begins at birth", that was formulated at the Jomtien (Thailand) World Conference on Education for All in 1990 by Robert Mayer seriously, and by that realize that development and learning are not two separate processes, but two sides of the same process. It is no coincidence that V.V. Davydov said that education is a form of development. This point of view logically follows from the idea of developmental education and Vygotsky's elaboration of such a strategy for building education that would not follow development, but would lead it.

In culture, there is a tendency to develop children's creativity, which, according to Vygotsky, is based entirely on the natural and suggests going beyond culture, in other words, going into the natural. With regard to preschool education, this desire translates into a desire to use the children's play activities for educational purposes. Thus, the problem of the natural and cultural in Vygotsky arises as the problem of his centrism and the objective in Jean Piaget, and this applies to both the child and the adult, both child behavior and the culture of the kindergarten. It is important to take these trends into account when building modern education.

In relation to the child, the egocentrism and naturalness of the culture are manifested in the initial assumption that the child is less educated and more limited in his/her abilities than an adult. Although there are current trends to equalize the rights of an adult and a child, there is an educational task to reveal properties of a child that show his/her ability to learn and create new things. In other words, the child acts as the bearer of the future, and in this sense, the adult, as a representative of culture, should provide the child with the opportunity to represent him/herself.

If we consider the problem of the play in the contexts of Piaget and Vygotsky, then it is given the status of the leading activity and the form in which the zone of the proximal development of the child is represented. In this case, the play performs an assimilative function. However, there is a tendency to turn the play into a form of learning (Singer, 2007; Van Oers et al., 2008). A new problem of the possibilities for the development of the child and the possibilities that the culture has for this arises.

In this regard, the problem of means and, in particular, the role of digital space in the lives of children and society acquire a special meaning (Säljo, 2016). It may also be time to consider play and learning not as two separate entities, but as a united process of great importance for young children's education.

The reader of the book will get a view of methodology that makes possible to unite up-to-date views based on Vygotsky and Piaget theories on child development and education.

Jean Piaget and Lev Vygotsky, two prominent childhood researchers, have had a significant impact on the understanding of child development. Jean Piaget viewed child development in the context of the conditions in which the child had to act. The child's behavior was understood as an adaptation to the current situation.

It should be noted that Piaget showed that seemingly such fundamental categories that Kant spoke about: space, time, speed, object constancy, and other concepts that are not innate, but are acquired by the child as he/she interacts with the situation. Of particular note is the clear demonstration that the development of the child is fundamentally different from its interpretation within the framework of associative psychology. New systems of tasks that have been developed showed the originality of children's thought. In fact, Piaget was one of the authors of modern cognitive psychology. A feature of Jean Piaget's approach to understanding development is associated with an analysis of the mechanisms of children's activity, which are of a dual nature: According to Piaget, balance is achieved through processes such as assimilation and accommodation. It is these mechanisms that began to be considered by a number of authors as tools for thinking. Of interest is the fact that the child is viewed as an active agent performing a system of actions. In this case, the very forms of activity of the child develop into a mathematical structure that describes the ability of children to achieve balance at the level of specific operations. In fact, Piaget describes how the intellect of a child is gradually transformed into an instrument of thinking activity subordinate to logic.

While Piaget considered the influence of the natural environment on child development, or the natural factor, Vygotsky—the influence of the social or cultural factor. According to Vygotsky, child development is due to the fact that he/she masters the ideal forms or samples of culture, which are offered by adults. The mechanism—that was proposed for child development—is imitation of the cultural forms. The cultural form itself is chosen in such a way that it is in the zone of proximal development of the child. This means that the educational process has to be built in such a way as to influence children's development, that is, to lead it. Thus, it was emphasized that without an adult, the development of a child cannot be effective. If we compare the points of view of Piaget and Vygotsky, it might seem that their approaches are fundamentally different. However, the objectives of our discussion of the two perspectives presented are not related to the search for differences, but rather to the desire to show their complementarity. For example, if we talk about the role of the environment in the studies of Piaget and Vygotsky, then we can say that Vygotsky took the cultural context of the child and the environment, and Piaget took the objective, physical context. If Vygotsky's child followed an adult in his development, then Piaget's child was an active researcher of the environment. Obviously, both Lev Vygotsky and Jean Piaget were constructivists, which only indicates another basis, which can be considered as a principle of the congruence of the two approaches. It should be noted that Piaget tried to reveal the child's capabilities as much as possible and limited the possible influence of an adult. Nevertheless, he convincingly showed that the child masters complex laws of logic. Unlike Piaget, Vygotsky tried to show the importance of an adult in child development.

Nevertheless, both Vygotsky and Piaget made transformations, according to which the child became not only a representative of a past, already established culture, but also a bearer of a future culture that was still emerging. The child's voice obtains shape in specific products that are important for peers and adults. The basis for this is the individualization of development due to the uniqueness of the social situation of development as a relationship between the child and his/her environment.

References

Kilhamn, C. & Säljö, R. (2019). *Encountering algebra: A comparative study of classrooms in Finland, Norway, Sweden, and the USA* (1st ed.). Springer.

Piaget, J. (1968). Piaget's point of view. *International Journal of Psychology, 3*(4), 281–299.

Samuelsson, I. P., & Fleer, M. (2008). *Play and learning in early childhood settings: International perspectives* (International Perspectives on Early Childhood Education and Development Book 1). Springer.

Säljö, R. (2016). Apps and learning: A sociocultural perspective. In N. Kucirkova & G. Falloon (Eds.), *Apps, technology and younger learners* (pp. 00–00). Routledge.

Singer, E., & de Haan, D. (2007) *The social lives of young children*. SWP Publishing.

Van Oers, B., Wardekker, W., Elbers, E., & Van der Veer, R. (2008). *The transformation of learning: Advances in cultural-historical activity theory*. Cambridge University Press.

Vygotsky, L. S. (1978). *Mind in society: The development of higher psychological processes*. Harvard University Press.

Vygotsky, L. S. (1981). The instrumental method in psychology. In J. V. Wertsch (Ed.), *The concept of activity in Soviet psychology* (pp. 134–143). M. E. Sharpe.

Prof. Nikolay Veraksa is a specialist in preschool education, works at Faculty of Psychology, Lomonosov Moscow State University, Moscow City University and Psychological Institute of the Russian Academy of Education, Head of UNESCO Chair in Early Childhood Care and Development, Honorary Doctor of the University of Gothenburg. He is a co-author of the most popular educational program in Russia for children in preschool "From Birth to School" as well as a program in English "Key to Learning." His main interests are development of child thinking and personality.

Ingrid Pramling Samuelsson is Professor in Early Childhood Education at Gothenburg She also holds an UNESCO Chair, since 2008 in ECE and Sustainable Development. She has been World President for World Organization for Early Childhood Education (OMEP) between 2008 and 2014. Her main research area is young children's learning and how teachers can provide the best opportunities for this in communication and interaction, in play as well as other activities in preschool. She has numerous publications and developed a preschool pedagogy labeled Development Pedagogy, based on many empirical studies. She is Honorary Doctor at Abo University in

Finland. She has also been a board member in Swedish UNICEF, and during later years engaged in research, development, and publications about ECE and ESD, and started an Network in Sweden for developing practice based in research.

Chapter 2
Vygotsky's Theory: Culture as a Prerequisite for Education

Nikolay Veraksa◉

Abstract In the twenty-first century, works of Lev Vygotsky continue to arouse steady interest among specialists. Understanding the theories of two famous thinkers in the field of child development, Piaget and Vygotsky, began with studying the differences between them (Lourenço, O. (2012). Piaget and Vygotsky: Many resemblances, and a crucial differenceɪo New Ideas in Psychology, 30, 281–295.). The differences were assessed as fundamental, since, according to Piaget, the child independently, individually, like Robinson on a desert island, creates his own knowledge. Vygotsky described the development process in a fundamentally different way, which directly follows from the general genetic law of cultural development, according to which every function in the cultural development of a child appears on the stage twice, in two planes, first socially, between people and then inside the child (Vygotsky, L. S. (1983). Problems of the development of the psyche (A. M. Matyushkin, Ed.). Pedagogika.). However, as noted by Orlando Lourenço, then a second period followed—a period of searching for lines of similarity between these points of view, including the development of the child, the role of action, the dialectic nature of the method of analysis, etc. It was prompted by the realization that Piaget's theory does not ignore social relations. The converse statements were viewed as a consequence of a misinterpretation of Piaget's approach. The third stage is again characterized by a search for differences. Speaking about the differences in theoretical constructions, Lourenço highlighted the fundamental non-obvious differences. He offered the following interpretation: "In short, whereas Piaget's theory continuously revolves around the subject's autonomy when she confronts her physical and social environment, Vygotsky's thinking turns around the subject's heteronomy as she is confronted with the existing diverse social structures" (Lourenço, O. (2012). Piaget and Vygotsky: Many resemblances, and a crucial differenceɪo New Ideas in Psychology, 30, 281–295., p. 292). At the same time, he emphasized that for both Vygotsky and Piaget, social contacts in child development play an important role.

N. Veraksa (✉)
Faculty of Psychology, Lomonosov Moscow State University, Moscow, Russia
e-mail: neveraksa@gmail.com

Psychological Institute, Russian Academy of Education, Moscow, Russia

© The Author(s), under exclusive license to Springer Nature Switzerland AG 2022
N. Veraksa and I. Pramling Samuelsson (eds.), *Piaget and Vygotsky in XXI century*,
Early Childhood Research and Education: An Inter-theoretical Focus 4,
https://doi.org/10.1007/978-3-031-05747-2_2

In the twenty-first century, works of Lev Vygotsky continue to arouse steady interest among specialists. Understanding the theories of two famous thinkers in the field of child development, Piaget and Vygotsky, began with studying the differences between them (Lourenço, 2012). The differences were assessed as fundamental, since, according to Piaget, the child independently, individually, like Robinson on a desert island, creates his own knowledge. Vygotsky described the development process in a fundamentally different way, which directly follows from the general genetic law of cultural development, according to which every function in the cultural development of a child appears on the stage twice, in two planes, first socially, between people and then inside the child (Vygotsky, 1983). However, as noted by Orlando Lourenço, then a second period followed—a period of searching for lines of similarity between these points of view, including the development of the child, the role of action, the dialectic nature of the method of analysis, etc. It was prompted by the realization that Piaget's theory does not ignore social relations. The converse statements were viewed as a consequence of a misinterpretation of Piaget's approach. The third stage is again characterized by a search for differences. Speaking about the differences in theoretical constructions, Lourenço highlighted the fundamental non-obvious differences. He offered the following interpretation: "In short, whereas Piaget's theory continuously revolves around the subject's autonomy when she confronts her physical and social environment, Vygotsky's thinking turns around the subject's heteronomy as she is confronted with the existing diverse social structures" (Lourenço, 2012, p. 292). At the same time, he emphasized that for both Vygotsky and Piaget, social contacts in child development play an important role.

In the course of a new stage, which began with an analysis of the works of Piaget and Vygotsky, Valsiner formulated the task of identifying the most promising ideas of Vygotsky in the contexts of the twenty-first century (Valsiner, 2021). Van der Veer proposed to consider Vygotsky's works in order to determine which of the ideas presented in them can have a positive impact on the development of scientific approaches that are adequate to modern problems. He emphasized, "The idea of understanding Vygotsky never was to glorify his work, which is necessarily constrained by the social and scientific context of his time, but to allow us to understand and extend his ideas and to see whether some variant of them can help us to develop our science further" (van der Veer, 2021, p. 795).

Vygotsky's views are usually considered in the context of the connection of his research with the study of the role of culture in the formation of the human psyche. It is important not to oppose the approach of Vygotsky and Piaget as two different views on the understanding of child development, but to show their commonality and even complementarity. Vygotsky analyzed culture as a system of ideal forms, the development of which leads to the formation of higher mental functions in a child (Vygotsky, 1996). A significant role in this process is assigned to the means developed in culture, aimed at controlling human behavior. Due to the development and usage of cultural means, natural mental functions (like natural perception that does not possess knowledge of form, size, and color) turn into higher ones (Vygotsky, 1983). However, in order to understand the issues that Vygotsky and Piaget studied in their research, it is necessary to understand the situation in psychology in which these outstanding authors acted. The chapter briefly examines the structure of the space of psychological knowledge and the features of actions in it by Piaget and Vygotsky and discusses the dialogue of their positions.

In this way, culture limits the nature of a person, assuming following social norms that apply to a person's behavior, his/her form of mental activity, including speech and thinking, interaction with other people and appearance. Education acts as a process of transferring cultural norms to the younger generation. In this sense, new members of society, sacrificing their individuality, obeying the established rules, ensure the stable functioning of social systems. According to Vygotsky, in order to develop and interact with other people, a person needs to master the culture (Vygotsky, 1996). Education in this case appears as an essential aspect of culture and, fulfilling the function of transferring knowledge, creates opportunities for the development of not only the individual, but also the culture itself.

However, there is a problem associated with the answer to the question: "How can a person carry out the process of cultural development?" One of the fundamental functions of culture is to ensure the process of broadcasting adequate forms of behavior. In this respect, adequate behavior characterizes the state of balance between the subject and the situation, which was paid special attention to in works of Piaget.

Each individuality requires a special relationship to itself that is different from that of others. In other words, individuality is self-centered in its essence. Society, however, prefers individuality that expresses the individualities of others. This implies the need to give individuals the cultural means to express themselves through forms that are accessible to other people. As such a tool Piaget named intellect, or rather the logic behind it as the basis on which logically adequate, non-egocentric reasoning is built. For Vygotsky, the entire system of higher mental functions or consciousness, as a derivative of culture, acted as such an instrument responsible for adequate free actions. In this situation, it became natural that logic, as a system that ensures the adequacy of judgments and culture in the form of social situations aimed at the development of arbitrariness and adequacy of social interaction, act as a prerequisite for education.

Thus, Vygotsky actually considered the transformation of the individual in the process of interaction with the universal, that is, with culture (Vygotsky, 1982a). In this sense, his approach can be considered similar to the approach of J. Piaget, who described the development of individuality also in the context of interaction with the universal, but with the only difference being that logical structures acted as universal in his research (Piaget, 1969). The dialogue between Vygotsky and Piaget was possible due to the fact that they solved similar problems, which consisted in explaining the transformation of the egocentric aspects of the personality into adequate forms of social behavior.

2.1 Introduction: L. S. Vygotsky's Cultural-Historical Approach

The purpose of this chapter, as seen by its author, is not to contrast L. S. Vygotsky's approach to understanding child development with Jean Piaget's formal operational thought theory, but to show their commonality and even complementarity. Vygotsky considered the problem of education in the context of studying the role of culture in the formation of the human psyche. In his research, culture acted as a system of ideal forms, the appropriation of which leads to the formation of higher mental functions in the child. An essential role is ascribed to the means developed in culture aimed at controlling human behavior. Due to the development of means, natural mental functions are transformed into higher ones. However, if we want to understand what caused the questions that the authors posed in their studies, it is necessary to characterize the space of psychological science with which they worked. There are reasons to believe that psychology forms a unified field, a system of interrelated theories, which does not prevent them not only from being different, but even contradicting each other. The emergence of a specific theory is explained not so much by personal characteristics of individual scientists, but rather by the possibilities that objectively arise within psychology at the time of the scientific activity of a particular scientist.

Thus, the first historically developed psychological approach was associative psychology. It consisted of various trends, but all associative psychologists relied on the same general principles in their description of mental phenomena. Alongside the principle of associations, these are principles of the conscious character, discreteness and closedness of the psyche to an external observer. The principle of consciousness was formulated by R. Descartes. The principle of discreteness has actually been known since the time of Democritus and was understood as atomism. The principle of the closedness of the mind for an external observer was very pronounced in the works of G. W. Leibniz.

Amid the psychological crisis indicated by Vygotsky, the limitations of associative psychology were revealed. At the end of the nineteenth and the beginning of the twentieth century, three powerful psychological trends originated simultaneously—behavioral psychology, gestalt psychology, and psychoanalysis. Behavioral psychology was based on the principle of accessibility of mental life to an external observer. It was opposed to the principle of the closed mind immanent to associative psychology. The behavior of humans and animals started to be considered the subject of psychology. The principle of structurality was contrasted to the principle of discreteness, and the principle of the unconscious was set against the principle of consciousness. All three theories can be considered a result of the transformation of associative psychology. In this case, the associative theory is a fundamental one, whereas behavioral psychology, gestalt psychology, and psychoanalysis are first-order theories.

The views of Vygotsky are usually considered within the context of the connection of his research with the study of the role of culture in the formation of the human psyche. He studied culture as a system of ideal forms, means and forms of behavior, the acquisition of which leads to the formation of higher mental functions in a child. Vygotsky wrote: «there is a relationship between the environment and the development of the child that is inherent only in the child's development and no other development at all. ... In the development of the child, what should come out of development, as a result of development, is already given in the environment from the very beginning. And it is not just given in the environment from the very beginning, but affects the very first steps of the child's development» (Vygotsky, 1996, p. 87).

Vygotsky explained this interconnection in this way: «In preschool age, a child still has a very limited and vague idea of the quantities. But these primary forms of children's arithmetic thinking interact with the already formed arithmetic thinking of an adult, i.e., again, the final form, which should appear as a result of the child's development, is already present at the very beginning of the child's development and is not only present, but actually determines and directs the first steps that the child takes along the path of development of this form» (Vygotsky, 1996, pp. 88–89).

Cultural means play a significant role in this process. The transformation of the inherent mental functions into higher mental functions occurs as a result of mastering cultural means. The process of turning inherent forms into cultural ones has a number of stages. Vygotsky distinguished two lines in the cultural development of a child: the mastery of tools and the use of signs. He explained that initially the world of external objects is alien to a child. But over time, a child gets closer to it and begins to master these objects, begins to use them in a functional way as tools. «This is the first stage in cultural development, when new forms of behavior and new techniques are formed to complement the innate and simplest acquired movements. The second stage of cultural development is characterized by the emergence of secondary processes in the child's behavior that reconfigure the child's behavior based on the use of such stimuli as signs. These behavioral tactics, acquired in the process of cultural experience, reconstruct the child's main psychological functions» (Vygotsky & Luria, 1993, p. 163).

According to Vygotsky, these two lines differ: «The most significant difference between the sign and the instrument, and the basis for the real divergence of both lines, is their different orientation. A tool mediates the influence of an individual on the object of his or her activity, it is directed outward, it must cause certain changes in the object, it is a means of external human activity aimed at conquering nature. A sign does not change anything in the object of a psychological operation, it is a means of psychological influence on the behavior – someone else's or one's own, a means of internal activity aimed at mastering oneself; the sign is directed inwards» (Vygotsky, 1983, p. 90). Vygotsky noted that «the transition to mediating activity fundamentally reconfigures the entire mental operation ... and immeasurably expands the system of activity of mental functions» (Vygotsky, 1983, p. 90). He designated the mental processes transformed by the sign with the term "higher mental functions" or "higher behavior".

Thus, at first, the child relies on the inherent mental forms, then begins to master the simplest functional actions, then proceeds to the acquisition of signs. Initially, the use of signs is inadequate, «then the child gradually masters them and finally outgrows them, developing the ability to use his own neuromental processes as means to achieve specific goals. Natural behavior turns into cultural behavior; the external tactics and cultural signs formed by social life become internal processes» (Vygotsky, & Luria, 1993, p. 204).

Vygotsky explained the genesis of this function using the example of the development of memorizing: «For the first stage of development it is characteristic that the child is able to mediate his memory only by resorting to certain external techniques …, preserving the memories based on external signs by an essential, direct, almost mechanical retention. At the second stage of development there is a dramatic shift: the external familiar operations as a whole reach their limit, but now the child begins to rebuild the internal process of memorization which is not based on external signs, so the natural process is now indirect, the child begins to use learned internal techniques… In the development of internal mediated operations, the phase of applying external signs plays a crucial role. The child shifts to the internal sign processes because he has made it through the phase when these processes were external…

In the described operations, we observe a twofold process: on the one hand, the natural process undergoes a deep restructuring, turning into an indirect, mediated act, on the other hand – the symbolic operation itself transforms, ceasing to be external and processing … into the most complex internal psychological systems» (Vygotsky, 1984a, b, p. 73). Vygotsky made the following conclusion: «Humans are social beings, so the socio-cultural conditions deeply transform them, developing a number of new forms and ways of behavior. A careful study of these forms of features is the specific task of psychological science» (Vygotsky & Luria, 1993, p. 204).

Vygotsky attached crucial importance to the social origin of the higher forms of behavior and mental functions: «The word "social" as applied to our subject is of great importance. First of all, in the broadest sense, it means that everything cultural is social. Culture is the product of human social life and social activity, and therefore the very formulation of the problem of cultural development of behavior already leads us directly to the social plan of development. Further, it could be pointed out that the sign, which is outside the organism, the same as a tool, is separated from an individual and serves essentially as a social organ or social means. Further, we could say that all the higher functions were not formed biologically, not along the purely phylogenetic history. The mechanism underlying the higher mental functions is an impression of the social. All higher mental functions are interiorized social relations, the basis of the social structure of an individual. Their composition, their genetic structure, their way of functioning – in a word, their whole nature is social; even when transformed into mental processes, it remains quasi-social. An individual as he is even by himself is retained by the function of communication» (Vygotsky, 1983, pp. 145–146).

Thus, according to L. S. Vygotsky, culture, being a universal medium of various forms of behavior, is a universal source of development. This fact brings his approach closer to that of J. Piaget. In his research, logical structures were considered as a universal form (Piaget, 1969). The dialogue between Vygotsky and Piaget was possible due to the fact that they were working on similar questions, aiming to explain the transformation of egocentric aspects of an individual into appropriate forms of social behavior.

2.2   Expansion of the Scope of Psychological Knowledge by L. S. Vygotsky and J. Piaget

As already mentioned, the first-order theories actualize the possibilities that were established by associative psychology, that is to say, they have emerged as a result of self-developing psychological knowledge. However, there is another way—to exploit not only the possibilities within the psychological science, but also other sciences. In particular, that was the path Vygotsky took. The singularity of Vygotsky's approach was that he merged the problematics of psychology with sociological problematics. In doing so, he created fundamentally new opportunities for the development of psychological science. Vygotsky argued: «the idea that higher mental functions cannot be understood without sociological study, i.e. that they are the product not of a biological but of a social development of behavior, is not new. But it is only in recent decades that it has received a solid factual basis in research on ethnic psychology and can now be considered an indisputable point of our science» (Vygotsky, 1983, p. 29). The concept of cultural means has become a cardinal one. Its inclusion in the psychological language led to the introduction of such concepts as "zone of proximal development" and "social situation of development". It is important to keep in mind that culture limits the nature of a person, implying adherence to social norms that apply to human behavior, his forms of mental activity, including speech and thinking, interaction with other people and appearance. Education acts as a process of transferring cultural norms to the younger generation. In this sense, new members of society, sacrificing their individuality, obeying the established rules, ensure the stable functioning of social systems.

In fact, Vygotsky investigated the influence of culture on child development. Culture acted for him as a universal social foundation of the psyche. Therefore, according to Vygotsky, in order to develop and interact with other people, a person needs to master the culture. In this case, education appears as an essential condition for culture and, performing the function of transferring knowledge, creates opportunities for the development of not only the individual, but also the culture itself.

Thus, Vygotsky expanded the scope of psychological knowledge using the possibilities presented by sociology. It is in this, before everything else, that we see the contribution of Vygotsky and the distinguishing feature of his cultural-historical theory, in the perspective of which he explored problems that were important for the associative psychology: the problem of thinking and speech, the problem of higher mental functions and the problem of human consciousness. The very fact that Vygotsky critically addressed behavioral theory, psychoanalysis, and gestalt psychology indicates that his theory was on the same level as the abovementioned approaches. At the same time, it should be taken into account that the theory of Vygotsky was, in our opinion, more powerful due to the breadth of the content involved, since it drew not only on the associative psychology, but also on sociology.

It is interesting that Piaget was also broadening the field of psychological knowledge. We find confirmation of this in the characterization given to Piaget by B. Inhelder: "The concept of mental development, as it is given in the works of my esteemed teacher, usually leaves the reader in some confusion, and not so much because of the given facts, but because of the terminology. Professor Piaget, being a zoologist by training, a specialist in the theory of knowledge by vocation and a logician by method, uses terminology that has not yet been used in psychology" (Zaporozhets & Venger, 1968, p. 58). It is obvious that by introducing terms from other fields of scientific knowledge, Piaget has also broadened the scope of psychological science.

2.3   Dialogue of Theories

Piaget and Vygotsky, as authors of theoretical approaches, expressed their attitude to both fundamental associative theory and first-order theories. Let us pay attention to the fact that Piaget specifically analyzed the principle of discreteness or atomism. He examined it in the context of the development of intellectual operations and cited the following as an example: "One of the remarkable examples of operational structures that depend on the subjects activity and were often observed even before the advent of the experimental method is atomism, discovered by the Greeks long before experimental study. A similar process can be observed in a child between 4–5 and 11–12 years in a situation where experience alone is clearly not enough to explain the emergence of a structure, and it is obvious that its construction involves an additive composition that depends on the subject's activity" (Obukhova & Burmenskaya, 2001, p. 110). This suggests that Piaget took into account the associative point of view in his constructions. Indeed, he wrote: «... the concept of association, which was used and abused by various currents within associationism (from Hume to Pavlov and Hull), arose as a result of the artificial isolation of one side of the whole process» (Obukhova, & Burmenskaya, 2001, p. 114).

Piaget saw the main disadvantage of the associative perspective in the limitations that the principle of discreteness imposed, to a large extent, on associative psychologists. In his work "The Psychology of the Intellect", he noted: «A mental operation can be compared to a simple action only if it is considered in isolation. But speculating on isolated operations is precisely the fundamental error of the "mental experience" empirical theories: a single operation is not an operation, but remains at the level of simple intuitive representations. The specific nature of operations, when compared to empirical actions, is, by contrast, that they never exist as discrete ones. We can only speak of a "single" operation as a result of an absolutely unjustified abstraction: a single operation could not be an operation, since the essence of operations is to form systems. That is at this point, where a particularly vigorous objection to logical atomism must be made, as its scheme was a heavy burden for the psychology of thought» (Piaget, 1969, pp. 93–94).

A consequence of the discreteness principle, known as atomism, was a method of psychological analysis, which consisted in the decomposition of complex mental entities into elements. Vygotsky emphasized that such an "analysis dominates traditional psychology, which is usually called associative psychology. In its essence, it was based on the atomistic idea that higher processes are formed by adding together known individual elements, so the task of any study was again reduced to presenting a higher process as a sum of simplest elements associated in a specific way. In fact, it was the psychology of the elements…" (Vygotsky, 1983, p. 91). He believed that such an analysis "is not an analysis in the proper sense of the word, in the perspective of the problem to which it is applied. Rather, we can consider it a method of cognition, antithetic to analysis and in a certain sense opposite of it. … the analysis of this kind, applied groundlessly in psychology, leads to deep misconceptions, since it ignores the aspect of unity and integrity of the process under study and replaces the internal relations of unity with the external mechanical relations of two heterogeneous processes that are alien to each other" (Vygotsky, 1982a, b, c, p. 14). In that regard, Vygotsky had a positive attitude toward the idea of the structural point of view with which W. Köhler, "having defeated atomism completely, established an independent and isolated molecule in the place of the atom" (Vygotsky, 1982a, b, c, p. 288).

Both Vygotsky and Piaget believed that the interpretation of behavior that is based on the concept of reflex and is developed within the context of the associative approach creates a limited point of view. Piaget explained his position as follows: "But if the existence of conditioned behavior is a real and even very significant fact, the interpretation of it does not require reflexological associanism with which it is too often linked. When movement is associated with perception, then it is already something more than a passive association, that is, an association established after only one repetition. Here, there is already a whole set of meanings, since in this case, the association is formed on the basis of a need and its satisfaction… In other words, there is no association in the classical sense of the term here, but rather the formation of such a scheme of building the whole, which is connected with the internal content" (Piaget, 1969, p. 147).

In our point of view, the position of Piaget happens to be very close to that of Vygotsky, who gave a similar characteristic to the reflexological approach: "It is necessary to study not the reflexes, but behavior–its mechanism, composition, structure. Every time we experiment with an animal or a human being, we have the illusion that we are investigating a reaction or reflex. In fact, we always investigate behavior, because we inevitably organize the behavior of our subjects in a specific way in order to ensure that certain reaction or reflex prevails; otherwise, we would not get anything… All this indicates the complexity of any reaction, its dependence on the structure of the underlying mechanism of behavior, the impossibility of studying the reaction in abstraction" (Vygotsky, 1982a, b, c, pp. 82–83).

Besides the criticism toward the reflexological approach to child development, the cited fragments also clearly present the authors' position on the structural point of view. Let us consider the attitude of Piaget and Vygotsky to gestalt psychology in more detail. Piaget specifically analyzed the gestalt theory. He noted: "It is necessary, however, to emphasize the essential part of the theory under consideration, namely, that the laws of organization are characterized by its proponents as independent of development and, consequently, as common to all levels. This thesis is unavoidable if we limit ourselves by considering only functional organization or a "synchronic" equilibrium of behaviors, since the necessity of such an equilibrium is a law for all stages of development, and hence the functional continuity that we have always insisted on. But usually such invariant functioning is opposed to sequential structures considered from the "diachronic" point of view, as changing from level to level. The essence of gestalt is to combine function and structure into a single whole under the name of organization and to consider its laws as unchangeable. Therefore, the proponents of the theory of form seek to show, using impressive scope of material, that the perceptual structures are the same not only in a small child and an adult, but in general in vertebrates of all categories, and that the only difference between a child and an adult consists in the relative importance of certain general factors of organization (for example, the factor of proximity), while in sum these factors remain the same, and the resulting structures obey the same laws" (Piaget, 1969, pp. 113–114).

Piaget acknowledged the validity of a holistic approach to the analysis of the phenomena of perception. Yet, he disagreed with gestalt psychologists' aspiration to explain the specificity of these phenomena through common physical foundations. Particularly, the questions of the immutability of such perceptual structures as constancy have not found experimental confirmation. Thus, Piaget, as a matter of fact, has been defending the notion that perceptual and intellectual structures are being constructed in the process of a child's development.

Piaget came to the following conclusion: "As a result, we come to the conclusion that the theory of form, which is clear in its definition of forms of equilibrium or well-structured entities, cannot, however, be accepted, since both in the perceptual sphere and in the sphere of intelligence it does not take into account either the reality of genetic development or the actual construction that characterizes this development" (Piaget, 1969, p. 123).

Vygotsky had rather similar views on gestalt psychology. He spoke of the need to overcome the one-sidedness of the structural point of view, which did not mean returning back to the principles of associative psychology, which built scientific knowledge on the atomistic, chaotic conjunction of elements. He emphasized: "The structural principle remains a great, unshakable conquest of theoretical thought, and when we criticize its application to the explanation of child development, we do not mean to say that the opposite principle is true .... It turns out that the structural principle is not so much wrong in its application to the facts of child development, but insufficient, relative, and limited, since what it reveals in child development is not specific to humans, but is common to humans and animals. And so the main methodological error in applying this principle to child psychology lies not in its fallacy, but in its undue universality, and therefore inability to reveal the distinctive specific features of human development as such" (Vygotsky, 1982a, b, c, p. 281).

This shows that, in a number of cases, Piaget and Vygotsky held very similar positions on the psychological approaches that took shape in the first half of the twentieth century, which speaks for the existence of a deeper common basis in the understanding of child development by these researchers.

2.4 Development and Equilibrium

Piaget viewed development as a stage process. According to his point of view, the development process "is understood as a sequence of structures that achieve a state of equilibrium, the form of which changes from one structure to another" (Piaget, 1969, p. 322). The state of equilibrium characterizes an already formed structure and marks the end of the development on the one hand, but at the same time, it means the beginning of a new period in the formation of the intellect. Piaget explained his point of view as follows: "Intelligence is a certain form of balance, to which all the structures formed based on perception and the skill of elementary sensorimotor mechanisms tend to gravitate. Indeed, it must be understood that if intelligence is not an ability, then this negation would entail the necessity of some continuous functional connection between the higher forms of thought and the totality of the lower varieties of cognitive and motor adaptations. And then intelligence will be understood as precisely the form of equilibrium to which all these adaptations tend" (Piaget, 1969, p. 65).

The notion of equilibrium means that a system is in equilibrium "if it has some sustainability or stability towards the forces influencing it from outside or from within" (Flavell, 1967, p. 318). Equilibrium is maintained by the processes of assimilation and accommodation.

Therefore, according to Piaget, the development is a balancing process during the transition from one structure of a child's intellect to another. In this process, the existing structure is the beginning of the formation of a next one of a higher level. The development of intellectual structures is viewed as a result of a child's own activity, which is based on the mechanisms of assimilation schemes and accommodation processes.

Piaget revealed a large-scale perspective: "The entire development of mental activity, from perception and to representation and memory skills, down to the most complex operations of inference and formal thinking, is thus a function of the ever-increasing scale of interactions. Thus it is a function of the balance between the organism's assimilation of an increasingly distant reality and its accommodation to it. It is in this sense that the intelligence with its logical operations provides a stable and at the same time flexible balance between the universe and thinking and continues and completes the set of adaptive processes" (Piaget, 1969, p. 67).

It seems to us that the idea of culture as a system of norms stabilizing the interaction of members of society in various situations stands behind the problem of equilibrium. If for Vygotsky, this issue is directly related to the interaction of people with each other, for Piaget it appears as the establishment of a balance between the subject and the environment.

When analyzing the development process, Vygotsky proceeded from the idea of structure, same as Piaget did. He emphasized that, in spite of all the complexities of the organization of the development process and the variety of its composition, it "is a single whole that has a certain structure; the laws of this structure, or the structural laws of age, determine the structure and course of each particular process of development included in this whole" (Vygotsky, 1984a, b, p. 256).

Studying development, Vygotsky took as a premise that "the child's personality changes as a whole in its internal structure, and the laws of this change determine the movement of each part of it" (Vygotsky, 1984a, b, p. 256).

In order to explain development, Vygotsky introduced the concept of the social situation of development. He wrote: "at the beginning of each age period, a completely particular, age-specific, singular, unique and unprecedented relationship develops between the child and the surrounding reality, primarily the social one. We call this relationship the *social situation of development* at a given age. The social situation of development is the starting point for all the dynamic changes that occur in development during a given period. It determines entirely the forms and the way in which the child acquires new personality traits, drawing on social reality as the main source of development, so that the social becomes individual" (Vygotsky, 1984a, b, pp. 258–259).

Thus, according to Vygotsky, a child's development is determined entirely by the social situation of development, i.e. the relationship between the child and his or her social environment. The important detail here is that this relationship persists throughout every age. In other words, this circumstance indicates the existence of a consensus or correspondence between the child's social environment and his or her developing personality.

Vygotsky showed it very clearly how the child's personality develops when the child acts in a social situation of development, which leads to a change in the entire system of his or her relationships with external reality and with himself. "At the end of a given age the child becomes a completely different being compared to what he was at the beginning of this age. But this also means that the social situation of development, established in its main aspects by the beginning of this age, must also change. For the social situation of development is nothing but a system of relations between a child of a given age and social reality. And if the child has changed radically, it is inevitable that this relationship must also be rebuilt" (Vygotsky, 1984a, b, p. 260).

On the basis of his analysis, Vygotsky formulated the law of age dynamics. "According to this law, the forces that drive the development of a child at a given age inevitably lead to the denial and destruction of the very basis of the development of this entire age period. There is an internal necessity, which determines the annulment of this particular social situation of development, the end of this era of development and the transition to the next, or higher age stage" (Vygotsky, 1984a, b, p. 260).

This law can be easily interpreted in the context of equilibrium and its disturbance. Indeed, it is not hard to notice that initially there is a balance between the personality of a child and his or her social environment, which allows us to consider the social situation of the development as adequate for a given age. The child interacts with the environment from within this equilibrium, which leads to the emergence of new formations in his or her personality, the restructuring of consciousness and an imbalance between the social environment and the personality of the child. Equilibrium is restored through the establishment of a new system of relations between the child and his or her environment. Here we see a certain similarity between the positions of Piaget and Vygotsky. There is an obvious difference however, that is, while Piaget's equilibrium shifts due to the individual activity of the child, the equilibrium of Vygotsky changes as a result of interaction with the social environment. In this regard, we could say that the positions of these two outstanding authors are complementary, since in the first case the object environment comes to the fore, and in the other case—the social environment does.

2.5 Sensorimotor Development

Among other issues, both Vygotsky and Piaget worked on the question of characteristics of sensorimotor development. The study of the genesis of a psyche at the initial stages (in addition to the theoretical problems faced by researchers) occurred within a range of approaches to child development by behaviorists, gestalt psychologists and K. Bühler. In particular, gestalt psychologists considered this process in the context of universal structures, in which the development of both a child and an animal obey the same physical laws of structure forming. Bühler offered another point of view. He wrote: "humans are not isolated in the world, they are related to animals. If we consider all meaningful, i.e. (objectively) purposeful forms of behavior of animals and humans, we will see a very simple and clear structure of three large stages; these three stages are instinct, training and intelligence" (Bühler, 1930, p. 30). Bühler studied the intellectual behavior of young children and came to the following conclusion: "It is said that speech comes first on the way to the transformation of a child into a human being; this may be true, but it is preceded by functional thinking, that is, the capture of mechanical connections and the invention of mechanical means to achieve mechanical goals, or, in short, before the development of speech, behavior becomes subjectively meaningful, that is, consciously purposeful" (Bühler, 1930, p. 88).

This point of view has been criticized by gestalt psychologists. Vygotsky has seen the main disadvantage of Bühler's psychological perspective in the fact "that there's nothing fundamentally new in the development of humans and human children, no new stage of behavior that distinguishes humans and is specific to them" (Bühler, 1930, p. 17).

Piaget emphasized that "the classical division of phenomena into sensory stimuli and motor responses, based on the scheme of the reflex arc, if considered in isolation, is just as erroneous as the concept of the reflex arc itself and relies on equally artificial results of a laboratory experiment. In fact, perception is influenced from the very beginning by movement, and movement, in turn, is influenced by perception. This is exactly what we have expressed, for our part, when we talked about sensorimotor "schemes" when describing assimilation; already in the behavior of an infant, such a scheme is both perceptual and motor" (Piaget, 1969, p. 143).

Analyzing the sensory and motor development of young children, Piaget raised the question of whether it was possible to explain children's progress in these areas through the trial and error mechanism proposed by E. Thorndike. The essence of this mechanism is that an animal attempts its trials randomly and blindly at first. Successful trials are retained and failed ones get removed. Over time, the animal gets closer to a successful set of actions. Piaget showed that this blind search is actually based not on the trial and error mechanism, but on assimilation. He concluded: "Thus, the accumulation of experience at all levels, from elementary learning to intelligence, seems to involve assimilating activity, which is equally necessary for structuring both the most passive forms of skills (conditioned behavior and associative transferences), and for manifestations of intelligence with their characteristic obvious activity (directed blind search)" (Piaget, 1969, p. 155).

Vygotsky also criticized the use of the trial and error method as an explanatory principle: "the idea of sensorimotor unity remains fully confirmed as long as we stay on zoological material, or when we are dealing with a young child, or with adults in whom these processes are close to the affective ones. But when we go further, there is a dramatic change. The unity of sensorimotor processes, that is, the connection in which the motor process is a dynamic continuation of the structure enclosed in the sensory field, is destroyed: motor skills become relatively independent in relation to sensory processes, and sensory processes are separated from direct motor impulses; more complex relationships arise between them" (Vygotsky, 1982a, b, c, p. 112).

Thus, it can be seen that the positions of Piaget and Vygotsky on the matter of sensorimotor development partially coincided. They both spoke about the initial unity of the sensory and motor components of the child's psyche. Yet there were also differences, as Vygotsky allowed for the possibility of independent developmental lines of sensorics and the motor sphere in the context of the development of arbitrariness while Piaget was interested in the sensorimotor period as an established independent structure.

2.6 Learning and Development

Piaget's position on this issue was based on his understanding of the difference between the processes of development and learning. One of the questions that he considered was how to determine the conditions for a child to master logical structures. Studies have shown that "in order to build a logical structure and learn how to use it, the subject must start with another, more elementary logical structure, within which he must differentiate and then supplement it. In other words, learning is nothing more than a part of cognitive development that is facilitated or accelerated by experience" (Obukhova & Burmenskaya, 2001, p. 126).

Piaget emphasized that "whenever we prematurely teach a child something that he could eventually discover for himself, we thereby deprive him of this discovery, and therefore deprive him of a complete understanding of this subject" (Obukhova & Burmenskaya, 2001, p. 127).

An interesting result was obtained by Inhelder and colleagues in the course of experiments aimed at identifying factors that contribute to the development of operational relationships. The obtained data showed that the successful performance depended on the initial cognitive level of the children. All children were ascribed a level: low, intermediate, or high. The high level was characterized by an understanding of the relationship of fluid quantity preservation; the intermediate level was determined based on hesitation in children's responses; the low level was assigned to children who showed the absence of the phenomenon of fluid quantity preservation. It turned out that the children who showed an intermediate level at the initial stage, later mastered the principle of conservation in the course of the experiment. "Their reasoning reached a genuine stability (in their last control tests, there were no phenomena of returning to the previous level)" (Obukhova & Burmenskaya, 2001, p. 128). The conclusion that Piaget has drawn was that learning depended on the level of cognitive development of the subject.

The position of Vygotsky in relation to learning and development was expressed in a number of statements. First of all, he said that "in one way or another, learning must be consistent with the level of the child's development - this is an empirically established and repeatedly confirmed fact that cannot be disputed" (Vygotsky, 1991, p. 383). Vygotsky also stressed that "we cannot limit ourselves to one definition of the level of development when we try to find out the real relationship of development processes to learning potential. We must determine at least two levels of the child's development. Without this knowledge we will not be able to find the right relationship between the course of the child's development and the learning potential in each particular case. Let's refer to the first level as the level of actual development. We mean the level of the child's mental functions development, which is a result of already completed developmental cycles" (Vygotsky, 1991, p. 384).

In addition, it is crucial to take into account not only the completed stage of development, but also the ongoing developmental processes. In order to assess the scale of what is developing in a given moment, Vygotsky proposed the concept of the zone of proximal development. He defined the zone of proximal development as the difference between what children can do on their own and what they can do with the help of an adult.

If we look more closely at the results reported by Piaget, we can see the following. The children who participated in the experiment could be divided into three different groups: those who had mastered the structure of the appropriate developmental level; those who were below this level, that is, were at the previous level; and those between them. Of particular interest were the children who scored for the intermediate position. One can say that they were on the border of the transition from the previous level to the next one. A child who is on the edge between two levels of development, has, in fact, finished the previous stage of development and has not yet gotten through the next stage. This means that the child is in transition, i.e., in the zone of proximal development, since the child sometimes is able to complete the task, and sometimes not. Thus, we could say that, in fact, both Piaget and Vygotsky, analyzed situations within which the learning was effective.

In other words, there is every reason to say that there is a similarity in the positions of Vygotsky and Piaget on learning and development. Vygotsky's point of view is more transparently presented. Vygotsky spoke about the leading role of learning in child development. In the zone of proximal development, the child masters cultural means in the process of understanding through imitation of the actions of an adult, and that's what causes the developmental effect.

It is to be noted, that J. Piaget also used the term "means" in his works. In his book "The Psychology of Intelligence", he said: "According to Claparede, feeling gives purpose to behavior, while intelligence is just providing behavior with means (techniques)" (Piaget, 1969, pp. 62–63).

When outlining the views of F. Buytendijk, Piaget wrote the following: "for a skill to form, the main condition is always the relation of the means to the end: actions are never a series of mechanically connected movements... Therefore, it is the relation "means x end" that defines intellectual actions" (Piaget, 1969, p. 145).

Examining the approach of E. Tolman and C. Hull, Piaget noted: "Hull insistently contrasts mental models involving means and ends with mechanical models of paving the way" (Piaget, 1969, p. 154).

Thus, we can conclude that there are elements of similarity between Piaget's and. Vygotsky's understanding of the role of learning in development. The similarity is that both authors considered this issue in terms of transition from one stage of development to another. But there are also differences. For Vygotsky, the key to the transition is the concept of means, which is acquired through the communication between a child and an adult in the zone of proximal development. For Piaget, the central point is establishing a balance between the processes of assimilation and accommodation. The developmental processes themselves acquire in one case a cultural, social, and normative character (according to Vygotsky), and in the other—an individual, natural, and creative sense (according to Piaget).

2.7 Affect and Intelligence

Piaget noted that "affective and cognitive life are ... inseparable, while also distinct. They are inseparable because any interchange with the environment involves both the implementation of structure and the creation of values ... but this does not make them any less different from each other, since these two aspects of behavior cannot be reduced to each other in any way" (Piaget, 1969, p. 64). Affectivity acts as the energy source of behavior, while the structure of behavior is determined by cognitive processes. Affective activity, same as cognitive activity, is an adaptation to arising situations, which involves the processes of assimilation and accommodation. Affective formations develop in parallel to the cognitive structures.

Vygotsky also spoke about the unity of affect and intelligence. He emphasized that "there is a dynamic semantic system that represents the unity of affective and intellectual processes" (Vygotsky, 1982a, b, c, p. 22). Vygotsky defined experience as a semantic unit of consciousness: "Experience is a unit, where, on the one hand, the environment (what is experienced) is represented in an indecomposable form, since the experience always is of something outside of the individual. On the other hand, it involves the way I experience it. That means that all the features of my personality and all the features of the environment are represented in the experience; all that is selected from the environment, all those moments that are relevant to my personality and highlighted in my personality, all those character traits and constitutional traits that are relevant to this particular event" (Vygotsky, 1996, pp. 79–80).

Thus, we can see that the approaches of Piaget and Vygotsky are partly similar, as they both speak of the unity of the affective and intellectual sides of the child's psyche. However, for Piaget it is the intellectual side that is important, because it represents the aspect of knowledge. For Vygotsky, the important point is the unity of an individual and the environment, because of its relevance for the development of cultural-historical theory and his aspiration to build a theory of emotions.

However, there is a problem related to the answer to the question: "How can a person carry out the process of cultural development?" It should be borne in mind that culture deals with individuals and each individual is different and self-centered in its essence. Society accepts only that individuality that expresses the individualities of others. Hence, the need to give the individual the tools to express himself/herself through the forms available to other people arises. This is one of the fundamental functions of culture—to ensure the emergence of adequate forms of behavior.

For Piaget, the intellect, or rather, the logic behind it, acted as such a tool as the basis on which logically adequate, non-egocentric reasoning is built. Vygotsky considered the entire system of higher mental functions or consciousness as a derivative of (the history of) culture as an instrument of adequate, free action. It is clear that in this case both logic, as a system that ensures the adequacy of judgments, and culture in the form of social situations aimed at the development of self-regulation and the adequacy of social interaction, act as prerequisites for education.

2.8 Conclusion

We tried to show that the works of Piaget and Vygotsky bear certain similarities, not just differences. Moreover, these similarities are not only external, but also substantial. In fact, both authors considered the development of a child's psyche as processes of formation of complex dynamic systems that are prerequisites for school education. Piaget saw these systems in terms of the object and subject relationships, while for Vygotsky they were determined by the child's interaction with the adults and peers around him.

Both Piaget and Vygotsky have been and still remain relevant authors who contributed to the development of psychological knowledge by expanding the scope of psychological science.

Responding to the criticism from Vygotsky, Piaget expressed deep regret, saying that "we could not come to an agreement on a number of issues" (Piaget, 1981, p. 188). Later, he distinguished two types of egocentrism: egocentrism in general (or cognitive egocentrism) and egocentric speech. Speaking of cognitive egocentrism, Piaget defined his position as follows: "For the knowledge to grow, the previous points of view have to be constantly reformulated, which happens through processes that also move backward as well as forward, constantly correcting the original systematic errors and thus slowly moving forward. This correctional process is subject to a certain law of development, the law of decentralization" (Piaget, 1981, p. 189). Piaget said about Vygotsky: "… I respect Vygotsky's position on the development of egocentric speech, even though I cannot agree with him on every issue" (Piaget, 1981, p. 191). Piaget appreciated Vygotsky's analysis of the development of egocentric speech: "…he proposed new hypotheses: egocentric speech is the starting point for the development of internal speech, which is found at a later stage of development and can serve for autistic inferences and logical thinking. I fully agree with these hypotheses. On the other hand, I think that Vygotsky failed to fully appreciate egocentrism as the main obstacle to cooperation and coordination of points of view. Vygotsky correctly reproaches me for not emphasizing enough the original functional aspect of these questions. But later, I did it" (Piaget, 1981, p. 192).

Piaget's answer to the criticism from Vygotsky shows that these authors used analytic tools that point to the congruence of their views on a number of issues of child development, which did not preclude them from disagreement. In this regard, it is interesting how Piaget explains his position: "…When Vygotsky concludes that the early function of language must be a function of global communication and that later speech is differentiated into egocentric and communicative, I agree with him. But when he claims that these two linguistic forms are equally socialized and differ only in function, I cannot agree with him, because the word "socialization" becomes ambiguous in this context: if individual A mistakenly believes that individual B thinks the same way as A, and if he does not try to understand the difference between the two points of view, then it will be social behavior in the sense that there is contact between the two, but I would call such behavior maladapted from the point of view of intellectual cooperation. This point of view is the only aspect of the problem that interested me, but did not interest Vygotsky" (Piaget, 1981, p. 192). This explanation clearly shows the complementarity of their positions.

In conclusion, we will consider the levels of theories of Vygotsky and Piaget within the system of psychological knowledge. In our opinion, after the emergence of the first-order theories, the second-order theories began to appear. Those are the theories that use the possibilities provided by first-order theories in their constructs. Second-order theories can adopt the principles of the first-order theories. In particular, this is representative of Piaget's approach. In his concept of grouping, he combined the principle of discreteness, structure, and actions into a single dynamic whole. This combination allowed him to build a unique understanding of intelligence development. The development of intelligence first follows the principle of external actions organized into sensorimotor intelligence (which is close to behaviorist descriptions). Then, according to the principle of gestalt psychology, goes the formation of pre-operational intelligence and, ultimately, they form intellectual structures of formal operations, in which images and classes of objects are the material of intellectual transformations. It is clear that the theory of Piaget could not have appeared without behavioral theory and gestalt theory. Even though Piaget began his work when these theories were just being developed, the operational approach emerged after both points of view were already clearly formulated. Thus, we see that the theory of Piaget is a second-order theory, while the cultural-historical theory is a first-order theory.

As a result of the analysis of the point of view of Vygotsky's approach to culture in comparison with the perspective of Piaget's approach, let us note that, in fact, both authors considered the transformation of individuality in the process of its interaction with the universal, that is, with culture. For Vygotsky culture acted as a system of social situations in which the child mastered non-egocentric forms of behavior, and Piaget described the development of individuality also in the context of interaction, but with the only difference that logical structures acted as the universal in his research. The dialogue between Vygotsky and Piaget was possible due to the fact that they solved similar problems, which consisted in explaining the transformation of egocentric aspects of personality into adequate forms of social behavior.

Acknowledgements   Research was supported by RSF grant# 19-18-00521-П.

References

Bühler, K. (1930). *The mental development of the child. A summary of modern psychological theory.* Harcourt, Brace.

Flavell, J. H. (1967). *Genetic psychology of Jean Piaget.* Prosveshenie.

Lourenço, O. (2012). Piaget and Vygotsky: Many resemblances, and a crucial differenceю *New Ideas in Psychology, 30,* 281–295.

Obukhova, L. F., & Burmenskaya, G. V. (Eds.). (2001). Piaget's theory. *Jean Piaget: Theory, experiments, discussions: Sat. articles* (pp. 106–157). Gardariki.

Piaget, J. (1969). *Selected psychological works: The psychology of intelligence. Genesis of the number in a child. Logic and Psychology.* Prosveshenie.

Piaget, J. (1981). Comments on critical remarks of L. S. Vygotsky on the books "Speech and thinking of a child" and "Judgment and reasoning of a child". In Yu. B. Gippenreiter & V. V. Petukhova (Eds.), *Chrestomathy in general psychology: Psychology of thinking* (pp. 188–193). Moscow University Press.

Valsiner, J. (2021). Understanding Vygotsky over three decades: A critical look. *Integrative Psychological and Behavioral Science, 55,* 705–707.

van der Veer, R. (2021). Vygotsky's legacy: Understanding and beyond. *Integrative Psychological and Behavioral Science, 55,* 789–796.

Vygotsky, L. S. (1982a). *Problems of general psychology* (V. V. Davydov, Ed). Pedagogika.

Vygotsky, L. S. (1982b). *Questions of theory and history of psychology* (A. R. Luria, & M. G. Yaroshevsky, Eds). Pedagogika.

Vygotsky, L. S. (1982c). *Questions of theory and history of psychology* (A. R. Luria & M. G. Yaroshevsky, Eds.). Pedagogika.

Vygotsky, L. S. (1983). *Problems of the development of the psyche* (A. M. Matyushkin, Ed.). Pedagogika.

Vygotsky, L. S. (1984a). *Child psychology* (D. B. Elkonin, Ed.). Pedagogika

Vygotsky, L. S. (1984b). *Scientific heritage* (M. G. Yaroshevsky, Ed.). Pedagogika.

Vygotsky, L. S. (1991). *Educational psychology* (V. V. Davydov, Ed.). Pedagogika.

Vygotsky, L. S. (1996). *Lectures on pedology.* Udmurt University Press.

Vygotsky, L. S., & Luria, A. R. (1993). *Behavioral history studies: Monkey.* Pedagogika-Press.

Zaporozhets, A. V., & Venger, L. A. (Eds.). (1968). *Child development* (M. S. Rogovin, Trans.). Prosveshenie.

Prof. Nikolay Veraksa is a specialist in preschool education, works at Faculty of Psychology, Lomonosov Moscow State University, Moscow City University and Psychological Institute of the Russian Academy of Education, Head of UNESCO Chair in Early Childhood Care and Development, Honorary Doctor of the University of Gothenburg. He is a co-author of the most popular educational program in Russia for children in preschool "From Birth to School" as well as a program in English "Key to Learning." His main interests are development of child thinking and personality.

Chapter 3
Learning and Development in a Designed World

Roger Säljö⊙ and Åsa Mäkitalo

Abstract The idea of appropriation of cultural tools as a central feature of human development is a cornerstone of the sociocultural/cultural-historical theory. Through the design of cultural tools, which are both physical and intellectual/conceptual, knowledge and skills are made available to new generations. During the past decade, young children in many countries have been introduced to digital devices (tablets, apps, games, etc.), first in their homes and later in preschool. From an early age (in fact, before the age of one), they engage with such devices in a range of activities and for extended periods during a day. Research shows that they are not necessarily under adult supervision when involved in digitally mediated activities. This contemporary reorganization of the daily practices of young children in many parts of the world raises interesting theoretical questions about how children appropriate knowledge under these circumstances, and how their thinking and world-views are shaped when accommodating to the affordances of digital environments.

3.1 Introduction

The background of this chapter is an interest in how to understand the relationship between child development and material culture. The argument is that development cannot be understood as the unfolding of capacities that are given through biology, but, rather, has to be seen as contingent on, and intimately tied to, the socio-material circumstances in which children grow up and make experiences. In contemporary society, children, from a very early age, learn to use complex digital artifacts for playing, communicating and for participating in a range of other tasks. Thus, it seems timely to ask how to construe development in a world which is designed, and

R. Säljö (✉) · Å. Mäkitalo
Department of Education, Communication and Learning, University of Gothenburg, Gothenburg, Sweden
e-mail: Roger.saljo@ped.gu.se

Å. Mäkitalo
e-mail: asa.makitalo@iped.uio.no

where children learn to engage in activities that have not been available to earlier generations.

In his keynote address at the centennial of the birth of Piaget and Vygotsky, Jerome Bruner (1997), when comparing the legacies of these intellectual giants, spoke on the joy of "celebrating divergence." Profiting from divergence implies wrestling with the richness of the "fruitful incommensurability" (p. 70) of the perspectives in terms of some of the basic assumptions they build on, and the various avenues of exploration they point us to when attempting to study development, learning and growth. Bruner contrasts the ambitions of the Piagetian project of searching for the "invariant logic of growth" (p. 63) during ontogeny, with the hermeneutically and socioculturally grounded Vygotskian attempts of understanding how people appropriate "higher order, culturally embodied symbolic structures, each of which may incorporate or even displace what existed before." Furthermore, these symbolic structures, in Vygotskian terms, are "cultural products" serving as "instruments of mind" (p. 68) of living and cognizing individuals acting in sociohistorically situated practices.

There are many elements of this fruitful incommensurability in the study of human development and learning that are interesting to explore. One of the central areas where the perspectives diverge concerns the role of culture, including material culture, in learning and development. The Piagetian version of development fore-grounds intellectual adaptation in a dynamic and changing world, and the achieve-ment of equilibrium through processes of accommodation and assimilation (Piaget, 1970). Piaget and his collaborators and followers in many of their experiments and interview studies certainly engage with significant features of the physical environ-ment in the sense that the evolution of children's conceptions of the structure and func-tioning of the material world is in focus (Piaget, 1973). Thus, the figurative (repre-sentations, imagery, language) and operative (active and transforming the world) aspects of intelligence are constitutive of how the growing intellect relates to and learns to conceptualize a complex external world that is both intellectual and material (Piaget & Inhelder, 1971). The reorganization of the intellect, to a large extent, is a consequence of interaction with a physical world and the instances of disequilib-rium encountered. However, the main knowledge interest is in the cognitive conse-quences of this interaction, i.e., how children and young people develop cognitive structures, or schemes, that allow them to cope with the surrounding world in increas-ingly specified and abstract ways. Logico-mathematical structures, reversibility and other features of the mature intellect in some sense liberate the mind from physi-cally interacting with the material world and from considering the specificities of its organization (cf. Müller et al., 2015).

The line of inquiry that we will follow takes its point of departure in the idea that materiality plays a crucial role as a constitutive element of human thinking. The material world is not merely something that is outside us and that contributes to intellectual development; materiality is embedded in the very activity of thinking, learning and knowing. The strong version of this position implies that we cannot study human development and learning without considering the material world and the impact of the artifacts that we learn to rely on in activities. Our intellectual capacities are not limited to what exists between our ears, nor are they determined by biology. Instead, they co-develop with our abilities to integrate increasingly sophisticated artifacts into our practices. Phylogenetically as well as ontogenetically, "material engagement" (Malafouris, 2013) is a fundamental source of knowing and human development at all levels.

In our opinion, the role of materiality in human development and cognition is important to raise in developmental research at this particular point in time. Through recent technological developments, basic elements of the daily activities of children and young people (and adults) have changed dramatically. New practices in the context of play, symbol manipulation, media use and communication have emerged through the omnipresence of digital tools and our constant online access to information, knowledge and activities. One consequence of this transformation of our daily lives is that the communicative and cognitive ecology of the daily practices of even very young children is undergoing rapid change. The issue of how to integrate such transformations of everyday practices with our understanding of learning and development is important to consider, if we want our theorizing to be relevant for socialization inside and outside formal educational settings in contemporary society.

3.2 Materiality, Cognition and Development

At one level, the background of our interest in the material nature of thinking is a brief comment made by Vygotsky (1981, p. 139), originally in a lecture, where he argues that an artificial tool often "abolishes and makes unnecessary a number of natural processes, whose work is accomplished by the tool." This comment, although made almost in passing, is very profound in the sense that it points to the intimate links between human cognitive practices and what Vygotsky refers to as "cultural tools." When tools change, our mental activities may be reorganized.

A telling illustration of such a reorganization of "natural processes" into something less natural is remembering. As has been shown in endless amounts of empirical research over the past 150 years, our capacity for keeping information in mind is, at one level, rather limited. The cognitive revolution in psychology in the post-war period was founded on the observation that our "processing capacities" or "span of immediate memory," as Miller (1956) put it, imposes "severe limitations on the amount of information that we are able to receive, process and remember" (p. 95). The title of Miller's seminal article refers to the observation that there is a "magical number seven plus or minus two" that describes our capacities for immediate recall of unrelated items of information, five to nine items of such information is what most people can handle.

There are of course ways around this limitation in our capacities. We can engage in repetition and memorization of the information presented (Ebbinghaus, 1885), and we can organize information in units or groups, so-called chunks (Miller, 1956), that are more easily recalled than individual items. We can also train our short-term (or working) memory capacities. As most other human capacities, people can excel if they practice a particular skill over time, and in this case, this implies that their performance on working memory tests increases, while these improvements do not appear to have any other significant effects on people's minds. As Melby-Lervår and Hulme (2013, p. 470) conclude in their meta-analysis of research, "memory training programs appear to produce short-term, specific training effects that do not generalize" to other intellectual capacities.

However, there is another obvious way around these limitations in "processing capacities" to use Miller's language: we invent technologies. The technology which revolutionized our capacities for remembering is writing. As a technology, writing implies that we document information outside the human body by using inscriptions on material objects. When we want to retain and recall information, we turn to the inscriptions—numbers, images, abstract symbols or whatever—and they serve as resources for recalling what we otherwise may forget. Use of inscriptions by humans goes a long way back in history, about 100 000 years according to recent archeological research (d'Errico et al., 2012). However, the earliest predecessors of what we now refer to as writing appeared in Mesopotamia in present-day Iraq and surrounding areas. The first inscriptions resembling written language were made on clay plates, and they were used in trade and social administration where they served as receipts, lists and registers by means of which transactions and other significant activities were documented (Schmandt-Besserat, 1989). Through the uses of such clay tokens with increasingly specified inscriptions in the cuneiform script appearing about 5 000 years ago, the burden of remembering no longer was on the human mind; it had been partially externalized, and remembering was now something that people did in collaboration with a material cultural tool. Through this invention, one of the most important in the history of human cognitive capacities, there were no longer any limits to how much information that could be retained in society. Material artifacts with inscriptions as repositories of information show few of the weaknesses that characterize the human mind when it comes to the specific problem of preserving information and extending the cultural memory.

In a sociocultural perspective, what we see in developments of this kind exemplifies the intimate ties between materiality and thinking, and between societal transformations and individual development. A material artifact, a clay token, a paper roll or a book, is designed, and when it is integrated into the flow of human activities, it begins to function as what Vygotsky refers to as a cultural tool. The cultural tool, thus, is both physical and "ideational" (Cole, 1996; Leontiev, 1972) in the sense that it involves the uses of signs that mediate information, insights and experiences of cultural communities; it serves as a material source for meaning-making that is integral to thinking, communicating, problem-solving and many other forms of social action.

Following the emergence of increasingly sophisticated technologies of writing and systems of documentation, new "memory practices" (Mäkitalo et al., 2017) emerged in society. The generic element of these new ways of remembering and organizing information is the increasing use of texts as cultural tools or as a "symbolic technology" as Donald (2010) puts it. All symbolic technologies involve the use of inscriptions (from rocks, clay tablets and parchment rolls to books and multi-media representations in recent digital documentation systems). One interesting point when we address issues of remembering and memory practices is that such artificial resources require adaptation of the human mind. Remembering as a "natural process" in Vygotskian terms, and without the use of material documentation, is a very different practice from remembering in coordination with cultural tools. In the latter case, systematic instruction, which may extend over years, is often a necessary preparation to become a competent user of the tool. Writing systems are human inventions and are very diverse in their design across cultures and societies. To read one has to be familiar with a range of conventions that have been integrated into the use of the tool. Scripts, the graphic form a writing system, differ with respect to the specific manner in which signs are written (alphabets, logo-graphic writing, syllabaries, etc.) (Coulmas, 1989), and learning how language is mediated in visuographic form takes time and requires training. Writing, in the sense of producing a message in an expected form, is an even more complex activity, which requires awareness of several features of language use such as vocabulary, grammar and expected genres of expression in relation to different audiences.

These uniquely human forms of communication thus rely on a particular combination of materiality and intent sign-making, and the cultural tool integrates both elements. Intent sign-making, in turn, is both a collective and an individual activity. As Barton and Hamilton point out (1999, p. 799), engaging in reading and writing is an internal, psychological activity, and, at the same, "writing is 'out there'; it exists along with other social artifacts of culture, and forms part of a broader social context." This dual character of the cultural tool implies that it serves many different functions such as documentation of events, communication with other people and as a tool for thinking and regulating one's own activities. In complex societies, cultural tools that rely on writing eventually become highly differentiated as they are integrated into different activities and institutions. Reading a diagram, a chemical formula or a table may require extensive training in order to understand how signs are to be used in expected manners.

Thus, there may be something disruptive in the reproduction of the cultural memory when new cultural tools become widely used. The invention of writing in Mesopotamia some 5 000 years ago resulted in the emergence of schools where systematic training of the intellect through instruction took place (Kramer, 1963). The impact of writing on the ancient Greek society illustrates another change from a predominantly oral culture to a society where literacy came to play an increasingly important role for institutions, such as science, education and philosophy, but also for daily life (Thomas, 2001). The literacy campaigns of the seventeenth and eighteenth centuries, including the introduction of mass education that followed the impact of book printing and the widespread circulation of books in Europe, is another example of how a disruptive technology was handled through major social and economic investments, affecting the daily lives of entire populations of nation-states and the access to knowledge and information of citizens. Again, the cultural tool of texts had collective/societal as well as individual/cognitive consequences.

In contemporary society, there is a wealth of cultural tools emerging in the wake of digitization, and some of these may be seen as having disruptive qualities. Even though many of the daily practices we engage in are literate in the sense that we read, write and manipulate information, other elements take us beyond traditional modes of engaging with text and other symbolic technologies. Search engines allow us to scan millions of documents in the flash of a second, and there is a wealth of "cognitive amplifiers" (Nickerson, 2005) that support our intellectual practices: calculators, digital dictionaries, word processors, spell and grammar checks, book-keeping software, pedometers and a world of apps supporting all kinds of tasks. The number of such resources is currently expanding rapidly, and they are becoming increasingly sophisticated in the wake of AI. Thus, a text or a printed table may be thought of as storing information, but digital documentation makes way for added affordances. The digital version of tables in spreadsheets makes it possible to organize, analyze and cross-tabulate information in complex ways, it is a tool to think with. It also facilitates specific forms of hypothetical thinking that Campbell-Kelly (2003) refers to as "what if" questions: What happens at the bottom of the table, if we insert another number in a specific cell? If we speculate that the interest on our mortgage will go up by half-a-percent, what will that imply for the future? Our capacities for considering alternatives and for hypothetical thinking about the future increase dramatically when we integrate such powerful cultural tools into our everyday activities.

3.3 Digital Tools and Developmental Trajectories of Children

It testifies to the depth of his theorizing that Vygotsky realized how the introduction of novel cultural tools may transform our capacities to think and to manipulate the world in symbolic terms. To use Vygoskian language, the emergence of new cultural tools in society may imply new forms of mediation that in turn will have consequences for how we think and how activities in society will be organized (Vygotsky, 1978). The map, the microscope and the abacus are powerful tools in different practices, but their use requires extensive adaptation through instruction and systematic training (Veraksa, 2014). A corollary of this insight is that the human mind operates in "*multiple mergers and coalitions*" (Clark, 2003, p. 7, italics in original) with external resources. Our mind is not a stand-alone device, but rather better conceived as a "hybrid mind" (Donald, 2018), flexibly coupled with dynamically evolving and increasingly sophisticated cultural tools.

Given this perspective on the inter-connectedness of minds and cultural tools, it is obvious that, today, children in many parts of the world become familiar with digital devices at a very early age, in fact before they can talk and long before they can read (see below). Tablets, smartphones and computers are physically present in the child's environment as everyday objects, i.e., as something they learn to recognize, relate to and, quite often, they trigger their curiosity. A reasonable question to ask is how these changes in the daily practices of children are to be conceptualized within a Vygotskian and sociocultural perspective recognizing the hybridity of our cognitive capacities. Are the forms of mediation introduced by digital tools significantly different from those characterizing print technology to substantiate claims that our accounts of development have to be modified? To answer this question, one has to take into account both the material and ideational side of the artifacts, and, in addition, consider the role they play in children's lives and what kinds of activities they mediate.

First, it should be noted that the materiality of such digital devices plays a significant role in broadening of the range of activities that children encounter and participate in in contemporary society. The introduction of the tablet around 2010, and the widespread use of it, implied major changes in terms of how children have access to information and experiences. Important technological/material elements of this remediation are innovations such as the touch screen, apps and constant connectivity. Thus, with a tablet it is no longer necessary to go through complicated procedures of logging on. The tablet connects to the Internet through the wifi as soon as it is turned on in the home. The combination of the touch screen and the app implies that a user can engage in a range of activities without being able to read in the traditional sense. Access to film clips, songs and other activities that children enjoy easily follows in this environment, and the role of adult assistance for these first steps into virtual activities is also limited. By using the app, the child enters a virtual world to be explored and enjoyed. As an example, YouTube, one of the most frequently used apps among young children (Statens Medieråd, 2019), quickly becomes a digital environment where children learn to navigate and find activities that interest them.

Second, children's engagement with the "ideational side" of the cultural tool implies that this link between the child and the artifact becomes a space where "higher psychological functions" (Vygotsky, 1977, 1978) such as thinking, symbol use, attention, voluntary memory and even self-regulation develop. It is obvious that children early on engage in practices that have the character of proto-reading. They learn to recognize symbols and patterns, and their search for activities is regulated by skills emerging in, and to some extent specific to, this environment. From an empirical point of view, it is interesting to explore the multitude of zones of proximal development (ZPDs) that characterize such settings, where children obviously will be acting on the edge of their capacities, and where they probably sometimes seek support from a more experienced person such as a sibling or adult to accomplish a task. Volitional activities and planning will also be constituents of engaging with digital tools. The interactivity of the cultural tool and the richness of the resources available make it necessary to develop strategies for how to navigate between activities in order to find objects of interest. Selectivity is an important element of engagement with the digitally mediated experiences. Somewhat later, and when the child begins to use digital devices for communicating with others by, sending messages, pictures and film clips, a range of higher psychological processes will emerge through such practices.

3.4 Trajectories of Participation in Digitally Mediated Practices

The pace of these social transformations, where children act as participants in digitally mediated activities, is very high as is evident from research in many countries (cf. e.g., UNICEF, 2019). One of the interesting observations is how Internet use is becoming a frequent element in the lives of even very young children. Using Sweden as a case in point, the proportion of children up to one year of age using the Internet has gone up dramatically during recent years. In the studies carried out until a few years ago (Statens Medieråd, 2019, p. 6), the youngest group included in studies of Internet use was two to four years of age. But, following observations from parents reporting that children younger than one year of age were using tablets, a new age category, 0–1 year, had to be included to reflect the impact of the Internet. In 2019, about 50% of the one-year-olds and between 75 and 80% of the two-year-olds were active on the Internet. It is now quite common to see infants, in fact babies, sitting in their strollers holding a smartphone while watching popular film clips of Babblarna and other children's comics or listening to nursery rhymes as their parents take them for a walk. At four years of age, 95% of the children use the Internet, at least occasionally (Statens Medieråd, 2019, pp. 11, 26; cf. Internetstiftelsen i Sverige, 2019).

Looking at the nature of activities that infants and children engage in, there appears to be a learning trajectory that is interesting from a sociocultural perspective. The earliest activities involve watching film clips, listening to music and playing games. Somewhat later, infants begin to use smartphones and tablets for activities such as taking photos, drawing, texting, creating personal contents and communicating with friends and relatives. From the age of six, when literacy skills increase, children begin to visit social media and communicate with friends and relatives via websites in addition to maintaining some of their earlier habits (watching clips, gaming) (Internetstiftelsen i Sverige, 2019). What is also interesting is that activities such as searching for information and using the Internet for doing school work emerge as important at about this age (six years and onwards). About 60% of children report engaging in activities of this kind. This implies that children learn to seek information when there is something they do not know or understand. Such practices, we may assume, have implications for how children think and engage in problem-solving in various settings.

In relation to our understanding of child development, it is thus interesting to take into account observations of this kind that concerns time, frequency and the nature of tasks that young children engage in in contemporary society. Children are introduced to digital devices at an early age and this takes place in the home. The latter observation indicates that the technology is an integrated part of family life. With age, the proportion of children using digital devices increases, and the proportion who uses them every day also increases. In addition, there seems to be a trajectory where children engage in increasingly diverse activities as they grow older and many end up in different social media communicating with their friends and absent family as they learn to read and write.

3.5 Digital Media and the Social Situation of Development

This evolution of children's daily practices at home and in preschools and early schooling is contingent on the availability of, and engagement with, digital artifacts. And, as we have argued, these devices have the character of cultural tools with specific physical and ideational elements in the sociocultural sense. This implies that they are not just technologies in a mechanical sense. Children inhabit a world in which they lead digital lives, and where they develop knowledge, skills and even identities. It is therefore better to think of these digital devices as digital media rather than as technologies (Lundtofte et al., 2021). In fact, many of the technological elements of the tools are hidden for the users, they are "blackboxed" as Latour (1999) puts it.

The observations reported above indicate that children meet these media in their home, they spend time using them from an early age and, as they grow, the nature of activities they engage in become increasingly diverse: watching film clips, playing, communicating and so on. They also begin to participate in communities that are separate from their families and other people they meet physically. In addition, digital media allow for both reception and production of messages in communicative encounters at an early age. One can produce film clips or drawings or take photos of activities and send them to friends and relatives with a specific communicative intent. Digital media thus become a sphere of social action and engagement is a way of living, we are not talking about a technical object.

Following the Vygotskian perspective on learning and development, the role of these cultural tools should not be seen as one that merely impacts on the child and his or her cognitive growth. Instead, at the heart of this theorizing lies the assumption that the "dual process of shaping and being shaped through culture implies that humans inhabit 'intentional' (constituted) worlds within which the traditional dichotomies of subject and object, person and environment, and so on cannot be analytically separated and temporally ordered into independent and dependent variables" (Cole, 1996, p. 103). Thus, there is no sharp line separating the cultural tool and the individual, nor is there any cause and effect relationship between them. Rather, it "is through tool use that individual/psychological and cultural/historical processes become intervowen and co-create each other" (Daniels, 2011, p. 21) in daily practices.

In order to analyze and theorize the role of cultural tools in children's activities, it is essential to consider Vygotsky's emphasis on what he referred to as the "social situation of development" (cf. Bozhovich, 2009, p. 66). The social situation of development points to the concrete social circumstances and relationships where children make experiences and learn to relate to others and to cultural tools within emotionally charged joint activities. Thus, the assumption is that the child is not a victim of his social environment but rather develops by actively engaging in practices that trigger interest and curiosity. As Karabanova (2010, p. 132) points out, when attempting to understand "development we have to define the meaning of surroundings to the child, child's attitude toward different sides of his surrounding, in other words, we have to expose the active-effective position of a child as regards his surroundings."

It follows from this perspective that the social situation of development is part of the child's lifeworld and a context where he or she engages in meaning-making. The social situation is not static, it will change as societies change and as new cultural tools and new activities emerge and begin to play a role in children's lives. In a historical perspective, the introduction of children's books, radio and television implied that the social situation changed with respect to the activities that children would participate in. Listening to a book being read by a parent, to a children's story on the radio or watching television are activities that have modified the social situation of development. Discussing the details or the gist of a bedtime story with an adult on a regular basis has consequences for the way in which children learn to understand and engage in "ways of taking" meaning from texts as the American anthropologist Shirley Brice Heath (1982, 1983) shows in her explorations of reading cultures in local communities. In her research on "literacy events" (1982, p. 50) that children engage in with their parents, some children were encouraged to articulate their understandings and their interests in relation to texts, while other children were not expected to do so. Thus, some children were encouraged to develop "mastery," in the sociocultural sense, of how signs are used, and what the expected and relevant reactions are. It is also reasonable to assume that such encounters with literature and other media under adult guidance create an interest in these kinds of literate and media experiences. The book or the television becomes a cultural tool that has implications for children's abilities to know about the world and to be involved in an emotional and affective sense; they are part of activities in which children appropriate "signs" (in the Vygotskian sense) that will have implications for their mastery of cognitive processes (Kravtsova et al., 2018). At the same time, and as we have alluded to, adult involvement and guidance of children may be very different in the case of digital media when compared to book reading.

As we have argued in this chapter, young children's lives have been infiltrated by digital media, and children spend considerable time using such cultural tools and the activities they afford. The consequences of these developments are ambiguous. As Veraksa et al. (2021) point out after extensive analyses in Russian settings, there is a dramatic change in the social situation of development in the sense that the use of a digital device without an adult is about one day a week. From a developmental point of view, Veraksa et al. continue, this raises questions of what happens in a child's development when interaction with an adult is replaced by interaction with a digial device. Thus, if the time adults and children spend in interaction in the social situation is reduced, this represents a shift in the extent to which the child will operate under adult guidance in developmental situations. On the other hand, it may well be that extensive engagement with such cultural tools implies that the child has access to a larger community of adults (absent family, grandparents) on a daily basis and at their own initiative. In the latter case, the child's ability to seek information and help in social situations of development will increase, as more conversation partners are available. It may also be that the presence of digital media in the family will increase joint activities when it comes to watching movies, playing games and organizing daily practices.

In our opinion, the observation that children engage in wide range of activities where digitized cultural tools play a central role, and that they do so more or less on a daily basis, raises important issues that have to be investigated through empirical research. If we agree with Vygotsky's claim that a cultural tool "abolishes and makes unnecessary natural processes," the cultural tools children encounter today, and that allow them to participate in practices to which earlier generations of children did not have access, represent interesting challenges for developmental research in the sense that there are many significant trajectories of learning to explore. At the level of history of ideas, the observation that the sociocultural perspective gives us a productive platform for pursuing such analyses testifies to the power of Vygotsky's intellectual achievements.

References

Barton, D., & Hamilton, M. (1999). Social and cognitive factors in the historical elaboration of writing. In A. Lock & C. R. Peters (Eds.), *Handbook of symbolic evolution* (pp. 793–858). Blackwell.

Bozhovich, L. I. (2009). The social situation of child development. *Journal of Russian & East European Psychology, 47*(4), 59–86. https://doi.org/10.2753/RPO1061-0405470403

Bruner, J. (1997). Celebrating divergence: Piaget and Vygotsky. *Human Development, 40*(2), 63–73.

Campbell-Kelly, M. (2003). The rise and rise of the spreadsheet. In M. Campbell-Kelly, R. Croarken, R. Flood, & E. Robson (Eds.), *The history of mathematical tables* (pp. 323–347). Oxford University Press.

Clark, A. (2003). *Natural-born cyborgs: Minds, technologies, and the future of human intelligence.* Oxford University Press.

Cole, M. (1996). *Cultural psychology: A once and future discipline.* The Belknap Press.

Coulmas, F. (1989). *The writing systems of the world.* Blackwell.

d'Errico, F., García Moreno, R., & Rifkin, R. F. (2012). Technological, elemental and colorimetric analysis of an engraved ochre fragment from the Middle Stone Age levels of Klasies River Cave 1, South Africa. *Journal of Archaeological Science, 39*(4), 943–952. https://doi.org/10.1016/j.jas.2011.10.032

Daniels, H. (2011). The shaping of communication across boundaries. *International Journal of Educational Research, 50*(1), 40–47.

Donald, M. (2010). The exographic revolution: Neuropsychological sequelae. In L. Malafouris & C. Renfrew (Eds.), *The cognitive life of things: Recasting the boundaries of mind* (pp. 71–80). The McDonald Institute for Archaeological Research, University of Cambridge.

Donald, M. (2018). The evolutionary origins of human cultural memory. In B. Wagoner (Ed.), *Handbook of culture and memory* (pp. 19–40). Oxford University Press.

Ebbinghaus, H. (1885). *Über das Gedächtnis: Untersuchungen zur experimentellen Psychologie* [On memory: Studies in experimental psychology]. Duncker & Humblot.

Heath, S. B. (1982). What no bedtime story means: Narrative skills at home and school. *Language in Society, 11*(1), 49–76.

Heath, S. B. (1983). *Ways with words: Language, life, and work in communities and classrooms.* Cambridge University Press.

Internetstiftelsen i Sverige. (2019). *Barnen och internet* [The children and Internet]. https://svenskarnaochinternet.se/rapporter/barnen-och-internet-2019

Karabanova, O. (2010). Social situation of child's development—The key concept in modern developmental psychology. *Psychology in Russia: State of the Art, 3*, 130–153.

Kravtsova, E., Veraksa, N., & Veresov, N. (2018). Contemporary research in early childhood: Roots and perspectives. In M. Fleer, B. van Oers B. (Eds.), *International handbook of early childhood education*. Springer. https://doi.org/10.1007/978-94-024-0927-7_18

Kramer, S. N. (1963). *The Sumerians: Their history, culture, and character*. University of Chicago Press.

Latour, B. (1999). *Pandora's hope: An essay on the reality of science studies*. Harvard University Press.

Leontiev, A. N. (1972). *Problems of the development of the psyche*. Moscow University Press.

Lundtofte, T. E., Odgaard, A. B., & Drotner, K. (2021). Making digital play work: Danish children's playful and creative production with digital media. In K. Kumpulainen, A. Kajamaa, O. Erstad, Å. Mäkitalo, K. Drotner, & S. Jakobsdottir (Eds.), *Nordic childhoods in the digital age: Insights into contemporary research on communication, learning and education*. Routledge.

Mäkitalo, Å., Linell, P., & Säljö, R. (Eds.). (2017). *Memory practices and learning. Interactional, institutional and sociocultural perspectives*. IAP.

Malafouris, L. (2013). *How things shape the mind. A theory of material engagement*. MIT Press.

Melby-Lervåg, M., & Hulme, C. (2013). Is working memory training effective? A meta-analytic review. *Developmental Psychology, 49*(2), 270–291. https://doi.org/10.1037/a0028228

Miller, G. A. (1956). The magical number seven, plus or minus two: Some limits on our capacity to process information. *Psychological Review, 63*, 81–97.

Müller, U., Ten Eycke, K., & Baker, L. (2015). Piaget's theory of intelligence. In S. Goldstein, D. Princiotta, & J. A. Naglier (Eds.), *Handbook of intelligence. Evolutionary theory, historical perspective, and current concepts* (pp. 137–151). Springer.

Nickerson, R. S. (2005). Technology and cognition amplification. In R. J. Sternberg & D. D. Preiss (Eds.), *Intelligence and technology: The impact of tools on the nature and development of human abilities*. (pp. 3–27). Erlbaum.

Piaget, J. (1970). Piaget's theory. In P. H. Mussen (Ed.), *Manual of child psychology* (pp. 703–732). Wiley.

Piaget, J. (1973). *The child's conception of the world*. Paladin.

Piaget, J., & Inhelder, B. (1971). *Mental imagery in the child*. Basic Books.

Schmandt-Besserat, D. (1989). Two precursors of writing: Plain and complex tokens. In W. M. Senner (Ed.), *The origins of writing* (pp. 27–42). University of Nebraska Press.

Statens Medieråd. (2019). *Småungar och medier* [Kids and media]. https://statensmedierad.se/publikationer/ungarochmedier/ungarochmedier2019.3347.html

Thomas, R. (2001). Literacy in ancient Greece: Functional literacy, oral education, and the development of a literate environment. In D. R. Olson & N. Torrance (Eds.), *The making of literate societies* (pp. 68–81). Blackwell.

UNICEF. (2019). *Growing up in a connected world in*. https://www.unicef-irc.org/growing-up-connected

Veraksa, N. (2014). Modern trends in early childhood education development in the natural vs cultural paradigm. *European Early Childhood Education Research Journal, 22*(5), 585–589.

Veraksa, A. N., Kornienko, D. S., Chichinina, E. A., Bukhalenkova, D. A., & Chursina, A. V. (2021). Correlations between preschoolers' screen time with gender, age and socio-economic background of the families. *The Art and Science of Television, 17*(3), 179–209. https://doi.org/10.30628/1994-9529-17.3-179-209

Vygotsky, L. S. (1977). The development of higher psychological functions. *Soviet Psychology, 15*(3), 60–73. https://doi.org/10.2753/RPO1061-0405150360

Vygotsky, L. S. (1978). *Mind in society: The development of higher psychological processes*. Harvard University Press.

Vygotsky, L. S. (1981). The instrumental method in psychology. In J. V. Wertsch (Ed.), *The concept of activity in Soviet psychology* (pp. 134–143). M. E. Sharpe.

Roger Säljö, Ph. D., Dr. h. c. mult., is Professor of Educational Psychology and specializes in research on learning, interaction, and human development in a sociocultural perspective, where he has published extensively. Much of this work is related to issues of how people learn to use cultural tools, and how we acquire competencies and skills that are foundational to learning in a socially and technologically complex society. He was Director of the Linnaeus Centre for Research on Learning, Interaction, and Mediated Communication in Contemporary Society (LinCS), a national center of excellence funded by the Swedish Research Council (2006–2018). He has been a Finland Distinguished Professor (FiDiPro) at the Centre for Learning Research at the University of Turku, Finland. Previously, he has been Visiting Professor at a number of universities, including Universität Konstanz, University of California San Diego, Rijksuniversiteit Utrecht, University of Oslo, Georg-August-Universität Göttingen, University of Agder, and University of Stavanger. He has supervised 52 students to their Ph.D. degrees at six different faculties.

Åsa Mäkitalo is Professor of Workplace Learning at the University of Oslo and part-time Professor of Education at the University of Gothenburg, where she currently pursues research on how digitalization transforms institutional practices with consequences in terms of conditions for learning, communication, and societal participation. Mäkitalo has extensive experience of interdisciplinary research leadership. From 2006 to 2018, she was a co-director of LinCS, a CoE in Research on Learning and IT. From 2010 to 2020, she established and coordinated the University of Gothenburg LETStudio, conducting interdisciplinary research on how technologies are intertwined in core activities in society with a focus on knowledge and learning practices. Her international publications amounts to about 30 peer-reviewed articles 35 book chapters and 65 conference presentations. Recent edited volumes include Memory practices and learning—interactional, institutional, and sociocultural perspectives. (2017) Information Age Publishing, and Designs for digital experimentation and inquiry. Approaching learning and knowing in digital transformation (2019), Routledge.

Chapter 4
Dialectical Thinking

Nikolay Veraksa⊙ and Michael Basseches

Abstract Lev Vygotsky noted that "all scientific thinking moves by dialectics." In works of Vygotsky, it manifests itself in contrasting fragments of content as opposites, in analyzing paradoxes, in identifying contradictions, in direct references to dialectics, in explaining with the help of its laws, and in pointing to dialectical logic.

The study of dialectical thinking as a special form of mental activity begun in the 1980s. Relations of the opposites were chosen as units of the analysis of dialectical thinking. They began to mean any content that could be mutually exclusive. It has been shown that opposites can relate to each other in different ways. The subject can make transformations of the opposites mentally, and then they act as dialectical mental actions that allow creative solutions of problems. Various dialectical actions were revealed: transformation, mediation, seriation, etc., which are organized into structures that can be described in the language of mathematics.

The development of dialectical thinking is seen as the formation of a mechanism for operating opposites. The first manifestations of dialectical thinking are associated with the development of figurative anticipation and the transformation of conflicting problem situations in preschool age. At primary school age, there is a restructuring of the mechanism of dialectical thinking, associated with the transition to the dominance of symbolic reflection of objects, which is manifested in a decrease in the success of solving dialectic problems by younger school children in comparison with children of preschool age. By older school age, the development of the mechanism of dialectical thinking is observed with the prevalence of a sign form reflecting the problem situation and the use of such actions as identification and closure. However, even in adult subjects, the mechanism of dialectical thinking is not fully formed.

N. Veraksa (✉)
Faculty of Psychology, Lomonosov Moscow State University, Moscow, Russia
e-mail: neveraksa@gmail.com

Psychological Institute, Russian Academy of Education, Moscow, Russia

M. Basseches
Suffolk University, Boston, MA, USA

This chapter shows that Lev Vygotsky and Jean Piaget used the dialectical method. In addition, we set the task to show the similarity of dialectical transformations that preschoolers make and which are presented in the works of Vygotsky and Piaget.

Dialectical thinking is of a cultural nature and is modeled in folk tales among various peoples. This indicates that dialectical thinking is addressed not only to adults, but also to young children. We have developed methods that made it possible to measure the ability of children to solve typical dialectical problems, such as creating a new one based on the example of constructing an original graphic image, resolving contradictions and understanding the simplest developmental processes. As the studies have shown, the solution of these problems is available to preschool children and is in the zone of proximal development.

Chapter focuses on how research on dialectical thinking founded in the work of Vygotsky and Piaget can be integrated, and the potential of bringing them together for informing early childhood development and preschool education.

4.1 Introduction

The task that we had in mind while writing the following chapter was not only to introduce the notion of dialectical thinking by J.Piaget and L.S. Vygotsky to the readers, but to show the similarity of their views on this issue as well.

Recognizing the existence of dialectical processes in nature and society calls for their adequate reflection in human thought, and thus, the problem of dialectical thinking needs to be formulated. The main difficulty is to distinguish the mechanisms of dialectical thinking against the background of the diverse content processed by consciousness. It should be noted that both Vygotsky and Piaget reflected on the dialectic nature of developmental processes. Piaget wrote: "…dialectical processes can be observed at all levels of both thinking and activity, in all situations where there is a need to construct new forms… dialectics is a logical derivative of all equilibration processes, while the balanced systems themselves leave room only for logical inferences. Hence the constant alternation, but with periods of various lengths between these two phases—dialectical construction and logical analysis" (Piaget, 1982).

Vygotsky pointedly wrote: "We are dialecticians." He emphasized that dialectical psychology should become aware of its own evolution and not abandon the "legacy" (1982a, p. 427) of other psychologists; that "all the truly scientific thinking moves through dialectics" (Vygotsky, 1983, p. 37) and "that the only legitimate application of Marxism to psychology would be the creation of a general psychology— its concepts directly depend on the general dialectics, for it is the dialectics of psychology…" (Vygotsky, 1982a, p. 419).

Piaget was certainly familiar with the dialectical method in the version used in Soviet psychology. Thus, Rolando García in his interview told how he introduced Piaget to Lenin's Philosophical Notebooks: "And there Lenin says: in order to build a theory of knowledge, you must first look at how a child constructs his idea of the world and then how science constructs its own ideas. So, I said to Piaget: look, Piaget is in front of you" (García, 2001, p. 3).

García also emphasized that in the third volume of "Introduction to Genetic Epistemology" (1950) there is a fundamental work "Different meanings of the concept of social totality." "Here Piaget makes a direct reference to Marx, to the organic concept of Marx. He did not repeat this again. I have never seen this work cited, but it is a very fundamental work. Piaget knew Marx's position very well" (García, 2001, p. 15).

In the book, published under the editorship of K.F. Rigel and G.K. Rosenward, famous American experts in the field of dialectical thinking, one of the chapters was devoted to the analysis of the dialectical method. It compared in detail the methodological foundations of the views of Soviet psychologists and Piaget's concept of the cognitive development of a child. The authors of the book concluded that, despite the differences between these approaches, they use a similar method, based on common structural foundations: "Differences of this kind should be sharply distinguished, however, from much of what is common to Piaget and the materialist dialectic approach underlying Soviet psychology" (Riegel & Rosenwald, 1975, p. 45).

The similarity of the positions of Piaget and Vygotsky manifested itself in the attitude of these thinkers to Plato. Garcia noted that he gave examples "in which Piaget is accused of Platonism" (García, 2001, p. 6).

At the lectures that D.B. Elkonin introduced at the Faculty of Psychology of Lomonosov Moscow State University, he said that Vygotsky was also actually criticized for his penchant for Platonism, since his explanations of child development included the interaction of the higher (ideal) and primary forms of consciousness.

At the same time, Vygotsky warned that dialectical materialism "is the most abstract science. The direct application of dialectical materialism to biological sciences and psychology, as is the case now, does not go beyond formal logical, scholastic, verbal classifications under general, abstract, universal categories of particular phenomena with unknown inner meaning and correlation" (1982a, pp. 420–421). What is said here is that dialectics can be applied in psychology both dialectically and metaphysically. That's what J.P. Sartre wrote about later, expressing a negative view on the scholastical use of dialectics: "The separation of theory and practice turned practice into ungrounded empiricism, and theory into frozen pure knowledge" (Sartre, 1993, p. 22).

The dialectical method has turned into a reproductive description of processes that follows the results instead of anticipating them. The formal, scholastic application of the dialectical method is a negative characteristic not of the method itself, but of those who applied it ineffectually. Perhaps this circumstance makes the problem of dialectical thinking less attractive yet does not cancel it.

We assumed that the mechanism of dialectical thinking includes ways of operating the opposite relations. It is the opposites that are the units of dialectical thinking and not the specific content to which they are implicitly inherent. This does not mean that dialectical thinking is substanceless and is reduced only to operating opposites, but the latter is, in our opinion, its characteristic, distinctive feature. The analysis of opposites as the invariants of dialectical thinking made it possible to define its psychological specificity: as thinking focused on the antithetic relationships.

The outlined approach made it possible to distinguish between formal and dialectical thinking and allowed to search for and identify invariant dialectical transformations. They were called dialectical thinking operations on the basis that each transformation has its own direction and can be associated with a certain invariant dialectical goal.

Due to limitations, the following dialectical thinking operations were considered: "transformation," "unification," "mediation," "seriation," and "conversion."

The thinking operation "transformation" is based on the fact that there are two opposites, and thus each of them has its own opposite. Therefore, the "transformation" operation is a mental transformation of the initial situation into a situation with the opposite meaning. The transformation contains a rip within itself. It records a "leap" from one extreme state to another. Each of the extreme states is the opposite of the other. This operation does not involve the consideration of transitional moments of changing situation. Let us denote symbols A and B as the opposite states of the situation or simply opposites, symbols AB and BA—as transitional states. The scheme of the operation is shown in Fig. 4.1.

Yet, another operation of dialectical thinking is what we call "unification." It reveals mutually exclusive properties, features, tendencies, etc., within a situation. The following formula can express the universal scheme underlying this operation: any unity is a relationship of mutually exclusive opposites. A scheme of this operation is shown in Fig. 4.2.

The third dialectical operation was called dialectical mediation. It seeks to find a unity within which opposites could coexist. A scheme of this operation is shown in Fig. 4.3.

Fig. 4.1 Scheme of the dialectical thinking operation of "transformation."

Fig. 4.2 Scheme of the dialectical thinking operation of "unification."

Fig. 4.3. Scheme of the dialectical thinking operation of "mediation."

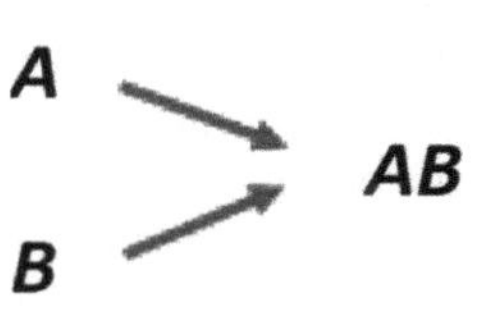

$$A \longrightarrow AB \longrightarrow B.$$

Fig. 4.4 Scheme of the dialectical thinking operation of "seriation."

$$B \longrightarrow BA \longrightarrow A$$

Fig. 4.5 Scheme of the dialectical thinking operation of "conversion."

There is also operation of dialectical seriation. The subject mentally imagines how one opposite gradually turns into another: not at once, but through a transitional state. A scheme of this operation is shown in Fig. 4.4.

The operation, which we call conversion, is basically a seriation, but performed in the opposite direction, i.e., the events are sequentialized starting from the opposite that was previously the endpoint. A scheme of this operation is shown in Fig. 4.5.

These operations are interconnected by the dialectical structural relations.

Let us note one of the essential features of dialectical thinking operations, which is that dialectical thinking is not isolated within itself, it keeps constantly turning to practical experience, to specific content reflected in ideas and concepts. Although dialectical operations are defined in a relatively abstract way as transformations of opposites, the opposites themselves exist as concrete contents entering into antithetic relations. Thus, the subject performing one of the dialectical thinking operations uses two perspectives simultaneously: the concrete one, since he takes into account the fragments of the content that have entered into a relationship of contraposition, and the abstract one, i.e., the intended transformations of this content.

In terms of dialectical thinking, we must distinguish between at least three things:

1. the dialectical thinking itself;
2. the developmental processes taking place in our surrounding reality;
3. the processes of development of the psyche as a whole and specific mental function, including perception, memory, attention, thinking, imagination, etc. All these processes can be expressly dialectical, but the dialectic nature of a process is not the same as a process of dialectical thinking. The fundamental feature of dialectical thinking is that it is arbitrary, deals with the opposites and is aimed at solving a dialectical problem. Unlike the process of solving a dialectical problem, any other process of objective or subjective character, albeit dialectical, is not regulated by the subject.

4.2   Dialectical Thinking as a Cultural Phenomenon

V.P. Alekseev, an anthropologist and historian, emphasized that irrationalism could not prevail in a primitive society: "an elementary analysis of the sphere of consciousness that encompasses empirical experience shows that this is a sphere of pure logic both in a primitive man, and in man of the developed modern society; so, within it, neither irrationalism nor associations based on seeming connections instead of real ones are not possible, otherwise empirical experience immediately ceases to be what it is, namely, a powerful stimulus for progress. Empirical observations, if interpreted irrationally, immediately plunge any primitive collective into the abyss of disasters and automatically exclude the possibility of its further development" (Alekseev, 1984, p. 244).

Therefore, according to Alekseev, humanity has been constantly facing developmental processes that determined its interaction with the outside world. In that case, an adequate form of thinking (that allowed to reflect the dynamic processes of transformation of objects, phenomena, and situations) should have been present from the very beginning of any social collective's cultural formation.

In view of this, it is logical to assume that dialectical thinking would be represented not only in classical philosophical works, but also in folk culture. To this end, we examined folklore, in particular, folktales. We assumed that in the folktales of peoples of the world, we would find structural constructions corresponding to the schemes of operations with opposites. Since folktales are linked to mythological tradition, and as Ya.Golosovker (1987) showed, the dialectics of myth corresponds to the logic of scientific discovery in some cases—then, with a high probability, one can expect similarities between dialectical transformations reflected in myths and folktales and the ones involved in scientific process.

So, as already outlined, the operation of dialectical unification is one of the dialectical transformations. It aims to establish mutually exclusive, opposite properties in an object. It was discovered that this operation underlies the folktale plot in a number of ethnic groups. The plot schema is in many cases just a way to illustrate the unification strategy. Usually in a folktale, the protagonist or another character finds some object that has mutually exclusive, opposite properties. Let us look at the Chinese folktale The Magic Pot as an example. A peasant finds a pot that makes ninety-nine copies of whatever gets into it. The greedy district governor takes the pot from the peasant, hoping to become immensely rich. But instead of wealth, he only gets trouble, as his old father falls into the pot. It is not difficult to see that the pot acts as an object which is a source both of wealth and ruin.

Not only something tangible, but also a quality or property that a person possesses can be such an object, as, for example, in the Maori folktale The Fate of Titia-i-te-Rangi about a young man who fell in love with a girl. In order to win her hand, he acquires a skill of killing men and women with his thoughts. However, while using this ability, he accidentally kills his beloved. It is characteristic that the plot of the tale is constructed precisely in such a way as to show the duality of given property. In this tale, the same unification strategy manifests.

The idea of unification is also presented in the Russian folktale about a fox. The fox asks a peasant for chickens as a reward. The peasant gives the fox a bag with dogs at the bottom and chickens on top. Thus, for the fox, the bag exhibits its opposite properties: both as a reward and as a punishment (Afanasyev, 1957). Of interest is the fact that if the man wanted to punish the fox, he could simply set the dogs on it. But in the folktale, it is precisely the idea of objects with opposite, mutually exclusive properties that is emphasized. In other words, the plots of folktales are not just built in accordance with the unification scheme, but aim directly at illustrating it.

The strategy of mediation is also expressed in folktales. The most typical example of mediation strategy is the following tale plot. A king sets tasks for a peasant. With the help of his daughter, the peasant finds the solutions. The king finds out that it was the peasant's daughter who was helping him. So he gives the most difficult task for her. In the Russian folktale The Wise Maiden, the king says: "Once your daughter is wise, let her come to me the next morning—neither on foot nor on horseback, neither naked nor dressed, neither with a gift nor empty handed" (Afanasyev, 1957, p. 247). The tale emphasizes that this is a "tricky task." Apparently, the cunning of the task, its originality lies in the nature of the requirements that a daughter must fulfill if she is smart. If we analyze the requirements, it is easy to see their contrasting character. Indeed, on foot and on a horse are opposites. In the same way, the opposites are naked and dressed, with a gift and empty handed. So the daughter must mediate these requirements, i.e., to come to the king with a gift and without a gift at the same time, and naked, and dressed, and on foot, and on horseback. Thus, this tale aims to illustrate the strategy of mediation.

This tale is found in various versions in a number of ethnic groups. In the Czech folktale The Quick-Witted Daughter, the king says to the shepherd: "So tell your daughter: if she comes to me neither on foot, nor on horseback, neither naked and nor dressed, neither by day nor at night, then I will marry her." Here, the scheme of mediation is presented similarly: the daughter needs to find a way that would meet, or rather, mediate the opposite demands. The daughter finds such a way: "So she came to the king neither at night, nor during the day, but at dawn!," "She wrapped herself in a fishing net, sat on a goat, riding on it, while stepping on the ground with her feet."

In an Italian folktale "The Inventive Girl," a king says to a fisherman's daughter: "Tomorrow you must come to me neither dressed nor undressed… and you will stay neither inside my palace nor outside." In this version of the tale, a scheme of mediation is also present: opposites are given in advance, you need to find a way to mediate them. This girl also "threw a fishing net over herself and rode a sheep to the king's palace. Arriving at the palace, she stopped the sheep so that it only half crossed the threshold of the royal hall." She then explained: "You see, I am not dressed, and one couldn't say that I am undressed, and my sheep stands neither inside nor outside your hall." Here we are interested in how the opposites "inside—outside" were mediated. The tale proposes mediation that uses a border separating what is inside from what is outside. This border is a threshold. The girl stopped at the threshold, i.e., she was both inside and outside. This is dialectical mediation. G.W.F. Hegel wrote: "The distinction of one thing from another one first lies in the border, as the middle ground between them, in which they both are and are not" (1971, p. 152). Thus, the girl from the folktale acted strictly according to Hegel. It is interesting that the tale was specifically constructed to illustrate the scheme of mediation. Analysis of this plot shows not only that it reflects dialectical mediation and models it, but also that this plot is not contingent. It is found in tales of various ethnic groups, thereby reflecting the strategy of mediation as an essential moment of dialectical thinking.

Transformation strategy is also presented in folktales. It consists in analyzing an object as its opposite. This operation is most vividly presented in the eastern folktale

"The Dragon." An evil and cunning dragon oppresses people. A brave young man goes to battle with a dragon, defeats him, and turns into a dragon himself. To defeat the dragon, he must see the dragon in himself.

For example, in some folktales plots, a poor one becomes rich, a rich one becomes poor, then they turn back. This does not just illustrate the scheme of dialectical transformation, but also emphasizes the need to analyze any state from the standpoint of transformation. There are folktales where a man turns into a woman, a woman into a man, an image into a real object, etc. This is a way to show that the most diverse opposites can transform into each other.

Folktales model both the operations of dialectical seriation and dialectical conversion. Dialectical seriation is the sequentialization of fragments of the transition process from one opposite object or state to another. As an example, we will turn to the well-known tale "The Turnip." The operation of seriation is modeled very explicitly in it. Indeed, the characters line up in a series from the largest to the smallest one, i.e., starting from one opposite (large) with a gradual transition to the other one (small).

Thus, folktales as a genre of folk culture display various dialectical thinking operations, which indicates that folktales are carriers of examples of dialectical thinking transformations. Folktales are addressed to children, which means that the use of dialectical thinking operations can be expected already in preschoolers. Traditionally, dialectical thinking was associated with three types of challenges: (1) creating an art product; (2) understanding the laws of development; (3) overcoming contradictions.

4.3   Experimental Studies on Dialectical Thinking Operations in Preschool Children

In accordance with the dialectical actions, we have developed three research methods: "Drawing an unusual tree," "Cycles," "What can be both at the same time?".

The "Drawing an unusual tree" method (Veraksa, 2006; Veraksa et al., 2021) allows to assess the child's ability to solve a creative problem. To complete it, children could apply both dialectical and non-dialectical transformations. One of the possible solutions was to use the dialectical thinking operation "transformation" to transform the object into its opposite. To complete the drawing, children were given a paper (A4 format) and a pencil. Children were given an instruction: "Draw an unusual tree, please." The test conductor did not give any additional instructions and did not comment on the drawing process. After completing the drawing, the child was asked to tell in detail what was unusual about the tree she or he had just drawn. The drawing was then considered as a result of the transformation of the image of an ordinary tree, which made it possible to analyze children's transformation strategies and to identify dialectical and non-dialectical strategies of approaching the task.

The "Cycles" (Veraksa, 2006; Veraksa et al., 2021) method evaluates children's ability to understand the simplest developmental processes. Children were offered three sets of five pictures each. Each set characterized an evolving situation. In total, three sequences were used: "Boiling water in a kettle" (Fig. 4.6), "The approach of a thunderstorm," "Dissolving sugar lumps in a glass" (see Fig. 4.7).

The child was given the task of arranging the pictures in such a way as to make a story. There could be only one correct set-up, conveying the accurate order of the situation development. Let us consider the progression of tasks for the teapot sequence. For the other two sequences, the order of tasks was similar.

As a first task, the child was asked to arrange all five pictures so that they would add up to a story (Fig. 4.8).

If the child had difficulties completing task 1, he or she was offered tasks 2 and 3. In tasks 2 and 3, the child was presented with three pictures reflecting only one

Fig. 4.6 A set of pictures corresponding to the sequence: "Boiling water in a kettle"

Fig. 4.7 Sets of pictures corresponding to the sequences: "Thunderstorm," "Dissolving sugar lumps in a glass"

Task 1. Initial arrangement of the pictures

Correct arrangement of the pictures

Fig. 4.8 The correct solution for the first task

half of the sequence (the initial or final stage), which the child also had to arrange in a way it tells a story (Fig. 4.9).

If the child still was experiencing difficulties, then he or she was given tasks 4 and 5. In tasks 4 and 5, the child was presented with two pictures from the set with the

Task 2. Initial arrangement of the pictures

Correct arrangement of the pictures

Task 3. Initial arrangement of the pictures

Correct arrangement of the pictures

Fig. 4.9 The correct solution for the tasks 2 and 3

missing middle picture. The child had to choose from the other three pictures and find the one that would correspond to the intermediate state of the process (Fig. 4.10).

The method "What can be both at the same time?" (Veraksa, 2006; Veraksa et al., 2021) is designed to assess the ability to overcome contradictions. It includes five questions that contain a conflicting pair of properties. Children were asked a question:

Task 4. Initial arrangement of the pictures

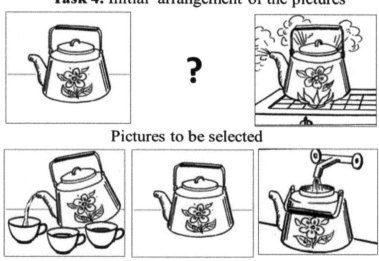

Pictures to be selected

Task 5. Initial arrangement of the pictures

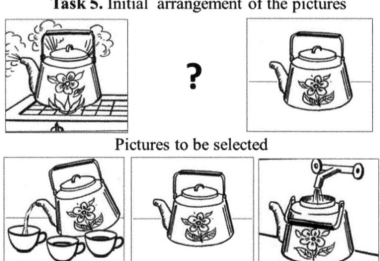

Pictures to be selected

Fig. 4.10 The arrangement of pictures in tasks 4 and 5

What can be at the same time:

black and white?
light and heavy?
big and small?
alive and inanimate?
the one and the other?

Let us consider in more detail, what mechanisms these methods are meant to identify. When analyzing the results of the "Drawing an unusual tree" test, we were primarily interested in the drawings that indicated the use of dialectical transformations. In order to draw an ordinary tree, the child must be able to perform the operation of dialectical seriation, i.e., to arrange the elements of a tree in a certain sequence:

4.3.1 ROOTS—TRUNK—CROWN

This Please confirm the section headings are correctly identified throughout the chapters sequence follows the structure of a regular tree. When a child is asked to draw an unusual tree, he or she must perform a transformation, since the word "unusual" is the opposite in meaning to the word "ordinary." If the child accepts this distinction, then we can expect a manifestation of a structural regularity in a drawing: that the transformation of the seriation would be its reversal. In this case, preschoolers would draw a tree with its crown down, roots up. Indeed, it turned out that there are preschoolers who draw inverted trees. The drawing of an inverted tree was typical (see Fig. 4.11).

So, the dialectical strategies for performing such drawings are based on spatial transformation of the tree and its fragments about the axis. In this respect, an interesting analogy with M.M. Bakhtin's analysis of carnival culture can be made (Bakhtin, 1984). Bakhtin shows that the same mechanism of swapping the "top" and "bottom" is engaged there to reflect the irregular character of what is unfolding. In addition to inverted trees, there are pictures where children turn their tree not 180, but 90 degrees. Some children change the direction in which branches grow etc (see Figs. 4.12 and 4.13). Thus, handling this task requires the operations of seriation $A \longrightarrow AB \longrightarrow B$., transformation $A \diagdown \longrightarrow B$ and conversion $B \longrightarrow BA \longrightarrow A$.

Let's look at the tasks of the "Cycles" method. In task 1, the child must arrange the pictures so that they tell a story. If we carefully analyze the correct execution of the task, it will become obvious that first, the pictures should be laid out based on seriation, then on conversion; that is, they lead back to the original state. Thus, this arrangement requires the use of two thinking operations: seriation $A \longrightarrow AB \longrightarrow B$. and Conversion $B \longrightarrow BA \longrightarrow A$.

With their help, the simplest developmental processes are reflected in the form of cyclical representations. Cyclic representations capture the unfolding of an event that

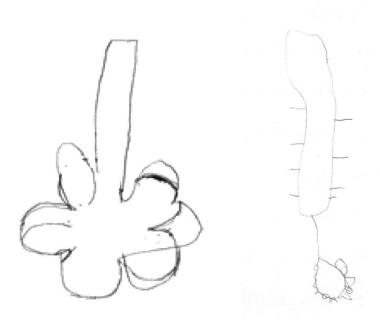

Fig. 4.11 The "dialectical" drawing of a tree—tree "on the contrary"—the leaves are at the bottom, and the roots are at the top

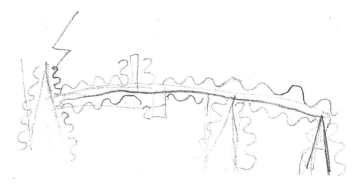

Fig. 4.12 Dialectical drawing of a tree, the trunk of which is horizontal. The drawing is built on the opposition of vertical and horizontal directions

begins and ends in the same way. The pictures were designed to show the development of the situation in two parts: the forward and reverse half-cycles (see Figs. 4.14 and 4.15).

Fig. 4.13 The child
transforms the branches of a
tree: an ordinary
tree—branches grow down
(B), an unusual
tree—branches grow up (A)

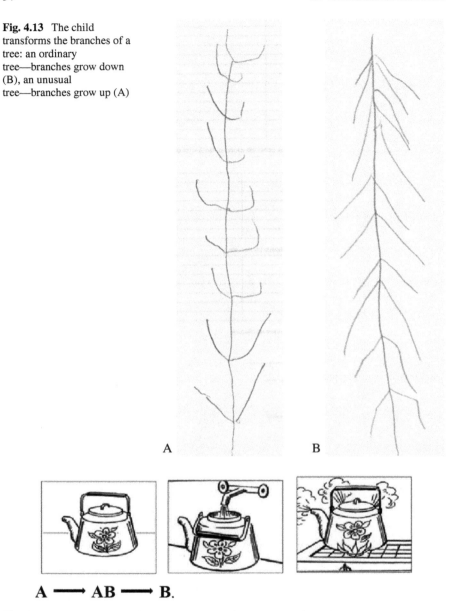

A   B

A ⟶ AB ⟶ B.

Fig. 4.14 The arrangement of pictures corresponding to the seriation schema

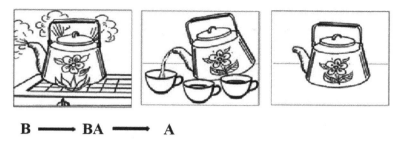

B ——→ **BA** ——→ **A**

Fig. 4.15 The arrangement of pictures corresponding to the conversion schema

An interesting fact is that if we look at the middle pictures of these two sequences, they turn out to be opposite in meaning. In other words, while performing these tasks, children face the same dialectical structural relationships and similar dialectical operations.

Some of the children coped with the proposed tasks. Preschoolers placed the pictures correctly and gave correct explanations. Here are some examples of explanations. The child arranged the cards as shown in Fig. 4.16 and explained: "First, water, then two sugars were added, then 3 sugars, then it dissolved and became an ordinary glass."

For drawings with a teapot, the explanations were as follows: "Mom took the teapot, poured water and set it to boil, then poured tea for the children, and put the teapot on the table (Fig. 4.17)."

For a set of drawings with the weather, there were such explanations: "At first the weather was normal, there was sun, then the wind began and the cloud flew in and heavy rain began, then it ended and the sun again (Fig. 4.18)."

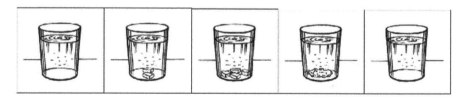

Fig. 4.16. xxxx

Fig. 4.17. xxxx

Fig. 4.18. xxxx

Fig. 4.19 The arrangement of pictures made by a child

Children's responses do not necessarily follow the logic of dialectical structural relationships. Let us give an example of such a response. The child arranged the pictures as shown in Fig. 4.19 and explained it as follows: "There was water, then they put salt, the sugar cooled down, and here there is ice and a lot of ices." It is clear that this explanation did not follow the structure of the dialectical transformations of the situation. It was based on the content of individual pictures and was not related to their supposed sequence.

The tasks of the "What can be at the same time" method requires the mediation of two opposites. Children have to imagine or find situations which include both properties indicated in the tasks. The scheme of the applied operation is as follows:

$$A \searrow$$
$$\qquad AB.$$
$$B \nearrow$$

However, in order to find such a situation or an object, the child must first perform the exact opposite operation. He must analyze objects determining opposite properties in them, i.e., applying the operation of dialectical unification $AB \searrow^{A}_{B}$. In this case, the child analyzes the situation in a different way, as he looks for opposites in it. Such an analysis requires a number of operations:

1. one has to remember which opposites are subject to mediation;
2. one has to apply the operation of dialectical unification onto analyzed objects;
3. one has to take into account that opposites must be in unity, that they must be mediated.

Here are examples of children's answers to these questions:

Black–White:
   There was a black fence—painted it turned white; gray, it refers to white and black; dark white; draw with two brushes at once, black and white.

Big–Small:

The child can be oldest, but small … I'm a middle child; a crack, it is small, spreads, and then it is again turned into a small crack by man; average person, because a person grows from small to large.

Light–Heavy:

Bucket in the middle of the water floating; artificial dumbbell, it is light—inflatable, and everyone thinks that it is real; even sizes on scales.

Alive–Nonliving:

A chameleon, he changes colors and freezes and everyone thinks that he is inanimate; fainted man; an interactive toy, if turned on, then alive, if not alive, then not turned on; robots; bears, when they sleep a lot in winter.

Same–Others:

The man cut his hair and people got used to the fact that he had different hair and did not recognize him; man moved to another house and another—what is home; a person who can transform and change clothes.

The following results were obtained with the "Drawing an unusual tree" method. Three types of tree drawings were identified: (1) normative; (2) symbolic; and (3) dialectical, which indicates the existence of various mechanisms for transforming the image of a tree. The normative drawing is a standard image of a tree: roots at the bottom, crown at the top. The symbolic image of a tree exhibits features that are not characteristic of an ordinary tree: it grants wishes, talks, etc.

An unusual tree was drawn by 87 (testing was carried out with an interval of 1 year). Table 4.1 shows a contingency table for the children's results in the senior and preparatory groups.

Generally, we can see that the number of children who draw a "normative" tree decreases (from 45 to 16). At the same time, most of the children (12 out of 16) who drew a "normative" tree in the preparatory group, also drew a "normative" tree [previously] in the senior group.

The number of children who drew a "dialectical" tree in the preparatory group is greater than in the senior group (16—preparatory, 6—senior). We note, however, that not a single child who drew a "dialectical" tree in the senior group drew the same type of tree in the preparatory group [one year later].

Table 4.1 Contingency table for the "Drawing an unusual tree" test results of the preschoolers in senior and preparatory groups

"Drawing an unusual tree," senior group		"Drawing an unusual tree," preparatory group			Total
		Normative	Symbolic	Dialectical	
	Normative	12	23	10	45
	Symbolic	4	26	6	36
	Dialectical	0	6	0	6
Total		16	55	16	87

The number of children who drew a "symbolic" tree increased in the preparatory group compared to the senior one (from 36 to 55).

The general conclusion may be that in the older preschool age, children are developing the ability to draw unusual trees. At the same time, it may be that the education "contributes" to the fact that some children who used to apply the dialectical thinking operation of transformation stop doing it.

The "Cycles" test was passed by 89 preschoolers in both the senior and preparatory groups (testing was carried out with an interval of 1 year). Table 4.2 contains the means, medians, standard deviations, maximums and minimums of preschoolers' scores in the senior and preparatory groups.

The distribution of estimates for the "Cycles" test is normal in both the senior and preparatory groups (Kolmogorov–Smirnov criterion), which allows the use of parametric criteria.

By using the student's t-criterion for paired samples, we found that the estimates of preschoolers in the senior and preparatory groups differed significantly ($t = 9,557$; $p < 0,001$)—the estimates were higher in the preparatory group.

The results obtained allow us to conclude that senior preschool age is sensitive for the development of dialectical thinking operations of seriation, transformation, and conversion. The development occurs intermittently. The last conclusion is based on the fact that the scores in the preparatory and senior groups are not correlated.

The "What can be at the same time?" test results are presented in Table 4.3. The test was passed by 88 preschoolers in both the senior and preparatory groups (testing was carried out with an interval of 1 year). Table 4.3 contains the means, medians, standard deviations, maximums and minimums of preschoolers' scores in the senior and preparatory groups.

The distribution of estimates for the "What can be both at the same time?" test is normal both in the senior and preparatory groups (Kolmogorov–Smirnov criterion), which allows the use of parametric criteria.

Table 4.2 The main psychometric characteristics of the total score for the "Cycles" test among preschoolers in the senior and preparatory groups

Group/ characteristic	Mean	Median	Standard deviations	Min	Max
Senior group	6,30	7,00	3,485	0	14
Preparatory group	10,38	10,00	2,516	4	15

Table 4.3 The main psychometric characteristics of the total score for the "What can be both at the same time?" test among preschoolers in the senior and preparatory groups

Group/ characteristic	Mean	Median	Standard deviations	Min	Max
Senior group	4,60	4,00	3,804	0	17
Preparatory group	9,17	9,50	4,718	0	18

By using the student's t-criterion for paired samples, we found that the estimates of preschoolers in the senior and preparatory groups differed significantly ($t = 7$, 645; $< 0,001$)—the estimates were higher in the preparatory group.

The results obtained allow us to conclude that senior preschool age is sensitive for the development of dialectical thinking operation of mediation. The development occurs intermittently. The last conclusion is based on the fact that the scores in the preparatory and senior groups are not correlated.

By using the Pearson correlation coefficient, it was found that the results of the "What can be both at the same time?" test in the preparatory group are linked with the results of the "Cycles" test in the senior group ($r = 0,305$; $p = 0,004$), which suggests that the success in the "Cycles" test in the senior group is a predictor for the success in the "What can be at the same time?" test in the preparatory group; that is, the degree of development of seriation, transformation and conversion is a predictor for the degree of development of mediation.

The results obtained show that preschoolers use dialectical thinking operations of transformation, seriation, conversion, unification, and mediation.

4.4 Conclusion

In conclusion, we want to show that both Vygotsky and Piaget used dialectical operations in their works. When reading Vygotsky's works, one really gets the impression that his analysis had a specific purpose: to establish opposite tendencies.

L.S. Vygotsky also exercised the operation of mediation. Moreover, he sought to rationalize the strategy of dialectical mediation. First, let us look at how Vygotsky understood what is meaning of a word. It is, according to him, a concrete form of the existence of the opposites: thought—speech. The whole point is that speech and thought are taken as opposites. This was quite clearly expressed by Vygotsky when he characterized notion of meaning: "What is it? Speech or thought? It is speech and thought at the same time, because it is a unit of verbal thought" (Vygotsky, 1982b, p. 17).

Let us consider one more example illustrating the application of the mediation operation. In Soviet psychology, the concept of "zone of proximal development" has played a large part for a long time. It is emphasized that the "zone of proximal development is of a more direct importance for the dynamics of intellectual development and the success in learning than the actual level of development" (Vygotsky, 1982b, p. 247). However, the essential characteristic of this concept is not always grasped correctly. The zone of proximal development is a specific form of the existence of opposites: learning—development. It captures the specificity of developmental learning. Without this category, developmental learning as an independent method loses its meaning.

Vygotsky's interpretation of scientific and everyday concepts also relies on the operation of dialectical conversion. According to Vygotsky, these concepts are opposite, since scientific concepts are strong "where everyday concepts reveal their weakness" (Vygotsky, 1982b, p. 263). The contraposition of these concepts follows from the reversal of their development: "For clarity, we could schematically outline the developmental paths of spontaneous and scientific concepts in a child as two lines going in opposite directions" (Vygotsky, 1982b, p. 261). These paths are, in a certain sense, opposite to each other (Vygotsky, 1982b, p. 260). In other words, we would like to emphasize that Vygotsky reprocessed the psychological legacy by systematically applying dialectical thinking that is based on dialectical thinking operations.

So, our analysis shows that Vygotsky's high productivity at solving psychological issues is largely due to the dialectical nature of his thought. A system of dialectical thinking operations played a special part in his work; with its help, he dialectically transformed the situations he studied. Based on the study of Vygotsky's work, it can be concluded that dialectical thinking is a special type of thinking activity, and that dialectical thinking operations can be considered a real psychological tool of scientific creativity.

Piaget studied dialectical thinking through the prism of the formal logical structures acquisition. Но мы показали, что Пиаже хорошо знал диалектический метод. Но кроме того он применял и диалектические операции.

It is rather difficult to single out the thinking mechanisms Piaget used in his work. However, in some cases this is possible. Let us consider the following dialogue between Jean-Claude Bringuier, a journalist, and Jean Piaget (1980, p. 9).

4.5 Bringuier: Please Continue. You Need to Finish Something

Piaget: No, that's all. It's better to stop in the middle of a sentence. Then you don't waste time getting started again. When I write, I always stop in the middle of a paragraph.

As one can see from this conversation, Piaget applied the operation of transformation here. He highlighted the "middle of the sentence" and "end of the sentence" fragments. It is clear that they are the opposites. The beginning of a sentence cannot be the opposite of the end of a sentence—since the beginning of one sentence is the end of the previous one. Therefore, if we say that we put a period at the beginning of a sentence, it will mean a period at the end of the previous sentence. In other words, it is the middle that is the opposite of the ending, which allows us to speak about the transformation operation here. But before that, Piaget had to perform the operation of equating the beginning of the sentence and the end of the previous one.

Bringuier: You have a peculiar office, one can rarely see something like this. I want to call it a disorder.

Piaget: As you know, Bergson said that there is no such thing that could be called disorder, but rather there are two kinds of order—geometric one and ordinary one. (Piaget, 2007, p. 9)

So, Piaget used the operation of transformation as well. He interpreted disorder as an "ordinary order", transforming disorder into the ordinary order or just order. The following fragment is also of interest.

Bringuier: At which level of life does the psyche emerge?

Piaget: I am convinced that there are no boundaries of any kind between life and the psyche, or between the biological and the psychological. (Piaget, 2007, p. 10)

A situation arises where Bringuier asks about the border that defines the origin of the psyche, and Piaget replies that there is no such border. This answer can be interpreted as a statement that there is no border, or as transformation of the question into its opposite.

Let us now consider the following statement by Piaget: "...science is based on itself. Scientific theory is rapidly becoming obsolete, but theories are supposed to have practical applications. In their improvement lies the progress" (Piaget, 2007, p. 20). This phrase can be read as follows: "The theory develops, then the development stops, but while the theory was developing, practical applications were emerging. And then the practice develops and influences the theory." This explanation suggests that these processes form a dialectical cycle of theory and practice. From the analysis of these interview fragments, it follows that Piaget used dialectical thinking operations, like Vygotsky.

We will give one more example to support this. Piaget wrote: "The physical, mathematical and other aspects of reality, which the intellect tries to cognize, can manifest in two ways: as states and as transformations. Each transformation proceeds from one state to reach another, therefore it is impossible to understand transformations without knowing the states; and, conversely, it is impossible to understand states without knowing the transformations that led to them and those for which they are the starting point" (Obukhova & Burmenskaya, 2001, p. 200).

This passage shows that Piaget highlighted the existence of two opposites in real objects: states (or completed products) and their transformations. They are in an antithetical relationship. Basically, this is one of the ways to use dialectical unification. Even though Piaget called it a classification, we emphasize the opposition of states and transformations. The point is that an object can be either in a certain state or in transforming, i.e., state and transformation are mutually exclusive. Therefore, it can be concluded that state and transformation are the opposites.

Another example belongs to the field of psychology. As Piaget emphasized, "there are such cognitive functions or aspects of these functions that correspond to descriptors: we are talking about aspects that are, essentially, associated with the configurations of the reality and can be called figurative. These are (1) perception, (2) imitation, and also (3) the type of internalized imitation that reproduces perceptual models more or less successfully, and which is called mental image. Generally, figurative functions 'capture' (reflect) a state; but when they are aimed at transformation, they also represent them in the form of configurations or states (for example, as a so-called good form). But on the other hand, there are cognitive functions, or aspects of these functions, which basically reflect transformations. These include: (1) operations and their sensorimotor mechanisms (sensorimotor schemes, including dynamic stereotypes), (2) internalized operations in their various operational forms, and (3) operations in a true sense of the word, i.e., internalized operations in their general form: reversible and coordinated into the structures of connected ensembles" (Obukhova & Burmenskaya, 2001, pp. 200–201).

It is clear that this is an operation of unification based on the antithetical relationship between the figurative and the operational aspects of thinking. In Piaget's works, this same relationship occurs between two sides of thinking (dialectical—logical, or balanced). Also, in his study of the concept of number (seriation—inclusion).

Let's take a look at one more passage. Piaget said: "in order to study the formation of the human psyche in a way that I believe is right, we must reconstruct the developmental stages from an ape to a man, the stages of the prehistoric man, the stages of the fossil man" (Piaget, 2007, p. 23). In addition the dialectical thinking operation of seriation presented here, let us pay attention to the fact that one of Vygotsky's works was called "Ape, Primitive Man, and Child." We can see here to what extent Piaget's thought is congruent to Vygotsky's thinking.

Summing up the problem of the development of dialectical thinking in childhood, we note that the analysis of the dialectical thinking processes is greatly influenced by the work of Piaget, who saw the development of intelligence as the formation of formal logical structures (Piaget, 1969). In this process, he also singled out dialectical aspects. Moreover, he spoke of special structural-dialectical transformations (Piaget, 1982).

It seems that at some point, Piaget began to see dialectical thinking not as an independent thought process, but as a developmental process. There are grounds for such an understanding, since development is dialectical. However, in this case, the processes of dialectical development and dialectical thinking got mixed up. Piaget's claim that dialectics exists at all levels7, from thinking to action (Piaget, 1982, p. 9) can be considered a result of that confusion.

Thanks to his works, the problematics of dialectical thinking was included in the context of the formation of formal intelligence. A special contribution to the interpretation of dialectical thinking was made by Riegel (Riegel, 1973), who emphasized that the peak of thinking cannot be reduced to a high level of formal intelligence. An adult faces very difficult questions in life. Therefore, an intellectual peak, understood as wisdom, implies that mature thinking is based not only on formal logical thinking, but also on dialectical thinking.

Basseches (Basseches, 1984) suggests that dialectical thinking should not be considered as a process of achieving equilibrium, but rather as a process that works with equilibrium. In this perspective, the equilibrium state of logical structures as understood by Piaget is a closed system of knowledge. Dialectical thinking allows us to break through this isolation toward new knowledge. Thus, the process of expanding knowledge remains thanks to dialectical thinking.

In Russian psychology, two approaches to understanding dialectical thinking were developed: the concrete approach (Davydov, 1972), which analyzes the development of the whole based on internal contradictions, and the structural approach (Veraksa, 1981, 1987). One of the goals of these studies was to establish formal dialectical operations that differ from those of formal logic. Moreover, since they are logical operations, they had to form some logical structure that would allow for a description in the language of mathematics, just as it was done by Piaget.

The understanding of dialectical logic and dialectical thinking rests on the realization that the opposites can form various relationships; that made it possible to consider the processes of transformation of objects in terms of these relationships. Thus, there was a real opportunity to link these transformations into a single logical structure. Transformations could be real transformations of real objects, as well as thinking transformations of imaginary objects. The former could be understood as processes occurring in inanimate and living nature, and the latter as dialectical thinking operations.

The identification of opposites and relationships between them with the use of dialectical thinking operations laid the basis for the structural and dialectical analysis method. The proposed method would be ineffective if its use was just to identify the antithetical relations while characterizing various objects. The main feature of the method is that it allows to describe possible transformations of both material and ideal objects in regard to the opposites inherent in their structure. The structural-dialectical method allows to understand the logic of possible transformations or changes of an object, which is what constitutes dialectical logic as the logic of possibilities and distinguishes its structural-dialectical interpretation from the traditional one (Bayanova, 2013; Veraksa et al., 2013).

In the course of the research, it was shown that dialectical thinking as a system of operations with the antithetical relations was part of the cultures of different ethnic groups and was represented through their folktales.

This study also showed that Piaget and Vygotsky used the apparatus of dialectical thinking, that is, a system of dialectical thinking operations.

Acknowledgements Research was supported by RSF grant# 19-18-00521-П.

References

Alekseev, V. P. (1984). *The formation of humanity*. Politizdat.

Afanasev, A. N. (1957). *Russian folk-tales*. State Publishing House of Fiction.

Bakhtin, M. M. (1984). *Rabelais and his world*. Indiana University Press.

Basseches, M. (1984). *Dialectical thinking and adult development*. Ablex.

Bayanova, L. F. (2013). Vygotsky's Hamlet: The dialectic method and personality psychology. *Psychology in Russia: State of the Art, 6*, 35–42.

Bringuier, J. -C. (1980). *Conversations with Jean Piaget*. The University of Chicago Press.

Davydov, V. V. (1972). Types of generalization in instruction. *Soviet Studies in Mathematics Education, 2*, 90–102.

Entrevista a Rolando García [Interview with Rolando García] (2001). *Piaget, las ciencias y la dialectica* [Piaget, science and dialectics].

Golosovker, Ya. E. (1987). *Myth logic*. Nauka.

Hegel, G. W. (1971). *Works of different years*. Musl'.

Obukhova, L. F., & Burmenskaya, G. V. (Eds.). (2001). Piaget's theory. *Jean Piaget: Theory, experiments, discussions: Sat. articles* (pp. 199–224). Gardariki.

Piaget, J. (1969). *The psychology of intelligence. Genesis of the number in a child. Logic and Psychology*. Prosveshenie.

Piaget, J. (1982). *Las formas elementales de la dialectica [The elementary forms of the dialectic]*.

Piaget, J. (2007). *What is the higher psyche?*. Aster-X.

Riegel, K. F. (1973). Dialectic operations: The final period of cognitive development. *Human Development, 16*, 346–370.

Riegel, K. F., & Rosenwald, G. C. (1975). *Structure and transformation*. A Wiley-Interscience Pablication.

Sartre, J. -P. (1993). *Question de method* [Question of method]. Progress.

Veraksa, N., Belolutskaya, A., Vorobyeva, I., Krasheninnikov, E., Rachkova, E., Shiyan, I., & Shiyan, O. (2013). Structural dialectical approach in psychology: Problems and research results. *Psychology in Russia: State of the Art, 6*, 65–77.

Veraksa, N. E. (1981). Peculiarities of the transformation of conflicting problem situations by preschool children. *Voprosy Psikhologii, 3*, 123–127.

Veraksa, N. E. (1987). Appearance of prerequisites of dialectical thinking in preschool age. *Voprosy Psikhologii, 4*, 135–139.

Veraksa, N. E. (2006). *Dialectical thinking*. Vagant.

Veraksa, N. E., Almazova O. V., Airapetyan Z. V., & Tarasova K. S. (2021). Heterochronicity of dialectic thinking development in preschool children 5–7-years-old. *Psychological journal* (in print).

Vygotsky, L. S. (1982a). *Questions of theory and history of psychology* (A. R. Luria, & M. G. Yaroshevsky, Eds.). Pedagogika.

Vygotsky, L. S. (1982b). *Problems of general psychology* (V. V. Davydov, Ed.). Pedagogika.

Vygotsky, L. S. (1983). *Fundamentals of defectology* (T. A. Vlasova, Ed.). Pedagogika.

Prof. Nikolay Veraksa is a specialist in preschool education, works at Faculty of Psychology, Lomonosov Moscow State University, Moscow City University and Psychological Institute of the Russian Academy of Education, Head of UNESCO Chair in Early Childhood Care and Development, Honorary Doctor of the University of Gothenburg. He is a co-author of the most popular educational program in Russia for children in preschool "From Birth to School" as well as a program in English "Key to Learning.". His main interests are development of child thinking and personality.

Michael Basseches is a professor emeritus, Psychology at Suffolk University, US. He works as a lifespan developmental psychologist with a focus on intellectual development, social development, and ego development.

Chapter 5
Social Representations of Play: Piaget, Vygotskij and Beyond

Bert van Oers(iD)

Abstract For the study and elaboration—in theory and practice—of sociocultural phenomena, it is important to realise that the content of many concepts are related to images that have been built during the long history of their use. These images are communicated from one generation to another, are included in academic and lay conversations and are very resistant to change. Such images are generally called 'social representations'. For the study of play, it is important too to reveal its social representations to better understand current discourses and applications of play in educational practices. This chapter analyses the social representations of play that can be found in the works of Piaget and Vygotskij, and their respective roots in the works of Rousseau/Schiller and cultural activity. It will be argued that both types of social representations need further elaboration to clarify meaningful learning in play and enhance the power of play for educational purposes.

> The more one attempts to reflect
> on play, the more enigmatic
> and questionworthy it seems
> to become
> Eugen Fink (1960/2016), Play as a symbol of the world. (p. 26)

5.1 Communicating About Play

Since ages, parents, authors, psychologists and philosophers have been deeply interested in the phenomenon of play in its cultural environments. When reading the

B. van Oers (✉)
Section of Educational Sciences, and LEARN! Research Institute,
Vrije Universiteit Amsterdam, Amsterdam, The Netherlands
e-mail: bert.van.oers@vu.nl

© The Author(s), under exclusive license to Springer Nature Switzerland AG 2022
N. Veraksa and I. Pramling Samuelsson (eds.), *Piaget and Vygotsky in XXI century*,
Early Childhood Research and Education: An Inter-theoretical Focus 4,
https://doi.org/10.1007/978-3-031-05747-2_5

literature on play, one cannot avoid being impressed about its quantity, richness and diversity (see King & Newstead, 2021; Mellou, 1994; Pramling Samuelsson & Fleer, 2009), and subsequently being discouraged by the lack of a clear conception of play from this proliferation of ideas.

Nevertheless, humans have always felt the need to communicate about play, both as a reference to children's engagements with the world, as adult ways of amusement, and as objects of study. Wittgenstein (1953, Section 64–77), however, warned us against too much optimism in finding the essence of play in the overwhelming diversity. In his view, there is no unique definition of play. We do recognize instances of play when they occur, but we cannot define them on the basis of one essential characteristic that belongs to all of them. Communications about play, according to Wittgenstein, cannot be based on a definition-based explanation. Actually, in his view, the meaning of 'play' depends on how people use the term in different situations. At best the phenomenon of play can be conceived of as a specimen of a cultural phenomenon that shares a series of overlapping similarities with other events called play, where no one feature is common to all of them. Actually, when facing an instance of human engagement like play in a certain situation, it is mostly sufficient to mention one or two characteristics (e.g. play is a self-chosen activity of children) in order to have a unambiguous conversation with others about play. Wittgenstein characterizes such notions as 'family-resemblances' (*Familienähnlichkeiten*, see Wittgenstein, 1953, Section 66, p. 57).

However, Wittgenstein's view was based on a *linguistic* analysis of how the word 'play' ('Spiel') is used. This ends up in what can be called 'linguistic relativism' (Eichberg, 2016). Such 'linguistic relativism', though, did not refrain people from continuing questioning and talking about play. At least we can communicate about play on the basis of what can be called an 'ostentative definition', i.e. a definition by giving an example, in addition to mentioning one or two characteristics and assuming that speaker and listener get a similar idea in mind about what is meant by 'play'.

This use-based definition of the word 'play' is nowadays still the dominant approach in discussions of play. As a result, numbers of academic articles were published for many decades without giving a clear conceptual definition of play, but only providing some pregnant characteristics and examples. Due to this circumstance, the progress in the theory of play is stagnating since long, leaving a number of serious gaps and burning problems in our understanding of play and hampering its potentials for implementation in (school) practices. Consequently, there is a lot of talk about '*playful learning*' without clearly explaining the relationship between play and learning. Similarly, there is much discussion about the (questionable?) *role of adults* (if any) in play, without convincing theory-based arguments about how adults may relate to play. And in what sense is play justifiably seen as *opposite to work*? How tenable is this criterion of productivity (work) versus 'free of external demands' (play)? And finally, a clear elaboration of *play beyond childhood* is often missing. What happens with play when children grow older? Is it only embodied in sports? Or in a playful attitude?

In this chapter, I want to explore a few ways of speaking about play and their elaborations, based on a *psychological* analysis. I will first discuss what social representations are and emphasize their predominantly descriptive function. Then two dominant social representations of play (an ontological one and a cultural one) will be discussed in relationships to historically established views of play. In line with these two types of social representations, I will address the works of Piaget and Vygotskij and how they transformed their descriptive views of social representations on play into theories of play. Of course, there have been comparative discussions about Piaget and Vygotskij before (see Tryphon & Vonèche, 1996), but they don't mention (let alone analyse critically) current conceptions of play. In this chapter, I will finally discuss briefly some of the possible dialogues that are needed to further develop a theory of play, with a focus on some 'burning problems' in the understanding of play.

The main aim of the chapter is to better understand the evolution of current views of play in both lay talk and academic talk, and by so doing, better understand current discourses and applications of play in educational practices. My analyses will be based on the notion of *social representation*, a theoretical notion for the understanding of social phenomena, developed in social psychology since the works of Moscovici (1961, 1981; see also Sammut et al., 2015a). Generally spoken, 'social representation' can be taken as way of representing a collection (a family) of ideas and propositions about a specific social phenomenon, without a strong internal systematic order. Social representations emerge and grow by adding together propositions and ideas to a certain notion during cultural history on the basis of their value for successfully communicating about the phenomenon. Unlike concepts, social representations often lack a strong and mandatory internal logic and structure. Hence, social representations are basically descriptive and might be compared to pseudo-concepts. As such they can be useful as a way of referring to shared ideas about a social phenomenon and support communication in a community.

In the present chapter, I shall use this notion of 'social representation' particularly for *characterizing* different ideas about play and their historical evolution. I will argue that a collection of different aspects of play can be seen as a social representation of play without a strong internal conceptual structure and which, by the same token, is different from theories of play. Both theories of play and social representations of play are ways of understanding play, that can be used to back-up communications about play and their related 'rethorics'. However, social representations *describe* some striking aspects of the phenomenon, theories *explain* the dynamics and interrelations of these aspects.

However, in modern discussions about play, there still remain many problems (like for instance in explaining 'playful learning', see, e.g., Hirsch-Pasek et al., 2009, p. 54, or justifying the role of the adult in children's play, see, e.g., Moran & Brown, 2017; Santer et al., 2007). Social representations of play remain impotent with regard to solving such problems. I will show how such problems can be solved in a cultural-historical theory of play.

5.2 Everyday Social Representations: The Case of Play

In a way, it is surprising that people can communicate so easily about play, when there is no clear-cut definition of it. As a start, it is useful to realise that this is not a unique circumstance. There are many notions in human cultures that are considered important, frequently used in interpersonal communications, but still lacking a clear generally accepted definition. Think of such notions as 'Truth', 'God', 'Love', 'Freedom', 'National identity', 'Child' and so on (see Sammut et al., 2015a, for more elaborated examples). From the numerous studies of such notions, it is obvious that they develop historically in the interpersonal communications of people within a specific community (see, e.g., de Dijn, 2020, about evolution of the notion of 'freedom'; Ariès, 1960, on the notion of 'childhood').

Since the studies of Moscovici (1961) on the views of psychoanalysis, it is common practice to refer to such historically evolved views as '*social representations*'. Social representations are inter-generationally transferred ways of speaking about certain cultural objects; they are historically established as appropriate within (sub)cultures in a community, and resistant to change. Social representations support common sense communications and circulate in social milieus. As Moscovici (1981) explains, social representations should be conceived of as 'collections of values, ideas and practices that serve to establish social order and facilitate communication'. They justify everyday human practices in a community. As widely agreed common sense within a community, social representations are highly indispensable for successful communication on phenomena that matter within a social group.

Likewise, we often can understand the notion of 'play' too as a social representation. The notion of play is often descriptively characterized as a multidimensional construct that varies in meaning across time, culture and contexts (e.g. Cohen, 2006). To understand the constitution of this social representation, though, it is useful to study how people—both lay and academic—have communicated about play during history. This history can be traced back deep into the past of human civilizations. In Plato's work, for instance, play is seen as a way of freely acting like children, worriless and without the need to yield any direct societal value (see, for example, *The Republic*, VII, 536–537). In Classical Greek, the word for play (paizein, παιζειν) also means 'act like a child' and is related to the word for 'child' (paίs, παις). It is important to keep in mind here that, according to Plato, play is not to be seen as 'childish' in the modern sense of the word. Rather, it is a free way of acting to explore the surrounding world and probe new inventions (see D'Angour, 2013). Remarkably, Plato also maintained a meritocratic view of play, as he saw it as a way of interacting with the world that benefitted those who succeed most in learning from their playful activities in childhood and youth. Play, according to Plato, selects those students who are *by their nature* best fit to learn disciplinary knowledge and fulfil the demands of the higher disciplined trades of their community. Obviously, and most significantly, in his Republic, Plato already introduced the distinction between free play (for young people) and disciplined work (for adults), and took play as a preparation for serious adult endeavours. We find this idea again in many twenty-century scholars, like Groos (1901) and among others Cassirer (1944, pp. 164–165), who explicitly refers to Schiller (discussed below).

Plato's view of play and his emphasis on freedom, serious engagement without pressures from the outside world, opposition between play and work, has continuously permeated western thinking on play ever since. Over the centuries, many authors have likewise discussed play as a child's activity, using different lists of characteristics to picture this phenomenon, and develop specific 'rhetorics' (Sutton-Smith's term, 1997) for communication about play. To mention just a few of them, see Bruce (2004) and Burghardt (2011). From the literature, we can summarize the following list of generally accepted characteristics that are generally taken as indicators of 'play' in the dominant social representation of play: (1) play is a self-chosen free activity of children; (2) play is based on intrinsic motivation, leading to high engagement in the players; (3) play is rule-based, but leaves room for creativity; (4) play follows the free imagination of the players; (5) play is free from external demands of following specific procedures and producing specific outcomes. Each of these characteristics describes an aspect of play as can be observed in playing children.

Reading this list, it is obvious that Plato's conception of play is still dominantly present in the modern social representations of play. We can find those indicators both in lay communications about play and in academic (research) literature. In addition to the listed aspects of play, many authors also emphasize 'pleasure' or 'fun' as indicatory for play, while referring to Huizinga (1938) as a source (see Singer, 2015), but these authors seldom explain why 'pleasure' should be seen as essentially defining play, rather than merely being a consequence of children's activity, organized according to the listed features. All in all, we may conclude, that most discussions of play are based on common sense social representations of play and don't represent a systematic theory of play. Most of such common sense social representations assume that *play and work* are essentially different activities, based on the general bias about externally provided rules and aims, deemed inconsistent with play. Moreover, many social representations are sceptical or ambiguous about the *participation of adults* in children's play, propagate *playful learning* without providing a theory of learning and fail to explain the *development of playing* during school age. Any theory of play should be able to explain these problems satisfactorily.

5.3 Classifying Social Representations of Play

As said above, my aim in this chapter is to outline and contrast the views of play and their roots in Piaget and Vygotskij. To explain how these views relate to common and contrasting social representations of play, I have to discuss first a classification of different types of social representations, based on incompatible, mutually exclusive assumptions regarding the roots of these respective views. Basically, it is claimed that two families of social representations can be distinguished, of which Piaget and Vygotskij are academic elaborations. The first family I have dubbed '*Ontological*', the second '*Cultural*'.

5.3.1   Ontological Social Representations of Play

Ontological representations of play can be traced back to the assumption that all play stems from the *nature of the human being*, particularly the child. Or as Fink (1960) once put it: 'Play belongs essentially to the ontological constitution of human experience; it is an existential, fundamental phenomenon' (Fink, 1960/2016, p. 18). We found this ontological-naturalistic assumption already in the works of Plato (see above), but many centuries later Rousseau (1712–1778) continued along this line, treating the child as an essentially natural creature, that should be educated by 'laissez-faire', i.e. by permitting it to be a free child. Any attempt to deliberately steer a child's development towards external (cultural) goals allegedly would inevitably lead to corruption of the child's being. Consequently, adults are advised to refrain from interfering in child's play. Equally explicit about human education and play is the German writer and philosopher Friedrich Schiller (1759–1805). In his writings about the aesthetical education of the human being, he states that 'play and only play is what completes the human being' and furthermore: 'The human being only plays, when he acts humanly in the full sense of this word, and he is only then completely human when he plays' (Schiller, 1794/1980; translation from the German by the author). The human beings' urge to play is what Schiller calls 'Spieltrieb' (play drive), which arises in an individual's natural attempt to harmonize the two basic drives: the drive to understand the world with available knowledge ('Formtrieb') and the drive to assimilate sensory experiences ('Stofftrieb'). In his attempts to become human in the full sense of the word, according to Schiller, the human being tries to harmonize these two drives and integrates them into one 'Gestalt'. This act of bringing the drives together in an harmonious whole is what can be witnessed in play (Schiller, 1794/1980, 15th letter; see also Theobald, 2011, for a more recent discussion). Analogies of this natural and playful balancing of two epistemic drives, we can see returning about 150 years later in Piaget's cognitive mechanisms of 'assimilation' and 'accommodation' in his explanation of play. I will discuss this further below.

The ideas of Rousseau and Schiller have influenced discourses on play for many years, maintaining the assumption that it is the nature of the spontaneous child itself and its 'life instinct' (Spieltrieb), which is expressed in playful engagements in the world, and which is even taken to explain the analogies between child play and play of animals (Buytendijk, 1932; Groos, 1898). In this ontological perspective, the main mechanism in human development is generally called '*maturation*'.

The ontology-based social representations of play have been highly influential in modern western pedagogical talk today, especially in the reform pedagogies of— among others—Pestalozzi, Fröbel, Montessori, Steiner ("Waldorfschools"). It is not mere coincidence that some of them have written anthropological treatises to explain the nature of the human being and to underpin their pedagogies accordingly. In Montessori (1913), for instance, the biological-medical essence of the human child is emphasized and taken as a regulatory principle for child development.

The ontological social representations of play contain a rich variety of ideas about the nature of children and their behaviour. Play is seen as a natural characteristic of the child and often seen as a way of natural learning and as a rich seeding ground for human maturation. The role of the adult is conceived of as someone who should refrain from interfering too much in children's play, and who should trust that learning will occur inevitably at the right moment in play. The adult's main role is to organise a rich and safe environment for children. When children grow older, play will be replaced by work activities as the core engagement of adolescents and adults, or it transforms into rule-driven games and sports. These widely accepted ideas about play inform the social representation of many lay people and academics. Since long, this representation is transmitted to new generations, through modelling, conversations and (academic) literature. Not all adherents of this social representation agree on everything regarding the ways of speaking about play. It is characteristic for social representations, that every adherent may extend it with new opinions, as long as the basic assumptions (regarding play as a process of harmonisation of thinking and experience, and regarding maturation as an explanation of development) are maintained.

An additional remark is in place here, with respect to the position of Brian Sutton-Smith, another influential scholar in the domain of play. In his seminal book on '*The ambiguities of play*' (1997), he also discusses different ways of speaking about play (what he calls 'rhetorics'). None of his seven presented rhetorics gives a clear definition of play, but they are only distinct in their assumptions about the consequences of playing for a child's development, like, for example, development of identity, or development of phantasy. There are views of play (which can be social representations) behind all communications about play, including behind Sutton-Smith's own rhetorics. Moreover, Sutton-Smith (p. 218) warns that 'The search for a definition […] is a search only for metaphors that can act as rhetoric for what might ultimately become adequate scientific processual accounts'. Finally, he pins down the notion of play in terms of 'adaptive variability' (p. 221 ff). Variability is the key to play, according to Sutton-Smith, (p. 229), which necessitates *adaptive* potentiation, i.e. a struggle for (cultural) survival of the child. This struggle rests on 'reinforcement of potential synaptic variability' and 'the imitation of the evolutionary process in which the organism models its own biological character' (p. 229). Actually, in the words of Sutton-Smith, 'play is a facsimilization of the struggle for survival' (p. 231). These latter statements unambiguously place Sutton-Smith within the ontological social representation of play.

Modern expressions of the ontological social representation of play are obvious in attempts to legitimate decisions about playing or not-playing, by referring to the child's nature as a playful being. Young children taking part in everyday role-play, in play in natural environments with loose parts, or in play with digital tools, they all can be permitted to explore freely, to manipulate unrestrictedly, to phantasize following their own imaginations, to follow their own will, to engage in activities without any obligation to produce specific external results. They are all treated from a natural perspective as described in the ontological social representation of play and the playing child.

5.3.2 Cultural Social Representations of Play

Notwithstanding the dominant status of the ontological social representation of play, a growing number of scholars in the twentieth century became increasingly critical of the naturalistic assumptions underlying this approach. In their view, play is not an inherent natural urge of the human being (or: the child, for that matter). It should be conceived as rooted in the culture of a child's (human being's) community. A prominent proponent of this point of view was the Dutch cultural historian Johan Huizinga (1938). In his view, play can be described as a kind of activity that is freely accomplished by the players, within the limits of a certain place and moment in time (Huizinga, 1938, p. 47). According to Huizinga, play is intrinsically connected to the human endeavours of life (like religion, administration of justice, warfare and the like) and enables participants in such practices to promote culture and cultural innovations. Culture, according to Huizinga, 1938, p. 224), is initially playfully accomplished: 'Culture does not emerge out of play like a living foetus detaching itself from the maternal body; culture develops *in* play and *as* play' (Translations from the Dutch by the author). So for studying play, we have to look at human practices and figure out how they are organised, innovate and integrate newcomers into this cultural context. Play is a way of appropriating culture and participation in complex cultural practices of the community.

In the same historical period, in another part of the world, Vygotskij independently from Huizinga developed a theory of human development and learning, that interpreted human activity also as a cultural-historical product (Vygotsky, 1978a). Vygotskij describes play as an activity accomplished by children, based on a self-created imagination of a cultural situation ('imaginary situation', see Vygotsky, 1978b, p. 93). Play on the basis of an imaginary situation always includes rules and allows the child to act more or less freely according to its own desires. In such play, a child can learn how to act on the basis of the personal sense ('smysl'[1]) attributed to the situation, rather than merely on the basis of direct perceptions of the objects in that situation. So the child then acts on the basis of its fantasies (Vygotsky, 1978b, p. 97) within his perceived environment. By acting with others in an imaginary situation, the child discovers what he/she cannot yet accomplish on his/her own. In the words of Vygotskij, play creates a zone of proximal development for the child.

---

[1] It is important to note here, that the English translation in 'Mind in Society' (Vygotsky, 1978b, p. 97) uses the word 'meaning', usually taken as referring the standard cultural meanings (značenie), while the original Russian text uses the notion of **'sense'** (smysl') which emphasizes the *personal* value attached to an object, action, etc. The latter fits better in an interpretation of play. Hence, the English translation is possibly misleading.

It is obvious that for Vygotskij, this is not a Schiller-like process of balancing, but a creative process of *enculturation*, modelled by adults, taking part in this situation. Life for Vygotskij is essentially a creative process (see Vygotskij, 1926/1991, p. 367). This is important to keep in mind when reconstructing Vygotskij's view of play. The cultural-historical approach to human development also holds true for many later understandings of play from the works of Vygotsky (1978b; and beyond: see among others Bodrova & Leong, 2007; Fleer, 2014).

5.4 From Social Representations to Theories of Play: Piaget and Vygotskij

Both types of social representations consist of a collection of values, views and practices and dominate in discourses about play until the first part of the twentieth century. By then a theoretical conceptualization of play is rarely undertaken. From these days, academics started to conceptualize play from a detailed psychological evidence-based theory about the mechanisms of human development. The ontological social representation of play was elaborated and transformed into an academic theory by Piaget, and his colleagues since the 1940s, especially with the publication of *La formation du symbol chez l'enfant* [Symbol formation in the child]. Nevertheless, Piaget's view sticked to a naturalistic assumption underlying his theory, viewing the child as the natural subject of play.

The cultural social representation was transformed by Vygotskij in the 1930s into an academic psychological concept, particularly in his article on '*The role of play in development*', written in 1933, published in Russian in 1966, and incompletely published in English in Vygotsky (1978a). Both Piaget and Vygotskij transformed social representations into *academic psychological theories of play*. For this reason, I will no longer refer to them as 'social representations' here, but as *theories* of play, since they built their approaches on the basis of systematic research and the construction of conceptual systems. They went beyond the traditional lists of descriptive characteristics of play. Academic theories are not just a list of characteristics, nor collections of ideas and values. Nevertheless, some elements of either theory have been isolated and adopted as elements of the discussed everyday social representations of play. The other way around is also true: the academic theories of play sometimes made decisions that seem to be based on the dominant social representation of play of their community, as we can see below.

Let's now turn to the reconstruction of the two theories of play.

5.4.1 Piagetian View of Play

From the beginning of his career, Piaget was interested in the question how an organism could adapt to his environment. In his numerous publications, Piaget propagated this balancing ('equilibrium') between the environment and the cognitive operations of an individual as the core issue of developmental psychology. This is a *natural process of equilibration*, comparable to homeostasis. Above, I pointed to the analogy between Schiller's view of the human play and Piaget's. But Piaget—unlike Schiller—was more demanding in his explanations, as he was looking for the psychological mechanisms that could explain play also on a theoretical level. For Piaget, (child) development should be interpreted as a self-regulating (genetic) structure. In his book 'Le structuralisme' (Piaget, 1979), Piaget explains that this structure 'is not a pre-given unity, but a process that organizes itself into an evolving structure. In his view, any genetic structure consists in a 'system of transformations', tends towards a consistent whole ('totality', Gestalt) and regulates itself to achieve this whole ('autoréglage'). This self-regulation is based on a process in which two mechanisms are central: assimilation (the process of taking in and transforming information from the external world to adjust inner processes) and accommodation (the process of transforming cognitive systems to make them fit for the exigencies of the external demands). In an ideal situation, these two mechanism are in balance ("equilibrium"). In cases of 'dis-equilibration', the self-regulating system strives for rebalancing by adjusting the cognitive system. This is what happens in cognitive development and learning. The reflection of Schiller's conception of play as rebalancing is obvious here.

Piaget (1951) further clarifies his approach by explaining his view of play in terms of his general psychological theory of development. To begin his explanation, he declares that play is not to be seen as a special type of behaviour per se, to be distinguished from other types. In fact, play 'is determined by a certain orientation of the behaviour' (Piaget, 1951, p. 147), in which assimilation of reality into the ego dominates. This is to be considered as distinct from more serious activities in which assimilation is in balance with accommodation to other persons or reality (p. 148). This latter situation occurs in work processes, oriented towards achieving goals imposed by the external world. For Piaget, play begins when assimilation dominates in the child's orientation to reality, including other persons. Since this dominance of assimilation over accommodation is typical for spontaneous behaviour in (very) young children, play occurs mostly in young children. However, the situation of disequilibrium between assimilation and accommodation can also occur in older people, play can also appear in older ages. In the later stages of development symbolic representations emerge as equilibration between assimilation and accommodation, which will guide most of the individual's behaviour.

From this exposition of Piaget's theory of play, we can speculate about Piaget's ideas regarding the burning problems of play theories as mentioned above. It is clear that Piaget acknowledges the fact that play develops from childhood. In adult ages, play is slowly taken over by work. While play in the young ages is predominantly orientated to practicing, when children grow older they will be more engaged in strictly rule-based play ('games') or symbolic play as in children's pretend play. Piaget definitely acknowledges the importance of the social environment (adult and peers), but denies the usefulness of instructing children towards the mastery of external goals. Adults do better not intrude into children's play in order to avoid contamination of the spontaneous quality of play. Adults may answer questions upon request, provide new challenging situations to children, but waive the imposition of strict rules. As demonstrated above, Piaget's equilibrium theory also opposes play against work, as the 'tendencies' of both activities are different. Finally, playful learning is the process of spontaneously changing existing operations or structures by switching from assimilation to accommodation to a context that allows the child to do so for a better adaptation to the play situation.

5.5 Vygotskian View of Play

Vygotskij is generally acknowledged as the founder of the Cultural-Historical Approach to human development. In this view, human behaviour and development are seen as a cultural product, resulting from sign-based interactions among adults and children in the context of cultural environments. Vygotskij's approach rejects the Piagetian idea that the development of human behaviour served the function of adaptation to reality. In Vygotskij's view, following Marx, human activity mainly aims at the *transformation* of the human being and reality. Vygotskij's psychological approach was essentially a *non-adaptive* theory (Asmolov, 1982).

Due to his early death, however, Vygotskij could not elaborate all the concepts that evidently underpinned his approach, among them the notion of 'shared activity' ('sovmestnaja detel'nost') and the notion of play. In the footsteps of the young Marx, Vygotskij frequently referred to (shared) activity, which should be seen as a fundamental notion in the Vygotskian approach (see Davydov, 1996). The notion of activity was elaborated by Vygotskij's colleague A. N. Leont'ev. This prominent place of 'activity' in the cultural-historical approach of Vygotskij is a compelling reason why we should prefer to call this approach the 'Cultural-Historical Activity Theory-approach', i.e. CHAT.

Vygotskij developed his ideas in the early decades of the twentieth century and was well versed in the international pedagogical and psychological literature in those days and in the by then prevailing social representation of play in the Soviet Union. In this revolutionary cultural context, he made a start with the construction of a theory of play that fitted in his cultural-historical view of human development. In this view, play is definitely a leading activity for children's development. 'The child moves forward'—he writes—'through play activity. Only in this sense play can be called a leading activity, i.e. an activity that determines the child's development' (Vygotskij, 1966, p. 75/Vygotsky, 1978b, p. 103). Play can promote development, because it creates a zone of proximal development (1966, p. 74/1978b, p. 102), which opens the need to appropriate new actions with the help of others (adults or more knowledgeable peers). Elsewhere in his work, Vygotskij claims indeed that imitation is the core of human development, in the zone of proximal development (Vygotskij, 1934/1982, p. 250). Obviously, he does reject a restricting definition of 'imitation' as copying individual actions. For Vygotskij, imitation was a *creative reconstruction of cultural activity*, populated by peers and (actual and historical) experts. This is exactly how imitation in play can promote a person's cultural development with the help of others and cultural tools.

In his only article on play and development (Vygotskij, 1966/Vygotsky, 1978b), Vygotskij starts out by saying, that any analysis of play should begin with clarifying the motivational drive for children to act playfully (Vygotskij, 1966, 63). In this respect he states, that the child is driven to play in order to act like a significant adult from its social environment. This is possible when the child can act on the basis of an 'imaginary situation' ('mnimaja situacija', Vygotskij, 1966, p. 65/Vygotsky, 1978b, p. 93), which the child creates and which allows it to act more or less freely in his emulations of adult behaviour in this situation. However, this freedom is never absolute, but limited by the acknowledged rules that belong to that situation (p. 66). By anchoring children's play in cultural environments, this play is rooted in culture and not in the ontological nature of the child! According to Vygotskij, this acting on the basis of an imaginary situation is the core of the definition of play and makes play activity essentially different from work.

However, as stated above, Vygotskij couldn't profoundly elaborate his view on play. In his view of the difference between play and work, he seems to follow the prevailing social representation of play by that time. It remains unclear how this difference in the eyes of Vygotskij can be explained in more detail. He admits that an adult may be part of the child's play activity, especially to provide help for the appropriation of the new actions in the child's zone of proximal development. It is not explained, however, under what conditions this adult participation is acceptable or not. It goes without saying, that Vygotskij accepts the possibility of learning within the context of play, but unfortunately, he doesn't pay attention to the conceptualization of the notion of playful learning. As to the development of playing during ontogenesis, it is clear that Vygotskij sees play as an activity of the young child, which may transform in ontogenesis into strictly rule-based activities like sports and labour. Moreover, in older age, play may change into a playfull attitude to reality (Vygotsky, 1978b, p. 104).

Vygotskij's reflections on play are further developed by D. B. El'konin, both with respect to the sociogenesis and the ontogenesis of playing. From El'konins opus magnum on *The Psychology of Play* (1978), there can't be any doubt about the sociogenetic perspective: role-play is a cultural-historical phenomenon, rather than a natural propensity of children (El'konin, 1978, Ch. 2/1989, p. 66). Therefore, El'konin rejects the theories of Groos and Buytendijk, with all due respect), especially because of their minimal attention to the human factors in play, like fantasy, imitation and emotions (p. 140). El'konin also rejects the Piagetian perspective on play and his periodization of development. With regard to Schiller's view, El'konin accepts the relationship between play and arts, seeing play as an aesthetic activity (El'konin,

1978, p. 16). But he interprets this too as an historically evolving kinship, not as a natural kind.

El'konin also critically discusses the work of the Russian pedagogue Ušinskij, who was a very influential pedagogue in the late nineteenth century and the first half of the twentieth century in Soviet Russia. Ušinskij's voice was undeniably present in the prevailing social representation of the child and its play by that time in the Soviet Union. He was deeply influenced by western pedagogical thinkers like Pestalozzi and Montessori, and also wrote a pedagogical anthropology to propagate his view on education, based on a view of the human being as a complex whole that must be studied from different points of view, including a cultural perspective. Ušinskij emphasized the importance of mastering the national language for the development of children. It must be notified here, though, that Ušinskij doesn't fit easily in a purely naturalistic social representation of play, although he sticks to the assumption of play as a quality of the child's nature, as opposite to work. Ušinskij is best seen as a mix between an ontological and a cultural social representation.

Although El'konin doesn't adopt the views of western pedagogical thinkers like Pestalozzi, Fröbel and Montessori, he accepts (like Vygotskij) Ušinskij's distinction between play and work (see Ušinskij, 1912/1978), and agrees with Ušinskij on the developmental importance of culture. Hence, he appears to agree with Ušinskij's view on the role of both proximal (teacher, parents) and distal influences (like administration, pedagogical literature) on the children's development (Ušinskij, 1857/1988). El'konin admits, however, that he couldn't find a clear definition of play in Ušinskij's writings. Remarkably, El'konin doesn't give a clear definition of play either, a definition that goes beyond what was already written by Vygotskij.

The most relevant contribution to the Vygotskian view of play is El'konin's (1977) explanation of the ontogenesis of playing. In our present discussion, it is highly significant to establish that El'konin connects play to specific stages of development, which are characterised as '*leading activities*'. Different leading activities are distinguished on the basis of the child's relationship to reality. So, after an early orientation to persons (in the baby period), the child's orientation to reality changes into a focus on objects, leading to manipulative play (around the age of three), then the child's orientation to reality changes again towards a focus on persons and the relationship among these persons' roles (leading to role-play). After that at the age of about 7/8 the orientation returns to a focus on objects again, especially driven by the need to know them. Here the playful character of children's activity changes drastically in a non-play learning activity. After this stage, the children's position in the world transforms again into a person-oriented relationship, which may have playful moments now and then, but is basically not play. Rather, it is dominated by interest in other peers (like in puberty). Finally, young adolescents enter the leading activity of societal useful work (labour). It is interesting to see how in El'konin's view, play slowly disappears as a mainstream developmental activity. Like Vygotskij, he admits that play remains in sports and a specific symbolic attitude to reality. Following Vygotskij, El'konin also accepts the idea of the important role of the adult in children's play, but again, he does not indicate the conditions under which this adult participation is allowed. As to playful learning, El'konin also does not provide a satisfactory explanation. Like in Vygotskij's work, it is still unclear what is meant exactly by 'imaginative situation'. How should we understand 'situation' here? It is obviously not just the physical surrounding of the playing child. But what is it?

From a genetic point of view, Vygotskij's and El'konin's perspectives have made a great step towards a cultural-historical theory of play. However, as we also have observed, there are still some issues left that call for a theoretical explanation. Building on the ideas of Vygotskij, Alexej N. Leont'ev (1944/1983) contributed to a further elaboration of the play theory from a Cultural-Historical Activity Theory (CHAT) perspective. In his view, most of the current theories of play were too generally formulated and needed concrete specifications at different points.

According to Leont'ev, the basic drive of children to act playfully is the desire to be like a significant adult, and he specifies this by referring to the content of an adult's actions (Leont'ev, 1944/1983, p. 305). More particularly, play emerges in the wish to adopt the *role* of an adult and use the tools of the adult in this role, learn the (hidden or explicit) rules that guide these actions. In fact, in emulating the role of adults, the child also obtains opportunities to learn how to deal with the objects that populate its environment (p. 304). Although it remains unclear as yet what kind of rules we should take in mind and how these rules relate to the player's wish to act freely, Leont'ev opens here the possibility to develop a CHAT-theory of play and playing, and definitely rejects a naturalistic (ontological) approach to play. Arguing from his activity theory, Leont'ev (1975) articulates that personal *sense* (smysl') which the child makes of the demonstrated actions and of the cultural *meanings* (značenie) is essential for all play (Leont'ev, 1944/1983, pp. 311, 323). It is through the child's fantasy and personal interests triggered within the situation, that personal sense emerges. Hence, Leont'ev, in my view, reasons towards an important specification of the imagined situation as a starting point for play. An imagined situation and its implied roles and rules is actually a (more or less) free and personal emulation *of adult cultural practices.*

By interpreting play in terms of an activity theory, Leont'ev made a big step in the development of a CHAT approach to play. However, some of the problems that haunt prevailing social representations and theories of play still remain unanswered.

By combining the ideas of Vygotskij, El'konin and Leont'ev, I elaborated a CHAT approach to play. Extrapolating from the positions of Vygotskij, Leont'ev and Huizinga, I propose to conceive of play as a special version of some cultural activity ('practice'). I have published several articles to explain this theory, so I will confine myself here to summarizing the main points from this play theory (for more see among others van Oers, 2013, 2014).

As Leont'ev correctly pointed out, it is particularly the way an activity proceeds, that we should study in order to characterize play as an activity. In line with this starting point, I argued that any cultural activity can be accomplished in different ways, depending on how the parameters of such activity are filled in. I have called this the format of activities and their implied actions. Since we talk about cultural activities here, we must acknowledge that any activity is basically social: there are always other (real of virtual) participants. The main parameters of the activity format are the following (van Oers, 2013):

- *the activity is regulated by explicit and/or implicit rules*; the types of rules can vary from social rules, technical rules, conceptual rules and strategic rules. The choice of the rule type depends on what the actor tries to do: correctly employing tools requires *technical rules* (e.g. how to use a stethoscope in a doctor's play, or how to find a clip on their iPad in a library play?). The required rules may also ask for *social* (e.g. moral rules), or *conceptual rules* (when the tool is based on theory-driven assumptions); if the actor tries to organize the interactions in acceptable ways, he may use social rules or even *strategic rules*, pointing out who will take what role? For how long?;
- the activity is in one way or another appealing for the player, which results in *engagement of the actor with the activity*; therefore, the participation must be voluntary;
- the activity allows some *degrees of freedom* to the actor(s); this freedom is not an absolute freedom, as Vygotskij pointed out, and may be used for the interpretation of the rules, the establishments of the goals of the activity, the ways of using the tools, the choice of the object of activity.

The value of each of the parameters depends mainly on the child's imagination of the cultural practice in which she/he can participate and which she/he wants to emulate within the acknowledged restrictions of the practice itself. In this imagination of the child, the need for new actions may arise. While playing, the child may become aware that she/he wants to reach a new goal within this practice which she/he cannot accomplish without help. This is exactly how play activities create new zones of proximal development (as Vygotsky, 1978a) stated.

From these parameters, it can be understood that play is always based on a cultural activity that highly engages the player, allows him/her ample degrees of freedom and is rule-based. Work, then, is distinct from play since the parameters are filled in differently: in work there are strict rules which cannot or may not easily be changed; moreover, there is a more limited degree of freedom for workers, as they have to follow the successful procedures, and high engagement is often not deemed necessary for carrying out the work successfully and satisfactorily in the eyes of the managers. However, the relationship between play and work may not be oppositional. Play and work are just different genres of cultural activity, basically connected through their kinship in cultural activity. That is why 'work' can contain playful moments, and play may switch momentarily to work, as long as this makes sense to all participants engaged in the play activity and does not eliminate one or more of the parameters mentioned above.

Considering the basically social nature of cultural activities (including played activities) it is obvious that adults also play roles in a child's play, provided they abide by the values of the play parameters and don't destroy the child's engagement, freedom or acknowledged rules (see van Oers, 2013). To put it more strongly, adults should somehow be represented in play activities in order to guard the nature of the cultural activity that underlies a particular play. They may be present as real co-actors, but they may also be virtually present in the rules or habits that the child has appropriated before.

When performing new actions within the emulated practice with or without help, it often turns out that the quality of actions changes. The actions become more fluent, more generalized, abbreviated, etc., driven by the need to become a better participant in the emulated cultural practice. The qualitative change of actions and repetition of these actions eventually lead to learning (cf. Gal'perin, 1976). Playful learning then is based on voluntary performing, being helped, and repeating *new versions of actions* in the context of play, driven by the wish to improve the practice and one's level of performance. Think, for example, about the boy who played cashier in a shared play-supermarket and who gradually improved his counting with the directive help of his peers. He gradually playfully learned new actions, which were culturally meaningful and made sense for him as it improved his ability to play the cashier-role.

And how about the development of playing? We can identify this development in the fact that the child acquires the ability to participate playfully in more and more complex and sophisticated cultural practices, using more and more conceptual and strategic rules. That is why play in school doesn't stop at the age of six or seven (as Vygotskij and El'konin suggest in the periodization of development), but continues in (for instance) the emulation of the practice of researchers, or craftsmen. Inquiry-based learning is actually embedded in a play activity ('playing researchers') with clear rules, some degrees of freedom (to suggest new and wild hypotheses for example), and high engagement when the pupils investigate their own questions.

And so continues the development of playing during ontogenesis.

5.6   Possible Dialogues

Although the common sense social representations of play (capitalizing on lists of characteristics of play), still have strong positions in the world of education, educational innovations and research, the influences of theories of Piaget and the Vygotskian CHAT are increasing too. It is reasonable to presume that further dialogues between 'Piagetians' and 'Vygotskians' (CHAT-ers) may be beneficial for the future formulation of a theory of play, based on critical conceptualisations and empirical research (see King & Newstead, 2021; Pramling Samuelsson & Fleer, 2009). As topics for such dialogues, we may first look at underlying social representations and how they may influence the theoretical decisions in the (re)construction of the theories. Above, I already referred to the continuation of Schiller's ideas in Piaget and of Ušinskij's in Vygotskij's treatment of the development of playing. Deeper analyses of such assumptions may be clarifying for our understanding of both theories and their (alleged) incompatibility. In the CHAT elaboration of a theory of play above, I addressed how the previously identified burning problems: 'playful learning', 'the role of adults in play', the 'relationship between play and work' and 'the ontogenesis of playing' are solved in this theoretical perspective. From a Piagetian perspective, these CHAT solution may not always be acceptable, particularly with respect to the influential cultural role of adults in play. Piaget's definition of learning (on the basis of equilibrating) may also be different, but an interesting question remains whether they are compatible and how this may change the innovation of educational practices. Deeper ongoing discussions are needed here for each theories' self-understanding. Moreover, it remains unclear how Piagetians look at the differences of play (based on concrete operations) and work, driven by more formally defined rules. It is obvious that the CHAT solution cannot easily be integrated into a Piagetian point of view. I guess that Piagetians accept the life-long evolution of rule-based playing (like in CHAT), but how varying degrees of freedom and different types of rules in (adult) play can be dealt with, remains to be explained.

Looking at the contrast between Piagetian and CHAT-based views on play may also be useful when discussing the twenty-first-century issues like inquiry learning. From a Piagetian viewpoint, this type of learning in primary school children is best represented in what has been called 'discovery learning' since the 1960s. This type of learning is based on autonomous explorations of problems and problem situation by pupils. Initially, Bruner (1961) followed this Piagetian view on learning and knowledge construction, but he rejected it later as too individualistic and solistic (Bruner, 1986). In the past decennia, further critique was levelled against discovery learning since it neglected the important steering role of the teacher (Kirschner et al., 2006) in educational matters in school.

However, critiques on the Piagetian discovery learning (e.g. by Kirschner et al., 2006) were most of the time not aware of the CHAT reconceptualization of learning by inquiry to which their critique was not valid or convincing. Hence, these authors could only solve the problems of discovery learning by explaining it away (i.e. by propagating direct instruction). Both discovery learning (in the Piagetian sense) and direct instruction can be contrasted by a CHAT approach to inquiry-based learning, in which learning (school-based knowledge construction) is based on participation in the cultural practice called 'science'. When children's activities (together with the teacher) are organized like a research group, in which the role of researchers are imitated, meaningful problems are addressed and solved with the help of hypotheses, data collection, concept application, model construction, dialogues and polylogues, then we get a view of inquiry-based learning that is based in the CHAT-theory of play (see van Oers & Dobber, 2013) that doesn't need to eliminate the role of adults. For the future, it might be very productive to analyse and contrast these views on school learning (Piaget, direct instruction, CHAT) for finding an appropriate and practically relevant view of inquiry-based learning, that accepts the role of the adults, as well as the potentially playful nature of inquiry.

Looking at the modern literature on this issue (e.g. King & Newstead, 2021) it becomes clear that further study of the role of the teacher is badly needed (see, e.g., Dobber, et al., 2017). Further professionalisation of teachers in using play as an activity format in the classroom is a core issue in the realisation of play-based curricula, not only for inquiry-based learning, but also for other cultural domains, like music education in young children (see Nieuwmeijer et al., 2019, 2021) and the use of social media for the improvement of subject matter learning in secondary education (e.g. Cunha, 2017).

Over the years we have learnt in our own research that a major dialogue between the Piagetian approach and the Vygotskian approach needs to be focused on their respective ways of systematising and upgrading the social representations of play in parents and teachers. By the end of the 1990s, I could start this dialogue, when I was a visiting researcher at CRESAS (Centre de Recherche de l'Éducation Spécialisée et de l'Adaptation Scolaire, i.e. Research Center for Special Education and Adaptation in Schools), then part of the Institut National de Recherche Pédagogique (INRP) in Paris. In this collaboration, we compared each of our theory-driven conceptions of education: Developmental Education (for the Vygotskians) and 'Pédagogie Interactive' (for the Piagetians). It turned out that the formulation of ideas about high-quality assistance of teachers within both approaches was of utmost importance for the innovation of education, the implied social representations of play, and the new conception of education (including play and playful learning). This required permanent mutual reflections on the way teachers should participate in children's learning and play, and avoid threatening the interests of the pupils (see van Oers & Pompert, 2021).

Last but not least, dialogues on play always need to be as explicitly as possible based on sound assumptions regarding play in theory, empirical research on play and play practices. Relevant elaborations of such cultural-historical approaches to play-based practices can be found in the works of Bodrova and Leong (1996), Fleer (2014), Kingdon (2020), Pramling Samuelsson and Fleer (2009), and Ridgway et al. (2020). Modern elaborations of Piagetian ideas in educational practice can be found in Acouturier (2017) and Wadsworth (2004).

Hence, for the benefit of all children all over the world, it is important to continue our dialogues on longstanding educational programmes, based on Piagetian, Vygotskian or other conceptualisations of play (see van Oers, 2018). Only in the slipstream of our close engagement with children and their playful interactions in their encultured worlds, educationalists can improve their social representations and improve their theories of play and contribute to the benefits and well-being of children.

References

Acouturier, B. (2017). *Agir, jouer, penser. Étayage de la pratique psychomotrice éducative et thérapeutique*. DeBoeck Superieur.

Ariès, P. (1960). *Centuries of childhood*. Penguin.

Asmolov, A. G. (1982). Osnovnye principy psichologičeskogo analiza v teorii dejatel'nosti [Basic principles of a psychological analysis in Activity Theory]. *Voprosy Psichologii, 28*(2), 14–27.

Bodrova, E., & Leong, D. J. (1996). *Tools of the mind. The Vygotskian approach to early childhood education*. Pearson Education.

Bodrova, E., & Leong, D. J. (2007). *Tools of the mind: The Vygotskian approach to early childhood education*. Pearson Prentice Hall.

Bruce, T. (2004). *Developing learning in early childhood*. Paul Chapman Publishing.

Bruner, J. S. (1961). The act of discovery. *Harvard Educational Review, 31*(1), 21–32.

Bruner, J. S. (1986). *Actual minds, possible worlds*. Harvard University Press.

Burghardt, G. M. (2011). Defining and recognizing play. In A. D. Pellegrini (Ed.), *The Oxford handbook of the development of play* (pp. 9–18). Oxford University Press.

Buytendijk, F. J. J. (1932). *Het spel van mensch en dier* [Play of men and animals]. Kosmos.

Cassirer, E. (1944). *An essay on man*. Yale University Press.

Cohen, D. (2006). *The development of play*. New York University Press.

da Cunha, F.R. (2017). *Online groups in secondary education: Communicating for changing educational practices* (Doctoral thesis). VU University, Amsterdam.

D'Angour, A. (2013). Plato and play: Taking education seriously in ancient Greece. *American Journal of Play, 5*(3), 293–307.

Davydov, V. V. (1996). Ponjatie dejatel'nosti kak osnovanie issledovanij naučnoj školy L.S. Vygotskogo [The concept of activity as a foundation of the research in the academic school of Vygotskij]. *Voprosy Psichologii, 5*, 20–29.

de Dijn, A. (2020). *Freedom. An unruly history*. Harvard University Press.

Dobber, M., & van Oers, B. (2015). The role of the teacher in promoting dialogue and polylogue during inquiry activities in primary education. *Mind, Culture and Activity, 22*(4), 326–345.

Dobber, M., Zwart, R., Tanis, M., & van Oers, B. (2017). Literature review: The role of the teacher in inquiry-based education. *Educational Research Review, 22*, 194–214. https://doi.org/10.1016/j.edurev.2017.09.002

Eichberg, H. (2016). *Questioning play: What play can tell us about social life*. Routledge.

El'konin, D. B. (1971/1989). K problem periodizacii psychičeskogo razvitija v detskom vozraste [On the problem of periodization in the psychological development of children]. In D. B. El'konin, *Izbrannye psichologičeskie trudy* (pp. 60–77). Pedagogika. Translated as: *El'konin* (1977).

El'konin, D. B. (1977). Towards the problem of stages in the mental development of the child. In M. Cole (Ed.), *Soviet developmental psychology* (pp. 538–563). Sharpe.

El'konin, D. B. (1978). *Psichologija igry* [The psychology of play]. Pedagogika.

Fink, E. (1960/2016). *Play as a symbol of the world, and other writings*. Indiana University Press.

Fleer, M. (2014). *Theorising play in the early years*. Cambridge University Press.

Gal'perin, P. J. (1976). *Vvedenie v psicholoiju* [Introduction to psychology]. Izd-vo Moskovskogo Universiteta.

Groos, K. (1898). *The play of animals*. Appleton.

Groos, K. (1901). *The play of man*. Heinemann.

Hirsch-Pasek, K., Michnick-Golinkoff, R., Berk, L. E., & Singer, D. G. (2009). *A mandate for playful learning in pre-school: Presenting the evidence*. Oxford University Press.

Huizinga, J. (1938). *Homo Ludens*. Tjeenk Willink.

King, P., & Newstead, S. (Eds.). (2021). *Play across childhood: International perspectives on diverse contexts of play*. Macmillan.

Kingdon, Z. (Ed.). (2020). *A Vygotskian analysis of children's play behaviours: Beyond the home corner*. Routledge.

Kirschner, P. A., Sweller, J., & Clark, R. E. (2006). Why minimal guidance during instruction does not work: An analysis of the failure of constructivist, discovery, problem-based, experiential, and inquiry-based teaching. *Educational Psychologist, 41*(2), 75–86. https://doi.org/10.1207/s15326985ep4102_1

Leont'ev, A. N. (1944/1983). Psichologičeskie osnovy doškol'oj igry [Psychological foundations of young children's play]. In A. N. Leont'ev, *Izbrannye Psichologičeskie Proizvedenija, T.1* (pp. 303–323). Pedagogika. Translated as: *Activity, consciousness, personality*. Prentice Hall.

Leont'ev, A. N. (1975). *Dejatel'nost, soznanie, ličnost'* [Activity, consciousness, personality]. Izd-vo Političeskoi Literatury.

Mellou, E. (1994). Play theories: A contemporary review. *Early Child Development and Care, 102*, 91–100.

Montessori, M. (1913). *Pedagogical anthropology*. F.A. Stokes Company.

Moran, M., & Brown, V. (2017). Play as a space for possibilities. In A. Woods (Ed.), *Child-initiated play and learning: Planning for possibilities in the early years* (pp. 95–107). Routledge.

Moscovici, S. (1961). *La psychanalyse. Son image et son public*. Presses Universitaires de France.

Moscovici, S. (1981). On social representations. In J. Forgas (Ed.), *Social cognition: Perspectives on everyday understanding*. Academic Press.

Nieuwmeijer, C., Marshal, N., & van Oers, B. (2021). Musical play in the early years: the impact of a professional development program on teacher efficacy of early years generalist teachers. *Research Papers in Education.* https://doi.org/10.1080/02671522.2021.1998207

Nieuwmeijer, C., Marshall, N., & van Oers, B. (2019). Dutch early years classroom teachers facilitating and guiding musical play: Problems and opportunities. *European Early Childhood Education Research Journal, 39*(6), 860–871. https://doi.org/10.1080/1350293X.2019.1678962

Piaget, J. (1951). *Play, dreams and imitation in childhood.* Norton. Translation of *La formation du symbole chez l'enfant* (1945).

Piaget, J. (1979). *Le structuralisme.* Presses Universitaires de France.

Plato, T. (2007). *The Republic.* Penguin Group.

Pramling Samuelsson, I., & Fleer, M. (Eds.). (2009). *Play and learning in early childhood settings: International perspectives.* Springer.

Ridgway, A., Quiñones, G., & Li, L. (Eds.). (2020). *Peer play and relationships in early childhood.* Springer.

Sammut, G., Andreouli, E., Gaskell, G., & Valsiner, J. (Eds.). (2015a). *The Cambridge handbook of social representations.* Cambridge University Press.

Sammut, G., Andreouli, E., Gaskell, G., & Valsiner, J. (Eds.). (2015b). Social representations: A revolutionary paradigm? In *The Cambridge handbook of social representations.* Cambridge University Press.

Santer, J., Griffiths, C., & Goodall, D. (2007). *Free play in early childhood: A literature review.* National Children's Bureau.

Schiller, F. (1794/1980). Über die ästhetische Erziehung des Menschen in einer Reihe von Briefe [On the esthetic education of humans in a series of letters]. In F. Schiller, *Werke in vier Bänden* (Bd. 4, pp. 361–439). Manfred Pawlak Verlag.

Singer, E. (2015). Play and playfulness, basic features of early childhood education. *European Early Childhood Education Research Journal, 21*(2), 172–184. https://doi.org/10.1080/1350293X.2013.789198

Sutton-Smith, B. (1997). *The ambiguity of play.* Harvard University Press.

Theobald, K. (2011). *Ästhetik, Spiel und Playing Arts* [Aesthetics, play, and playing arts]. Diplomarbeit in Erziehungswissenschaft (Sozialpädagogik). Johannes Gutenberg Universität.

Tryphon, A., & Vonèche, J. (Eds.). (1996). *Piaget—Vygotsky: The social genesis of thought.* Psychology Press.

Ušinskij, K. (1857/1988). Tri elementa školy [Three elements of school]. In K. D. Ušinskij, *Pedagogičeskie Sočinenija, T.1* (pp. 177–193). Pedagogika.

Ušinskij, K. (1912/1978). *Čelovek kak predmet vospitanija: opyt pedagogičeskoj antropologii.* Translated as: *Man as the object of education: An essay in pedagogical anthropology.* Progress.

van Oers, B. (2013). Is it play? Towards a reconceptualisation of role-play from an activity theory perspective. European Early Childhood Education Research Journal, 21(2), 185–198. https://doi.org/10.1080/1350293X.2013.789199.

van Oers, B. (2014). Cultural-historical perspectives on play. In L. Brooker, S. Edwards, & M. Blaise (Eds.), *SAGE handbook of play and learning in early childhood* (pp. 56–66). Sage.

van Oers, B. (2018). Longstanding and innovative programs in early childhood education: An introduction. In M. Fleer & B. van Oers (Eds.), *International handbook of early childhood education* (pp. 969–994). Springer.

van Oers, B., & Dobber, M. (2013). Communication and regulation in a problem-oriented primary school curriculum. In D. Whitebread, N. Mercer, C. Howe, & C. Tolmie (Eds.), *Self-regulation and dialogue in primary classrooms. British Journal of Educational Psychology. Monograph Series, No. 10* (pp. 93–110). BPS.

van Oers, B., & Pompert, B. (2021). Assisting teachers for curriculum innovation: An international comparative study. *New Ideas in Child and Educational Psychology, 1*(1), 43–76. https://doi.org/10.11621/nicep.2021.0303

Vygotskij, L. S. (1926/1991). *Pedagogičeskaja psichologija* [Pedagogical psychology]. Pedagogika. Translated as: *Educational psychology.* St Lucie Press.

Vygotskij, L. S. (1934/1982). Myšlenie i rec. APN. In *Sobranye Sochinenij, Vol. 2. Pedagogika,* 1982. Translated by L. S. Vygotsky, *Thinking and speech.* Springer 1987.

Vygotskij, L. S. (1966). Igra i eё rol' v psichičeskom razvitii rebёnka [Play and its role in the psychological development of the children]. *Voprosy Psichologii, 6,* 62–76. Partly translated in Vygotsky, 1978b.

Vygotsky, L. S. (1978a). *Mind in society: The development of higher psychological processes.* Harvard University Press.

Vygotsky, L. S. (1978b). The role of play in development. In L. S. Vygotsky, *Mind in society: The development of higher psychological processes* (pp. 92–104). Harvard University Press.

Wadsworth, B. J. (2004). *Piaget's theory of cognitive and affective development: Foundations of constructivism.* Longman.

Wittgenstein, L. (1953). *Philosophische Untersuchungen* [Philosophical investigations]. Suhrkamp.

Bert van Oers is professor in 'Cultural-historical theory of education' in the department Research and Theory of Education at the VU University Amsterdam. In 2004 he was awarded a honorary doctor's degree by the University of Jyväskylä in Finland. His research approach is based on Cultural-Historical Activity Theory (CHAT) and his main research interest is play as a context for learning (mathematics, literacy, music). He was one of the founders of the Dutch play-based curriculum 'Developmental Education' for primary school. In addition to his publications in Dutch, he published many articles and book chapters in English: *Developmental Education for Young Children* (2012), *Narratives of Childhood* (2003), and co-edited books, like *The Transformation of Learning: Advances in Cultural-Historical Activity Theory* (2008) and *The International Handbook of Early Childhood Education* (with Marilyn Fleer, Australia). He is member of a number of editorial boards of English and Russian journals in early childhood education.

Chapter 6
Children's Perspectives Informing Theories and Nordic Preschool Practice

Camilla Björklund and Ingrid Pramling Samuelsson

Abstract In this chapter, we aim to explore and discuss how the notions of child perspective and children's perspectives can be traced back to Piaget's and Vygotsky's theories, but we also relate this to a later approach based on empirical studies in the context of preschool, called *developmental pedagogy*. Developmental pedagogy has its origin in a methodology called phenomenography, focusing on describing the learner's perspective of the world around them—and through this centering the child's perspective in teaching and learning in early-years education. The question we focus our discussion on is how a child perspective and children's perspectives can be understood in Piaget, Vygotsky, and developmental pedagogy, as well as what the implications for Nordic preschool practice are.

6.1 Introduction

In this chapter, we aim to bring to the fore the notions of children's perspectives and child perspective, as key in the scientific knowledge of children's learning and development in Piaget's and Vygotsky's theories as well as developmental pedagogy. A *child perspective* is defined by Sommer et al. (2010) as what teachers believe is the best for the child based on his or her knowledge; in other words, an adult's idea about the child's world. *Children's perspectives*, on the other hand, are children's own expressions and ways of seeing their surrounding world. The two notions are thus very different concerning whose voice is foregrounded, but they are seldom distinguished from each other in research or practice. Children's perspectives are often taken-for-granted, as if it would be sufficient to attend to what concerns children, with adults keeping in mind a child perspective. In this sense, preschool has traditionally always had a kind of child perspective—its education focused on the child rather than the

C. Björklund (✉) · I. Pramling Samuelsson
University of Gothenburg, Gothenburg, Sweden
e-mail: Camilla.Bjorklund@ped.gu.se

I. Pramling Samuelsson
e-mail: Ingrid.Pramling@ped.gu.se

subject matter to be learned (Pramling Samuelsson & Asplund Carlsson, 2014). This may often differ from the perspectives held by the children themselves, however; that is, the children's perspectives. While the difference between these notions and their significance for children and childhood experiences have only recently received attention in debates about early childhood education, we can see how this interest has been influenced by Piaget's and Vygotsky's work as early as the beginning and middle of the last century, and is specifically highlighted in the more recently developed developmental pedagogy. Developmental pedagogy has its origin in a methodology called phenomenography where focusing on describing the learner's perspective of the world around them is key and through this centering the child's perspective in teaching and learning in early-years education. In this chapter, we will therefore focus on these three approaches regarding their taking a child perspective and children's perspectives as key to understanding children's development and learning. Here, we would like to refer to Chapman (1992), who states that the significance of a theory should be measured not in its completeness but in the importance of the problems it poses. Thereby, in this particular discussion, we will not try to cover the whole depth and breadth of these theories but rather to highlight how children's perspectives and a child perspective have run through the most influential theories on child development of our time as well as contemporary education. The chapter will start with an inquiry of how the child's perspective come through in Piaget's studies of children's development, followed by Vygotsky's cultural-historical theory seen from a Western educational perspective. We then describe developmental pedagogy as it is implemented in Swedish early childhood education and the traces of Piaget's and Vygotsky's theories that can be recognized in the pedagogy.

6.2   What We Learn from Piaget's Studies of children's Development

A young Jean Piaget worked with intelligence testing of young children. It is well known that this woke an interest in him to understand why children answered non-logically to given tasks. He devoted a tremendous amount of time and effort to studying and describing the intellectual development of the child, building a model of description for this development in terms of cognitive processes and stages. Children's perspectives were present from the beginning of Piaget's work, with an aim to understand how the child reasons and how intellectual skills develop. He did this by developing methods—so-called clinical observations and clinical interviews—through which a trained observer or interviewer was able to reveal the context of the child's answers and solutions, whether based on reflection, beliefs, play, or even irrelevant chatter (Piaget, 1973). Children's expressions are thus taken seriously, and multiple observations and interviews build the foundation of Piaget's universal theory of intellectual development.

6.2.1 Central Concepts in Piaget's Theory

Piaget's primary goal in his lifelong work can perhaps be summarized as a search for how knowledge is constructed and transformed in development (Inhelder, 1992). The main objective then becomes to study transitions from less effective toward more effective and valid knowledge.

Piaget's studies of children's development pay attention to the individual child. He had a great interest in getting to know how the child perceives his or her surrounding world and made extensive efforts through multiple investigations and publications to unravel the child's cognitive progress. In his book *Play, Dreams and Imitation in Childhood* (Piaget, 1962), he explicitly states that, in order to study the beginnings of children's representations, he dedicates himself to studies in which individual processes dominate the collective factors, particularly in imitation and symbolic play.

Piaget's background in biology can be discerned in his explanation of how the main condition for development is the strive for *equilibrium* as a continuous process. The child develops an idea of something in reality, into which he assimilates other experiences. When the child has new experiences that do not fit into his or her thinking process, this results in a state of disequilibrium. The child now has to either assimilate the new experiences to attain equilibrium or accommodate the new idea. This process of adaptation is the basis of cognitive development, here viewed as a changed way of thinking, which takes place when the child is able to make an accommodation to a new reality (Piaget, 1976). In Piaget's studies, we see how the core concepts of the theory, *assimilation* and *accommodation*, come together in the symbolic function that can be observed in children's play. Play, in Piagetian terms, is heavily influenced by the assimilation process. During play, the child cares little about objects' physical features—a building brick can be a phone or a wooden stick can be a sword. The objects are assimilated to the child's needs and earlier experiences to fit the purpose of the play. Imitation play, on the other hand, bears accommodative features as the goal is to reproduce actions that are defined by external circumstances. To construct this highly theoretical model for describing intellectual development, the researcher needs to apply children's perspectives, whereby the child's imagination is taken seriously and regarded as an expression of how the child understands the world.

Piaget regards the child's intellectual development as a continuum of transition from less to more valid knowledge (Inhelder, 1992), but also describes it as qualitative changes in perceptions. He describes the development in stages, but there are never any abrupt transits between the stages. The first stage is characterized by reflexes and the child's acts, which gradually shape schemas that help the child organize his or her interaction with the environment (Piaget, 1973). Gradually, the child learns that the environment consists of objects independent of him- or herself. This means that the child realizes that objects exist even if he or she does not perceive them in the immediate space and time. Observations of children's acts, particularly repeating actions and the coordination of actions, may reveal emerging cognitive structures (or schemas); that is, the meaning behind children's actions, utterances, or other expressions (Nutbrown, 2011). The pre-operational period in thinking is the stage most often described within the preschool ages. This is characterized by an increasing ability to recapitulate actions, for instance when the child is able to determine a number of items as equal even if the items have been physically rearranged, but is not yet able to draw conclusions, mentally manipulate ideas, or extract general rules from systematic investigations. What is essential in Piaget's theory of intellectual development, however, is that knowledge and intellectual development do not occur spontaneously or through maturation but rather have to be constructed through an adaptive process, which also means that knowledge is never transmitted directly from the environment to the child but is instead constructed from the child's subjective perspective (Piaget, 1952).

Piaget studied children's actions as expressions of the child's thoughts and understanding. Interpreting the aim of the child's play and acts then became important for understanding the developing mind of the child. In fact, Piaget studied interactions between children and other people as a source of knowledge construction. Their coordination of viewpoints and intersubjectivity was considered to be the origin of objective knowledge (Inhelder, 1992). However, in Piaget's theory development is described in terms of the child's cognition, whereby social, environmental, and cultural influence are said to have the role of pointing the child's attention to certain objects or phenomena (Beilin, 1992). Thus, in Piaget's line of reasoning, social environment, interaction, and cooperation are necessary conditions for intellectual development but the construction of knowledge is an individual process.

Children's perspectives are present throughout Piaget's theory as the basis for his ambition to form a general theory of intellectual development but are perhaps the most explicit in the notion of *egocentrism*. At the beginning of the intellectual development, the child is considered to be highly egocentric in his or her thoughts. This is observed in the way children reason and reflects upon the world, for example, as discussed in Piaget (1973, p. 170):

(Excerpt from interview with child aged 6 years 6 months)

Interviewer:	Have you seen the clouds moving?
Child:	Yes.
Int:	Can you make them move yourself?
Child:	Yes, by walking.
Int:	What happens when you walk?
Child:	It makes them move.
Int:	What makes them move?
Child:	We do, because we walk and then they follow us.
Int:	What makes them follow us?
Child:	Because we walk.
Int:	How do you know that?
Child:	Because when you look up in the sky, they are moving.
Int:	Could you make them go the other way if you wanted to?
Child:	By turning round and walking back.

| Int: | And what would the clouds do then? |
| Child: | They'd go back. |

Piaget claims that these kinds of dialogues make it possible to identify the nature of the child's ideas. In this example, his interpretation of the child's ideas is that the child perceives him- or herself as participating in actions along with the sun and the clouds, whereby his or her intentions or will are coordinated with the will of the other. During the first years of life, the child does not differentiate him- or herself from the environment; but gradually, as in the reasoning in the example above, the child's perception of the relationship between his or her actions and changes in the environment become more dynamic (Piaget, 1973). Decentration is thereby fundamental for intellectual development. As long as the child is egocentric in his or her thoughts, assimilation dominates the adaptive process and the child only develops a subjective knowledge of the world. Flexibility between different views about a phenomenon is thereby necessary in order to enable accommodation and thus a better balance between what is known and what is new. Piaget's great interest in and efforts to explain the child's way of perceiving the world focus on the child's own experiences of the world and how objects and the child him- or herself relate to one another. More recent research has offered evidence of children's ability to decentrate already at an early age, and to take the other person's view that is different from theirs, when encountering familiar problem situations (see, e.g., Donaldson, 1978; Mauritzson & Säljö, 2001). Whatever the interpretations may result in, Piaget's attention to children's perspectives on the world has inspired many researchers to replicate his studies and challenges the knowledge of the child's intellectual development and learning.

Thus, Piaget has made a significant contribution to the attention in research and practice directed at *the mind of the child*, further explored in contemporary research in psychology as well as education. His interest is in the universality of competences and features of the developing mind and thought (Beilin, 1992). What Piaget accomplished is thereby a general picture of the intellectual development among children, based on empirical observations of their acts and interaction, which are interpreted by taking the child's way of understanding as the outset. In sum, in accordance with Chapman's argument regarding the validity of a theory (1992), we find that the questions Piaget raised should perhaps be seen as more relevant for early childhood education than the specific model he outlined. Theories are often regarded as being developed in reaction to dominant paradigms, and in Piaget's case, his empirical work and detailed documentations of children's intellectual development represent an argument against the insufficiency of nativist or empiricist views, which he found could not help in the understanding of development. That is, knowledge cannot be imported directly from the outside; nor is development pre-determined. His work arose from a genuine interest in children's perspectives and resulted in a general theory on intellectual development. The individual child thus became invisible in favor of the general and abstract child (Piaget, 1985), but has nevertheless informed preschool education by affording a child perspective based on scientific inquiries into the child's perception of the world.

6.2.2   Consequences of Piaget's theory for preschool education

Piaget focused on *discovery processes* in the child (Inhelder, 1992), and rarely used the term "learning". To Piaget, learning meant instructive actions such as showing the child that a number of objects are equal in number when rearranged, which does not necessarily lead to a developed concept of numbers. Instead, to acquire new knowledge, the child has to actively construct the knowledge him- or herself when facing some kind of contradiction (to the child's conception), or encounter some surprising event that triggers adaptive efforts to obtain equilibrium again.

The Piagetian child is a *"scientist", an exploring child*. This metaphor stems from the conjecture that children construct knowledge when searching for coherence, consistency, and application of experiences (Case, 1992). Athey (2007) also describes this development based on multiple observations in terms of schemas; that is, repeating actions coordinated with other actions, constituting a form of thought in the child. In education, these forms of thought are nourished by encounters with content that extends the particular form of thought. A child's interest in, for example, circular objects may thus be enriched by circular actions that extend the child's understanding and form of thought.

Even though Piaget and his colleagues wrote sparsely about education, his theory has influenced the discourse on teaching and learning in research and practice in the US and other parts of the world. Murray (1992) states that this should not come as a surprise, as Piaget's work was the only theory before the 1960s to actually deal with how children understand the content and concepts that are included in most curricula, such as arithmetic, geometry, time, and space.

This influence can be found, for instance, in a highly popular children's TV show in Sweden (inspired by the American show *Sesame Street*) during the 1980s, called *Five Ants are More than Four Elephants* (our translation). The show had the educational intention to teach children literacy and numeracy concepts, framed in short, humoristic sketches accompanied by songs and animations. The discovery of concept meanings by contrasting, for example, different ways of categorizing a set of objects, was the basic framework. The title of the show also clearly flirts with the Piagetian description of children's conception of conservation as a central feature of developing number concepts (Piaget & Szeminska, 1977/2001)—the size of the objects to be counted should not interfere with the number of objects. That is, the abstraction of numerical relationships depends on the ability to differentiate physical features, such as size, from numerical ones. In this particular show, we can see actors mirroring seemingly naïve perceptions of worldly phenomena and concepts, which other actors contrast with other, more advanced explanations of relationships or meaning, in a child-oriented and playful setting. Children's different ways of perceiving the world are thus highlighted and contrasted, to help the viewer (the child) recognize his or her own perspective and encounter other perspectives, resulting in the adaptive process that stimulates intellectual development.

In line with Piaget's view (according to Youniss & Damon, 1992), teaching entails supporting children in developing intellectual instruments to coordinate knowledge, rather than developing procedures. This has led to an emphasis on group work and active discovery, rather than teaching in a master-pupil fashion. The most well-known implementation of Piaget's theory in early childhood education is perhaps the High-Scope program. In the US in 1970, an initiative was taken to develop early childhood education that would support children at risk of educational failure, by establishing the HighScope Educational Research Foundation. The HighScope program includes a scientifically based curriculum and program for instruction with observation-based assessment tools for preschool children. The cognitively oriented curriculum is characterized by teachers interacting with children, both individually and in small groups, to support learning at the child's own level of cognitive development. Piaget's theory provided the foundation for this model, based on the assumption that mental growth occurs through children's active exploration and manipulation of their environment (Weikart, 1981). Today, the HighScope program can be found in several countries outside the US as well. Its main feature is a large number of goals, such as notions that children should learn, but also the process of "plan-do-review", whereby each child is to plan and tell the teacher what he or she intends to do (playing role play, working with construction materials, working with creative arts, reading books, etc.). After a set time, the child returns to the teacher and retells what he or she has done (Sanders & Farago, 2018).

In Sweden, for example, we do not find preschool programs similar to those in the US (e.g., HighScope), because of differences in the educational system and childcare traditions. There is a national curriculum that manifests the intentions of the Education Act (SFS, 2010:800) by formulating goals for children's development and learning within academic areas of knowledge, as well as values and norms to strive for; but there are no achievement goals, and the preschool teachers who are responsible for carrying out the pedagogical practice according to these goals are free to choose how to orchestrate their teaching. Thus, we find a diversity of approaches to teaching in contemporary Swedish preschool education. Nevertheless, in Swedish childhood and preschool practice, we find indications of Piaget's contribution from a historical perspective, for example, in the *Barnstugeutredningen* (Survey of Preschools, Ministry of Health and Social Affairs, 1972) in the 1970s. This survey aimed to renew the content and organization of preschools in Sweden. It was a reaction to an increasing number of working parents, both mothers and fathers, creating a demand for the government to aid in the care of young children. Preschools began to expand dramatically within only a few years (Johansson et al., 2018). The renewal of the preschool came to be based on Piaget's theory for the cognitive aspects of development, and on Homburger-Eriksen for the social-emotional aspects. Communication became a key notion, as did the organization of different physical areas where children could freely explore and experiment. One can conclude that children's perspectives were put on the agenda, inspired by Piaget's many studies in which children's own ideas were made visible (Pramling, 1983). A practical consequence was that, in order to understand the child's world, teachers had to be skilled in communicating with children (Doverborg & Pramling Samuelsson, 1985/2012). This can be seen as the beginning of an increasing interest in children's perspectives in education as well as seeing the child's subjective world, which in turn directs awareness to children's own rights. For a short period of time, this approach was called dialogue pedagogy (Schyl-Bjurman & Strömstedt-Lind, 1976; see also Pramling Samuelsson, 2003). However, the emphasis on communication led to a decreasing prominence of the content for learning in preschool.

6.3   Vygotsky and the Cultural-Historical Theory from a Western Perspective

If Piaget is understood as directing attention to the individual child, Vygotsky is often described as attending to the social child. Nevertheless, Vygotsky's view on children's development is very much based on an interest in children's perspectives, which can be seen not least in his thorough investigations of concept development among children, for instance reflected in the well-known quote: "children have their own preschool arithmetic, which only myopic psychologists could ignore" (Vygotsky, 1978, p. 84). Our interpretation of the quote, based on our reading of Vygotsky, is that the child always has a reason and logic behind their actions and speech, but it may be different from the adult's logic.

6.3.1   Key Concepts in Theory Based on Vygotsky

There are certain notions that are associated with Vygotsky (1987) and the cultural-historical theory he developed, which many recent researchers have further developed and added new notions to. Here, we will briefly discuss some of them, which have direct implications on how this theory is used in preschool education in the Nordic countries and that reflect Vygotsky's attention to children's perspectives.

The first and most widely used notion is *zone of proximal development* (ZPD), which relates to the development of children's higher cognitive and psychological functions (Vygotsky, 1978). These functions concern language and writing, as well as number concepts, logical conclusions, remembering, and selective attention. ZPD is the relationship between what the child can do by her- or himself (individually) and what the child can manage along with a more competent adult or peer (socially). Here, the focus is on the child's way of knowing and mastering, and what he or she is able to do in the near future. Here, we find children's perspectives treated as essential, in that it is necessary to identify the child's way of knowing in order to define where the child is on his or her developmental path. ZPD is a notion that connects the individual and social aspects of learning. The child's development is said to proceed through the mechanism of *mediation*. Higher mental processes are mediated by psychological tools such as language, signs, and symbols; thus, mediation can be seen as the process in which the teacher is involved when challenging the child's cognitive understanding. Today, mediation is by Wertsch (2007) also bringing emotional aspects into the learning process, although Vygotsky's theory already included emotions in the notion of "perezhivanie" (Fleer et al., 2017).

The Vygotskian tradition specifically emphasizes semiotic mediation; that is, the child is coming into contact with and starting to take over cultural tools (appropriation) that will shape—mediate—how he or she perceives, thinks, etc. Language thus came to be specific in the child's development of knowledge. On the other hand, in her doctoral thesis Os (2019) points to the notion of mediation as being close to many other notions—for example facilitating, supporting, promoting, fostering, scaffolding, and involvement—and shows how mediation is a common interactive process among toddlers, who due to their young age have limited language skills but nevertheless strive to make themselves understood through other expressional modes than verbal ones. In toddler groups in Norway, teachers involve themselves in children's play and mealtimes and mediate meaning by making individual children's ideas visible. Mediation can thus be indirect or direct, in relation to an individual child or a group of children. Indirect mediation targeted at a group of children offers more space for them to continue their joint play, while the opposite, direct mediation in relation to one child, often stops the play between children. Thus, for the mediation process to succeed, there has to be an awareness of the child's understanding and directed attention; yet again, the children's perspectives become the key to describing and interpreting learning and development. This is perhaps particularly evident in observations of toddlers—that is, very young children—who strive daily to understand and make themselves understood through other expressional modes than verbal ones. This directs attention to the notion of *intersubjectivity*, introduced by Rommetveit (1974); that is, how the participants manage to establish joint attention, which is thereby related both to the child's and the adult's coordinated perspectives. The notion of intersubjectivity has become important for understanding the communication between child and teacher, but also between children in play (see Pramling et al., 2019).

When a child grows increasingly more familiar with a praxis, such as mealtimes or how to play games, and the tools connected to these practices (Säljö, 2005), this implies that he or she can see something as specific but also possible to view in different ways. This process is called *appropriation,* a notion developed by more recent researchers in the cultural-historical theory (see Wertsch, 1998) and can be viewed as a question of how mankind has developed (and still is developing) *cultural tools* for preserving and mediating insights and experiences. Wallerstedt et al. (2014) state that these tools may comprise intellectual tools, including language categories and distinctions, narratives and other language genres—sometimes called discursive tools—and physical tools (also known as artefacts) such as books, music sheets, mobile telephones, instruments, watches, compasses, or maps. Appropriation is then the active acquisition and formation of such cultural tools.

Mediation and appropriation are both dependent on language and the child's involvement in the negotiation of meaning. The cultural-historical theory is *non-dualistic*; that is, the world around the child cannot be separated from his or her experienced world. In this way, the communication process is always related to something that is communicated about, a content experienced by the communicating partners. Mediation then includes both a content that is focused on and how the meaning of this *something* is mediated. Thus, "what" cannot be separated from "how". On the other hand, Elkonin (2005), a colleague of Vygotsky claimed that children have different *activity directions*, or goals for their activities, at different ages. This can be viewed as equivalent to the Piagetian perspective of stages, although Piaget relates these to mind and inner motivation while the cultural-historical perspective views the actions as related to the social world. Elkonin (1972) sees emotional and intellectual development as closely related, and criticizes a view on child development that most often separates them. The first period in a young child's life concerns how children relate to other humans through direct personal and emotional activities. Children then become increasingly more focused on physical objects to manipulate, objects that carry social meaning related to adults, which leads to role play. This period of role play is viewed as necessary for the child to move into the next period of human activities and sees them as social and meaningful, which is the foundation for knowledge development and learning in school.

6.3.2   Implications of the Cultural-Historical Perspective in Preschools

If we look at preschool education in the Nordic countries today, we see a strong emphasis on communication and interaction, and a tendency to organize activities in smaller groups for short periods of time during the day (Pramling Samuelsson et al., 2015; Sheridan et al., 2015). We can also see the influence of a cultural-historical perspective, in that language has been the dominant topic in early childhood education as well as, for example, in the goals in Sweden's revised preschool curriculum (National Agency for Education, 2019). However, this does not necessarily reflects a view entailing participating in activities along with more advanced peers or adults, by which meaning and cultural tools could be mediated. This is apparently a challenging task, as it goes beyond working on a joint project with others and highlights the need to establish and maintain intersubjectivity and thus adhere to different perspectives.

In the book *A Cultural-Historical Study of Children Learning Science* (Fleer & Pramling, 2015, p. 171), communication around skeletons, which the children are learning about and are asked here to make a drawing of, is represented and analyzed:

Polly: Can I paint the hair?

Teacher:	You can maybe all paint these (points to the ribs). He has these ones, you see. And then the chest here. Under the head.
Eva:	But can I do a man, me?
Teacher:	Feel free, paint a man here.
Malin:	I'm painting my Mum!
Teacher:	Are you painting your Mum's skeleton?
Malin:	Mmm.
	(—)
Teacher:	Look, Richard has done that too. Look, it looks just like that too (points to the skeleton).
Richard:	That's me! That's me!
Teacher:	Is it your skeleton?
Richard:	Yes!
Teacher:	It looks just like that.

In the empirical example above, we can see how every child's perspective is high-lighted and constitutes the ground for the teacher to understand what the children express, for instance that they have grasped that every body has a skeleton. In other words, the children's perspectives are necessary for the teacher to know what her next step should be in challenging the learning process, in terms of ZPD.

Os (2019) claims that a misunderstanding of the cultural-historical perspective has led to teachers sometimes acting with the belief that if they communicate with children, in general terms, the children will consequently develop skills and knowledge. There are also examples in Os's study that show how the teacher unintentionally destroys the play through her mediating actions focusing on only one child at a time. Mediation between peers is often more positive, which means that the play continues when a group of children is the focus of the mediation. As appropriation and mediation take place when adults or more advanced peers communicate *about what they are doing*, communication becomes the most central aspect of preschool pedagogy. However, teachers then have to listen to children in order to know how to challenge them within their ZPD. However, this is a much more vague and general view on applying the idea of ZPD in preschool education than the idea Vygotsky once developed, in which he measured the individual child's knowledge before and after mediation to evaluate the learning that had taken place.

The notion of *active participation* is often (mis)used in practice claiming to take a cultural-historical perspective in both research and practice. It may signal to teachers that it is sufficient to activate children in something for learning to occur (Sheridan et al., 2009). Active participation is very seldom used the other way around, with *teachers* being active in the children's world, which would be much closer to the original idea of ZPD. Thus, the difference is again obvious when one considers whether it is a child perspective or children's perspectives that are foregrounded.

6.4   Developmental Pedagogy—Placing the Children's Perspectives and Content Focus at the Center of Attention

Developmental pedagogy advocates a pedagogical approach aimed at developing children's values, skills, and understanding as knowledge formation. It is a research-based approach that has been used in early childhood education for the last 30 years, mainly in Sweden. The pedagogy, grounded in phenomenography (closely linked to phenomenological approaches in European philosophy), has developed through multiple empirical studies in Swedish preschools (see Pramling & Pramling Samuelsson, 2011). At the center of this pedagogy is the notion of children's perspectives; but also, in line with the theoretical framework it is based on, the notion that to understand someone's perspective of something one needs to know what that something is, which leads to a focus also directed at the content for learning. Learning is always the learning of something; thus, children's ways of experiencing or perceiving this something is essential to pedagogical practice. Developmental pedagogy is characterized by the teacher participating as a partner in children's learning and nurturing the children's development by listening to their voices while still taking an active role in order to understand and extend their thinking. This is why play is also an essential feature of developmental pedagogy. Play and learning are different, but are interconnected through common features, which is reflected in the notion of "the playing, learning child" (Pramling Samuelsson & Asplund Carlsson, 2008).

6.4.1   Key Concepts in Developmental Pedagogy

Developmental pedagogy is based on a phenomenographic research approach developed by a research group under the leadership of Professor Ference Marton at the University of Gothenburg in the 1970s. The research began to focus specifically on the subjective world of the learner, and it soon became clear that students do not understand or misunderstand but rather create a variety of understandings, which researchers came to describe as a variation of meanings (Marton, 1981). This led to many studies in which people expressed their understandings in interviews with open-ended questions (Marton & Booth, 1997). The focus of the methodological framework for investigation was initially university students, but it soon led to classroom studies and then to studies of children's experiences, of which *The Child's Conception of Learning* was the first (Pramling, 1983). The results of Pramling's study showed different stages of children's thinking and their talk about their own learning related to age. There was a resemblance to Piaget's qualitative levels of understanding, but in Pramling's study it became obvious that the content in focus complicated the qualitative levels and had a great impact on the child's ways of experiencing the content in question.

The ontological foundation of phenomenography and thus developmental pedagogy is non-dualistic; that is, the subject (the child) and the object (the surrounding world) are perceived as being included in an internal relationship, making one composite whole of the child's understanding and his or her context. This means that one important aspect, with educational implications, is that a phenomenon appears different to different people because they discern different aspects of it. Thus, it is essential to determine the *qualitatively different ways* in which a phenomenon can be distinguished by children. By describing the various ways children think and express themselves, it is possible to reveal the child's understanding and describe these differences in terms of critical aspects (Marton, 2015). In order to help children discern and focus on critical aspects of a certain phenomenon, a teacher has to contribute to creating the necessary pattern of variation and invariance that liberates new ways of seeing the phenomenon. Simultaneity and variation are thereby central notions in the pedagogy, both for understanding the child's learning process and for orchestrating for learning by offering the child experiences that extend his or her way of seeing phenomena in the surrounding world. Variation and simultaneous experiencing are furthermore fundamental to several aspects of cognitive development in childhood, including the ability to distinguish one learning object or phenomenon from another. This, in turn, is fundamental, for instance, to the categorization process. For example, for a young child to be able to understand the concept of animals, rather than simply designating a single animal an animal it is necessary for the child to experience a variety of animals in order to distinguish the essential features that constitute what we call an animal. However, it is not sufficient to let the child experience a variety of animals. He or she also needs to experience that an animal differs from other living things, such as humans or plants. Gradually, the child will come to understand the concept of a type of animal, also distinguishing the critical features of a dog or a bird from those of other animals.

The notions that constitute the framework of developmental pedagogy have emerged based on both theoretical conjectures of the nature of knowledge and learning and empirical conclusions from a large number of studies. Children's perspectives and ways of experiencing phenomena in their surrounding world are at the center of the theoretical framework and pedagogy. Key notions for describing the learning and teaching of young children are: open-ended communication, content of the teaching as a learning object, the strategy for learning (the learning act), qualitative differences in understanding or expanding concepts, variation (as both a result of teaching and a source for teaching), metacognition, and finally the playing, learning child. All these notions reflect an interactive, reflective educational practice whereby the content to be learned, or rather how the content appears to the learners, is important to consider as it is related to how this content can be learned (and taught).

For grasping children's perspectives, *open-ended communication* is a must. Listening to children and challenging them in open-ended tasks will give them room to express different ideas and their own views. This strategy has to be related to the fact that the teacher is sincerely interested in what the child has to say—rather than seeing if they can produce a correct answer. Consequently, communication on many levels is an important feature of this pedagogy; not only to encourage children to think and reflect, but also for the teacher to turn the communication to a meta perspective and make the children aware that they think and talk from different perspectives— that is, to use a *metacognitive approach* and turn the children's attention toward their own way of thinking and their own learning (Pramling, 1983). Communicating and creating meaning from the child's perspective is not restricted to verbal communication alone but can also be viewed in drawing, solving tasks, or other situations like play.

In all communication there is something that is communicated about, and in preschool there is curriculum content that is to be worked on. When we talk about content we do it in a broad sense, for instance mathematics as the area as such, but when we label it *learning object* it refers to the particular object focused on in the teaching at hand, which could be number concepts, size, or patterns as part of the mathematics. We call the way children learn the *act of learning*, and this can include many different strategies. But the specific strategies related to teaching are particularly communication, metacognition, and *variation*, which come from the theoretical source of phenomenography. There are always different ways of understanding among members of a group, and this is then what is used in teaching, in order to make various ways of thinking or understanding something visible to the children—that is, to make the children aware of the specificity and generality of their own way of thinking by encountering a variation of ways of understanding the same content. Of course, some ways of understanding something are more powerful and developable than others. This is for the teacher to deal with and determine, by focusing on critical aspects. The starting point is always the children's subjective experiences of the object of learning, and the end point is also the children's experiences of the same learning object, which will have changed as new notions or ideas have emerged.

Finally, the perspective of viewing the child as a *playing, learning child* also needs to be emphasized; that is, not separating playing from learning but rather viewing children as playing, learning children (Pramling Samuelsson & Asplund Carlsson, 2008, 2014), which also has to do with how the teacher allows room for the child to bring his or her own world into the curriculum and teaching situation. The notion of the playing, learning child centers around children's perspectives and emphasizes the idea of not seeing a child as playing for one part of the day and learning during another. We wish to picture a child who plays and learns simultaneously. Like learning, as defined in the phenomenographic framework, children's play is always focused on something—an objective (what they want to play). There is also an enacted aspect, when they arrange and negotiate in the process, and a lived object, which might be the result (what they end up playing), which can be seen in how they experience the content in focus of their play. Another similarity between play and learning is variation as the source of both the play and learning—variation that can be used spontaneously by children or as a tool and strategy for teachers in challenging children in their learning.

6.4.2 Teaching Within the Framework of Developmental Pedagogy

The main features of developmental pedagogy outlined above entail that the teacher makes use of variation as a strategy for making particular knowledge, skills, ideas, or phenomena visible to the child. This demands teachers who are able to adjust their perspective or capture the children's interest in order to share views on the same learning object. A precondition is that the teacher is able to focus the children's attention on the learning objects they want them to develop an understanding of, whether this takes place in spontaneous play or in planned teaching situations. Integrating play and learning in a goal-orientated preschool means not only seeing the playing, learning child and making room for the children's creativity, choices, initiatives, reflections, etc. (thus taking the children's perspectives), but also being aware of the objects of learning that appear to be meaningful *for the children* and making use of occurrences throughout the day and any activities to develop the child's understanding of different aspects of the surrounding world, by adhering to the children's perspectives.

In developmental pedagogy, the teaching is based on children's own ways of communicating and thinking. The objective is to highlight the variation in ways of thinking, which leads to the children being challenged to relate their own ways of thinking to those of other children's. Each child's taken-for-granted way of thinking is thereby challenged through *metacognitive dialogues*. Thus, the teacher must make an effort to listen to and observe the children and be willing to see what the child sees, and to interpret this as a touchdown in time, expressed knowledge that is related to what is made explicit there and then.

A number of studies have been conducted in collaboration between teachers and researchers, with the teachers being educated in how to apply the principles of developmental pedagogy in practice. The prosperity of the approach has been evaluated by following these teachers as they work with specific content and comparing children's learning outcomes with those of other child groups in which their teachers have been working with the same content. For example, for a year, children at one preschool were involved in book reading, visiting the museum of natural science, and other activities that offered to them experiences highlighting different aspects and meanings of the ecological cycles, in line with the principles of developmental pedagogy. These children developed a much more advanced understanding, on a group level, of the complex phenomenon of ecological cycles than did children from preschools following traditional practice, with more focus on learning by doing without reflection or the specific metacognitive approach that characterizes developmental pedagogy (Pramling, 1991, 1994, 1996).

In Swedish preschool, the focus has long been on the *act* of learning rather than *what* children should develop their knowledge about. While there have obviously always been content areas for learning—that is, something the teacher intends the children to work with—the content as such has not been considered to be of great importance. In a recent project, the idea of teaching as part of participating in preschool children's play was put to the test and theorized (Pramling et al., 2019). Following the principles of developmental pedagogy, it is important to embrace the learning objects that are meaningful to develop for the children's play. This places serious demands on the teacher to read the play situation and determines what content is made relevant to extend and explore, by contrasting meanings and perspectives. In the following, we see an example of how the children's play and the content of the play are made into learning objects (Björklund et al., 2018, p. 476):

(three children are playing "school", with the teacher participating in the role of "little sister")

Alice:	Aa … I'm seven years and I'm in zero[1] … in first grade.
Teacher:	So you're in first grade?
Alice:	You'll start in the zero.
Teacher:	Zero! But that's nothing! She says that I'll start in the zero.
Lisa:	They're next to us.
Alice:	The zero *in school*!
Teacher:	Is there a zero in school?
Alice:	Yes, there's a zero.
Teacher:	Aha.
Alice:	Yes, that's zero and I'm in the one.
Teacher:	Yes, and you're in the one.

Throughout the example, the teacher acts in her role as little sister and the children in their roles as big sisters. In the dialogue, "zero" becomes an object of exploration, with the teacher highlighting the possibility to interpret the expression in different ways. Numbers imply different things in different situations, and by saying "Zero! But that's nothing!" in the context of the talk, the teacher makes visible two dimensions of how the numeral zero can be used, both as the identification of a grade in school and as a quantity. In this example, the teacher and children work together in an intellectual way to solve the problem of what zero means, and the children contribute to the explanation by saying "The zero *in school*" and "Yes, that's *zero* and I'm in the *one*". The teacher's role is of certain importance, as the two dimensions of "zero" would not have been challenged if the teacher had not brought in the contrasting meaning.

Teaching based on attending to children's perspectives and extending their experiences aims at changing the child's way of seeing the world (and thus altering his or her perspective). This further means that the focus is simultaneously on the teacher's ability to adhere to the children's perspectives and the appropriateness of the teaching setting for offering the best possible opportunities for the children to gain such experiences that will facilitate a more advanced understanding. The preconditions for an early childhood education built on children's perspectives, or the ways they experience different phenomena, are thereby set by their teachers' pedagogical skills and knowledge.

---

[1] The preparatory year before Grade 1 in primary school starts is locally called "the zero" ("nollan" in Swedish).

6.5 Traces of Piaget's and Vygotsky's Theories in Developmental Pedagogy

In this chapter, we have aimed to highlight children's perspectives in theories with implications for preschool education. However, the child perspective and children's perspectives can also be related to the UN Convention on the Rights of the Child (1989), in which a child perspective is related to what adults believe is the best for a child, while children's perspectives relate to hearing their voices and taking their ideas seriously. Listening to children and entering into communication with them is considered to be a key factor for high-quality preschool teaching today (Björklund et al., 2018), which can also be related to Vygotsky's theory.

General theories of learning, or rather development, such as those by Piaget or Vygotsky, focus mainly on the act of learning and thus on a child perspective. Certain ways of working with children are thus seen as more appropriate than others, and the pedagogy is adapted to the child's level of development based on children's expressions of their understanding. This is clearly a manifestation of the importance of a child perspective—trying to do what one thinks is best for the child according to what we know from children's own expressions.

Developmental pedagogy also attends to the act of learning, but intertwined with the object of learning. The object of learning is a key toward which the interaction between teacher and children is directed in a teaching situation. Both Piaget's and Vygotsky's theories focus on child development from a psychological perspective; that is, from experimental situations. Developmental pedagogy, on the other hand, derives from studies conducted in preschool praxis and thus contextualized—avoiding to adapt research into practice as the praxis and theory are developed simultaneously. Furthermore, children's perspectives dominate the approach and it can be viewed as an approach to preschool education in which the content for learning is also important. Piaget and Vygotsky were concerned with child development more generally, while research in developmental pedagogy is concerned with children's learning of various content areas, which makes it focus more on education than psychology.

One can claim that Piaget already long ago put children's perspectives on the agenda for preschool practice, perhaps even being the first to take a serious interest in the children's subjective world. His observations and interpretations laid the groundwork for his theory of intellectual development. However, his reasons for studying children were based on his interest in epistemology. Vygotsky, on the other hand, had a greater interest in the child becoming a member of cultural and social practices; but he also based his theoretical framework for explaining development on observations and interpretations of children's ways of understanding their world —which is visible in children's perspectives. This is demonstrated not least in the notion of ZPD. Both Piaget and Vygotsky thus had an interest in children's perspectives as a *basis* on which theoretical conclusions of development could be drawn. Developmental pedagogy, on the other hand, focuses on children's perspectives as a *strategy* for early childhood education—the child's perspective is both the foundation for preschool education and the outcome of the education.

One other point to consider is that Piaget focuses on children *as a group*, while Vygotsky talks about children *in a group*. In developmental pedagogy the focus is on both: in research it is on the variation in ways of understanding the world around them, which results in qualitatively different conceptions, while in practice the challenging task for the teacher is to use the diversity of ways of understanding in communicating in the group to influence the children's learning.

In contemporary Nordic preschool practice and curriculum there might be a stronger relation to the cultural-historical theory, considering the emphasis on language and communication, but the explorative approach that is found in Piaget's way of indulging in the thoughts of the child is in many ways an inspiration that helps teachers interpret children's perspectives. This is central in preschool education based on developmental pedagogy, in which the content for learning and how it appears to the children is the core of the teaching practice. Shared experiences are considered important, for instance in play and exploration, but planned situations in which new experiences can be attended to are also important. In this need for experiences that extend the children's views on the world, all three theoretical approaches come together, embracing the children's own perspectives. A reason why children's perspectives have been more in focus in the twenty-first century may be that both research and education respect young children and their views more than earlier generations—thanks to the results of research.

References

Athey, C. (2007). *Extending thought in young children: A parent-teacher partnership* (2nd ed.). Sage.

Beilin, H. (1992). Piaget's new theory. In H. Beilin & P. Pufall (Eds.), *Piaget's theory: Prospects and possibilities* (pp. 1–17). Lawrence Erlbaum.

Björklund, C., Pramling Samuelsson, I., & Reis, M. (2018). Om nödvändigheten av undervisning i förskolan – exemplet matematik [The necessity of teaching in preschool—The example of mathematics]. *Barn, 3–4*, 21–37.

Chapman, M. (1992). Equilibration and the dialectics of organization. In H. Beilin & P. Pufall (Eds.), *Piaget's theory: Prospects and possibilities* (pp. 39–59). Lawrence Erlbaum.

Case, R. (1992). Neo-Piagetian theories of intellectual development. In H. Beilin & P. Pufall (Eds.), *Piaget's theory: Prospects and possibilities* (pp. 61–104). Lawrence Erlbaum.

Donaldson, M. (1978). *Children's minds*. Fontana Press.

Doverborg, E., & Pramling Samuelsson, I. (1985/2012). *Att förstå barns tankar – Kommunikationens betydelse* [Understanding the thoughts of the child] (4th ed.). Liber.

Elkonin, D. B. (2005). On the historical origin of role play. *Journal of Russian and East European Psychology, 43*(1), 49–89.

Elkonin, D. (1972). Problemet med periodisering av barns psykiska utveckling. In L.-C. Hydén (Ed.), *Sovjetisk barnpsykologi – en antologi* [Soviet child psychology—An anthology]. Natur & Kultur.

Fleer, M., González Rey, F., & Veresov, N. (Eds.). (2017). *Perezhivanie, emotions and subjectivity: Advancing Vygotsky's legacy*. Perspectives in Cultural-Historical Research, 1. Springer.

Fleer, M., & Pramling, N. (2015). *A cultural-historical study of children learning science*. Springer.

Hundeide, K. (2006). *Sociokulturella ramar för barns utveckling – barns livsvärldar* [Socio-cultural frameworks for children's development]. Studentlitteratur.

Inhelder, B. (1992). Foreword. In H. Beilin & P. Pufall (Eds.), *Piaget's theory: Prospects and possibilities* (pp. xi–xiv). Lawrence Erlbaum.

Johansson, J.-E., Pramling, N., & Pramling Samuelsson, I. (2018). Förskolans utveckling och barns tidiga lärande. In W. Klintberg & G. Nyberg (Eds.), *Lärande och bildning. Hundra år i Göteborg* [Learning and education: One hundred years in Gothenburg] (pp. 178–203). Carlssons.

Marton, F. (1981). Phenomenography—Describing conceptions of the world around us. *Instructional Science, 10*, 177–200.

Marton, F., & Booth, S. (1997). *Learning and awareness*. Lawrence Erlbaum.

Marton, F. (2015). *Necessary conditions of learning*. Routledge.

Mauritzson, U., & Säljö, R. (2001). Adult questions and children's responses: Coordination of perspectives in studies of children's theories of other minds. *Scandinavian Journal of Educational Research, 45*(3), 213–231.

Ministry of Health and Social Affairs. (1972). *Betänkande avgivet av 1968 års barnstugeutredning* (Survey of Preschools). SOU 1972:26–27. Socialdepartementet.

Murray, F. (1992). Reconstructing and constructivism: The development of American educational reform. In H. Beilin & P. Pufall (Eds.), *Piaget's theory: Prospects and possibilities* (pp. 287–308). Lawrence Erlbaum.

Nutbrown, C. (2011). *Threads of thinking: Schemas and young children's learning* (4th ed.). Sage.

Os, E. (2019). *Voksnes mediering av jevnaldringsrelasjoner i barnehager. En undersøkelse av voksnes bidrag til samhandling mellom barn under tre år* [Adults' mediating peer relations in child care]. Det utdanningsvitenskaplige fakultet. Oslo Universitet.

Piaget, J. (1952). *The origins of intelligence in children*. International Universities Press.

Piaget, J. (1962). *Play, dreams and imitation in childhood*. Norton.

Piaget, J. (1973). *The child's conception of the world*. Granada.

Piaget, J. (1976). *The grasp of consciousness*. Harvard University Press.

Piaget, J. (1985). *The equilibration of cognitive structures*. The University of Chicago Press.

Piaget, J., & Szeminska, A. (2001). Abstraction, differentiation, and integration in the use of elementary arithmetic operations. In J. Piaget (Ed.), *Studies in reflecting abstraction* (pp. 33–53) (Edited and translated by Robert L. Campbell, orig. 1977). Psychology Press.

Pramling, I. (1983). *The child's conception of learning*. Acta Universitatis Gothoburgensis.

Pramling, I. (1991). Learning about "The shop": Approach to learning in preschool. *Early Childhood Research Quarterly, 6*, 151–166.

Pramling, I. (1994). *Kunnandets grunder. Prövning av en fenomenografisk ansats till att utveckla barns förtåelse för sin omvärld* [The foundations of knowing: Test of a phenomenographic effort to develop children's ways of understanding the surrounding world]. Acta Universitatis Gothoburgensis.

Pramling, I. (1996). Understanding and empowering the child as a learner. In D. Olson & N. Torrance (Eds.), *Handbook of education and human development: New models of learning, teaching and schooling* (pp. 565–589). Basil Blackwell.

Pramling Samuelsson, I. (2003). Dialogpedagogikens uppgång och fall? [The rise and fall of dialogue pedagogy]. *Vägval i skolans historia, 3*(1), 6–7.

Pramling, N., & Pramling Samuelsson, I. (Eds.). (2011). *Educational encounters: Nordic studies in early childhood didactics*. Springer.

Pramling Samuelsson, I., & Asplund Carlsson, M. (2008). The playing learning child: Towards a pedagogy of early childhood. *Scandinavian Journal of Educational Research, 52*(6), 623–641.

Pramling Samuelsson, I., & Asplund Carlsson, M. (2014). *Det lekande lärande barnet – i en utvecklingspedagogisk teori* [The playing learning child – in a developmental pedagogical theory] (2nd ed.). Liber.

Pramling Samuelsson, I., Williams, P., Sheridan, S., & Hellman, A. (2015). Swedish preschool teachers' ideas of the ideal preschool group. *Journal of Early Childhood Research, 14*(4), 444–460.

Pramling, N., Wallerstedt, C., Lagerlöf, P., Björklund, C., Kultti, A., Palmér, H., Magnusson, M., Thulin, S., Jonsson, A., & Pramling Samuelsson, I. (2019). *Play-responsive teaching in early childhood education.* Springer. https://link.springer.com/book/10.1007%2F978-3-030-15958-0

Rommetveit, R. (1974). *On message structure: A framework for the study of language and communication.* Wiley.

The Swedish National Agency for Education. (2019). *Curriculum for preschool* (Rev. ed.). National Agency for Education.

Sanders, K., & Farago, F. (2018). Developmentally appropriate practice in the twenty-first century. In M. Feer & B. van Oers (Eds.), *International handbook of early childhood education* (Vol. II, pp. 1379–1400). Springer.

Sheridan, S., Pramling Samuelsson, I., & Johansson, E. (Eds.). (2009). *Barns tidiga lärande. En tvärsnittsstudie om förskolan som miljö för barns lärande* [Children's early learning]. Acta Universitatis Gothoburgensis.

Sheridan, S., Williams, P., & Pramling Samuelsson, I. (2015). Group size and organizational conditions for children's learning in preschool: A teacher perspective. *Educational Research, 56*(4), 379–397.

Schyl-Bjurman, G., & Strömstedt-Lind, K. (1976). *Dialogpedagogik* [Dialogue pedagogy]. Studentlitteratur.

Sommer, D., Pramling Samuelsson, I., & Hundeide, K. (2010). *Child perspectives and children's perspectives in theory and practice.* Springer.

SFS. (2010:800). *Education Act.* Ministry of Education.

Säljö, R. (2005). *Lärande och kulturella redskap. Om lärprocesser och det kollektiva minnet* [Learning and cultural tools]. Norstedts Akademiska.

UN Convention of the Right of the Child. (1989). UN. https://www.ohchr.org/en/professionalinterest/pages/crc.aspx

Wallerstedt, C., Lagerlöf, P., & Pramling, N. (2014). *Lärande i musik. Barn och lärare i tongivande samspel* [Learning music: Children and teachers interplaying]. Gleerups.

Weikart, D. (1981). Effects of different curricula in early childhood intervention. *Educational Evaluation and Policy Analysis, 3*(6), 25–35.

Wertsch, J. V. (2007). Mediation. In H. Daniels, M. Cole, & J. V. Wertsch (Eds.), *The Cambridge companion to Vygotsky* (pp. 178–192). Cambridge University Press.

Wertsch, J. V. (1998). *Mind as action.* Oxford University Press.

Vygotsky, L. S. (1978). *Mind in society: The development of higher psychological processes.* Harvard University Press.

Vygotsky, L. S. (1987). *The collected works of L. S. Vygotsky, Volume 1: Problems of general psychology, including the volume thinking and speech.* Plenum.

Youniss, J., & Damon, W. (1992). Social construction in Piaget's theory. In H. Beilin & P. Pufall (Eds.), *Piaget's theory: Prospects and possibilities* (pp. 267–285). Lawrence Erlbaum.

Camilla Björklund is Professor in Education at the University of Gothenburg, Sweden. She is involved in research projects concerning play and learning in early childhood, often within the field of mathematics education. Her research is characterized by practice-oriented research questions and project designs in which teachers are participating in joint commitment to develop educational practices. Research areas of interest are mathematics learning and teaching in the early years of preschool and primary school, and teachers' professional pedagogical development. In addition to scientific reports and articles, she has frequently published books for teacher students and practicing teachers, particularly within the field of teaching about numbers and arithmetic in play-oriented preschool practice.

Ingrid Pramling Samuelsson is Professor in Early Childhood Education at the University of Gothenburg, Sweden. She also holds a UNESCO Chair, since 2008 in ECE and Sustainable Development. She has been World President for World Organization for Early Childhood Education (OMEP) between 2008 and 2014. Her main research area is young children's learning and how teachers can provide the best opportunities for this in communication and interaction, in play as well as other activities in preschool. She has numerous publications and developed a preschool pedagogy labeled Development Pedagogy, based on many empirical studies. She is Honorary Doctor at Åbo Akademi University in Finland. She has also been a board member in Swedish UNICEF, and during later years engaged in research, development, and publications about ECE and ESD, and started a Network in Sweden for developing practice based research.

Chapter 7
Preschool Children's Pretend Play Viewed from a Vygotskyan and a Piagetian Perspective

Polly Björk-Willén

Abstract Pretend play can be seen as a breeding ground for children's socialization and it plays an important educational role during the preschool years. To make pretend play work socially, children need to share a co-constructed interactional framework that refers to the pretend world (alternate reality) as well as to the real context (actual reality). Both Piaget's and Vygotsky's ideas about children's development, talk and imagination have had great influences on Swedish preschool practice during the years. The present chapter aims to examine some *empirical examples* of children's pretend play adding a Vygotskian and a Piagetian perspective, and to further discuss what topicality Piaget's and Vygotsky's diverse ideas about children's *talk* and *pretending* in social peer play has for the preschool practice of today.

7.1 Introduction

When I was qualifying as a preschool teacher in the 1980s, Jean Piaget's stage theory about children's development was the predominant approach to our (future preschool teachers') understanding of the child's development and acting. Play, according to Piaget, was the child's way of adapting to the world, assimilating and understanding it (compare Bert van Oers' concept of "ontological representations of play" in Chapter 4). Piaget's work shows how the child develops the ability to represent the world through a series of stages in which assimilation and accommodation are increasingly coordinated. As preschool teachers, we encouraged and provided the child with pedagogical material and toys in accordance with Piaget's thinking about the child's own driving force to test and explore the world (see Chapter 10). This might, for example, be construction toys and building blocks, with which the children could experience different forms and functions on their own. We also learnt that knowledge about children's development stages could be a pedagogical tool to understand what to expect from the child at various ages (National Board of Health

P. Björk-Willén (✉)
Linköping University, Linköping, Sweden
e-mail: polly.bjork-willen@liu.se

© The Author(s), under exclusive license to Springer Nature Switzerland AG 2022
N. Veraksa and I. Pramling Samuelsson (eds.), *Piaget and Vygotsky in XXI century*,
Early Childhood Research and Education: An Inter-theoretical Focus 4,
https://doi.org/10.1007/978-3-031-05747-2_7

and Welfare, 1987). At the same time, Lev Vygotsky's theoretical framework about children's development and learning was underway. Though he was a contemporary of Piaget (both were born in 1896), Vygotsky's theories didn't reach the western world until the 1960s–1970s. Both Piaget and Vygotsky were interested in children's thinking and cognitive development and their pioneering work, highlighting, and recognizing the child, has had a great impact on Swedish preschool practice.

Piaget (2008) was interested in what processes lay the foundation for children's reasoning and concept formation. Despite most of his studies being conducted in western settings, he saw the child's development as universal. Like Piaget, Vygotsky (1999) also believed that the child actively learnt from experiences and play, though he viewed the child's development as *culture specific*, and he stressed that the child is part of a social and cultural context (see "cultural social representation of play" in Chapter 4). Piaget's failure to consider cultural differences has brought his theory some criticism (Babakr et al., 2019). So has the fact that Piaget didn't considers children's language use in his experiments (Rommetveit, 1974). Furthermore, Piaget has been criticized for his view on young children's lack of perspective-taking (see for example Johansson, 2000). In step with increasing criticism of Piaget's theory, Vygotsky's culture-driven theory has gained more impact on teaching, and today Vygotsky's theoretical influence on the Swedish preschool curriculum and practice dominates, especially when it comes to the support and scaffolding of children's learning. Many of Piaget's ideas are however, quite unreflectingly, still incorporated in everyday preschool practice, especially when evaluating a child's maturity and what a child can or cannot do. It is, for example, common to divide children into age-groups during teacher led activities, a division that can be derived from a stage theoretical view. This sometimes prevents the preschool teacher from recognizing and challenging the individual child's experiences and skills.

However, the two theorists, albeit in different ways, suggest that children's play forms an important aspect of learning and development (Aronsson, 2010). Therefore, it can be of interest, along with the use of a multimodal interactional approach, to examine how Piaget's and Vygotsky's ideas can be applied and understood *empirically* within the preschool practice of today, specifically in relation to children's *social interaction* and *pretend play*. The term pretend play denotes a play scenario where the outside realities are transformed and set up on the children's conditions and under their control. Hence, this chapter aims to highlight children's *talk* and social interaction during pretend play scenarios.

7.2   Children's Talk and Imagination According to Piaget and Vygotsky

In much of his early works, Piaget (1945) had a phenomenological focus, manifested in a series of *ethnographic studies* of children's actions. His studies of children's acting and thinking resulted in a theory about children's cognitive progress, in which he divided the child's cognitive development into four consecutive stages (Piaget, 1973). The stage relevant for this chapter is the second, named the pre-operational stage, where he placed preschool children from two to six years old. This stage is characterized by children beginning to think symbolically, which is mirrored by their language and imagination. According to Piaget, children's thinking during this stage is *egocentric*, which means they have difficulty in taking another person's perspective, because their normative starting point derives from themselves and they do not make any distinctions between their self and others (Piaget, 1973). In contrast to Piaget, Vygotsky (1999) views the child as *social from birth* and claims that language fulfills a social function through dialogue with others. It should be added that Vygotsky's statements were built on theoretical assumptions and not taken from discourse examples, in contrast to Piaget's approach. However, Vygotsky shared an interest in the dialogue with Bachtin (1981), seeing social dialogue as central for the development of the child's thinking. Vygotsky suggests that the child's thinking is closely connected to the input of language and that the *thinking proceeds in language*, as opposed to Piaget, who views language as a product of the child's cognitive development. The question still is: what comes first, the chicken or the egg?

7.2.1   Egocentric Talk or Social Speech

In children's early ages, they often talk out loud during play. Ragnhild Söderbergh (1988), a Swedish linguistics researcher, paid early attention to children's talking aloud when they were playing alone and highlighted that their talk often accompanied the ongoing activity. She called this phenomenon accompanied monologue, and she saw this as the child's way of narrating, though she also pointed out that sometimes the child's talk could also complement their acting. Piaget's (1973) term for this self-talk out loud is *egocentric speech*, and he viewed it as a sign of cognitive immaturity. He thought that egocentric speech would later, after a child has gained a fair amount of cognitive and communicative skills, develop into fully mature and effective speech, *social speech* geared to others' needs, and as such more dialogic and empathic. Consequently, children's egocentric speech will decrease with increasing age. Piaget, however, found that a child's egocentric speech was more common together with a parent than it was with peers, where he found it more social. He also suggests that the child's socialization is twofold: Together with peers the children are able to discuss (negotiate) and cooperate, which develops their social thinking. On the other hand, along with their parents they can get answers to their questions, and in that sense the adults represent the knowledge authority rather than a socializing party (Piaget, 1973).

Vygotsky (1999) acknowledged Piaget as being the first to pay attention to the child's egocentric speech and who gave this everyday phenomenon a theoretical value. But he also suggests that Piaget was blind to the real meaning of egocentric speech. According to Vygotsky, egocentric speech is in part *vocalized social speech*, geared toward solving problems, that develops into *inner language*. He felt that egocentric speech is not an accompaniment but rather an independent melody that aims to raise awareness and works as a tool to overcome difficulties. Vygotsky (1978) further proposed that language provides the shared experiences necessary for cognitive development, and he also stressed that play is the vehicle for communication and for children to build thinking and cognitive skills. This view is also closely connected to Vygotsky's well-known term, the *Zone of Proximal Development* (ZPD) (see also Chapters 6 and 10), which means "the distance between the actual developmental level as determined by independent problem-solving and the level of potential development as determined through problem-solving under adult guidance, *or in collaboration with more capable peers*" (Vygotsky, 1978, p. 86, my italicizing). In the context of children's pretend play, the final part of the definition is of particular importance (Bewemyr & Björk-Willén, 2016).

7.2.2 Imagination and Play

Piaget (1945) claimed that cognition involves a constant balancing (equilibration) between the known and the unknown. The child therefore repeats, recombines, and experiments with what is not yet quite mastered. Piaget (1951) describes play as a developmental path that goes from the simple to the complex and from the concrete to the abstract. According to Piaget, fantasy play is primarily an aspect of young children's early learning, where the play's content often varies because the children have difficulties organizing the play consistently. Vygotsky (1995), on the other hand, argued that children's play is influenced by cultural and social understanding. He also claimed that children's imagination continues to develop all through the school years, and he asserted that their imagination and creativity increases as they appropriate more knowledge of the world. Vygotsky further highlighted that imagination leads children's development to a higher cognitive level, as it enables them to imagine possibilities and to think beyond their actual existence (Reyes & Ebbeck, 2010). It is quite clear that Piaget and Vygotsky present two ways of understanding children's imagination and pretend play and how it could be explained. Since their time, many other scholars have studied children's play, especially pretend play, which I will shortly review below.

7.3 Pretend Play

The Swedish preschool curriculum emphasizes that playful learning at preschool has a positive impact on children's learning and further school success (National Agency for Education, 2018). As mentioned above, both Piaget and Vygotsky believed that children's play is an important means for children's learning and development. But children's play can also be seen as a breeding ground for children's everyday social organization at preschool and as such joyful, hard work, and deadly serious (Björk-Willén & Cromdal, 2009; Danby, 2000).

Children's *pretend play* is a scenario where children's social and verbal skills are made visible and at the same time develop. Sidnell (2011) treats children's make-believe as a form of social interaction, which gives children the epistemic right to talk about the pretend world within the play domain. He also shows how proposals are used by children in joint pretend play, in order to orient them to shared epistemic rights when talking about objects and events. Below I will further emphasize some overall features from earlier research that characterize pretend play. The pretend reality is mainly created by children through talk, but also through gestures, prosody and transformative manipulation of objects (Sawyer, 1997). In social pretend play, children need to share a co-constructed interactional framework that refers to both the pretend world (alternate reality) and to the real context (actual reality) (Butler, 2008; Sidnell, 2011). They also need to share a "contextualization cue" (Gumperz, 1982) which signals when they are within the pretend play frame, i.e., *in frame*, or in the real context, i.e., *out of frame*. For instance, bilingual children can use their different languages as a contextualization cue to signal when they are *in* versus *out of frame* (Guldal, 1997; Halmari & Smith, 1994; Kyratzis, 2014). Björk-Willén (2012, 2021) also shows that children's use of tense can serve as a contextualization cue. Like in the example (excerpts 1–6) below, children can use the past tense (preterite) to signal a pretend world alongside reality (Strömqvist, 1984). Use of the past tense is also consistently exploited by children to display the factual past event status. It signals to the co-players that there is a matter that cannot be altered. In contrast, the use of present and future tense is utilized to make bids for upcoming events (Björk-Willén, 2012, 2021). Björk-Willén (2012) further points out that, in addition to talk, gestures, bodily positions, and movement, material as well as imaginary objects are used to configure both nearness and distance in children's interaction and relationships during a pretend play activity. However, Sawyer (1997) emphasizes that the borders between in and out-of-frame can sometimes be blurred, a level which she names *blended frames*. For example, the child speaks as a play character but is at the same time referring to out-of-frame objects, and vice versa. The narration of children's pretend play also exposes how the play content is built on their earlier experiences from the "outside world" that they insert into their pretend play, and the play script is a mixture of reality and fantasy (Corsaro, 2018).

7.4 Methodological Considerations

7.4.1 Setting and Participants

The example in the chapter derives from a project about children's language environment at Swedish preschools.[1] Children's play and social interaction was video-recorded during "free" play activities. In Swedish preschools, the term "free play" refers to children's activities that take place outside instructional events (Ivarsson, 2003). The current examples are taken from one of the studied preschools and the children recorded were at the time of the research 3–5 years old. Both the parents and children were asked for consent prior to the study. The parents gave their written permission, and in addition, the children were informed orally at the preschool when the study was about to begin.

7.4.2 Procedure and Analysis

The analytical framework of the study has been influenced by ethnomethodological work on social action (Garfinkel, 1967). This means that I have tried to view the recordings from the perspective of the participants (compare chapter 6 about children's perspectives) analyzing their methods of carrying out social activities and making sense of them (Björk-Willén, 2012, 2021). Further, the analytical focus has been on the children's multimodal interaction, which means that I have considered both verbal and embodied resources to elucidate how children co-construct their interactional framework (Goodwin, 2000). The present analysis is partly based on earlier analyses which deal with how the children's transformation act from the real context to the pretend world is accomplished, and vice versa. Within the framework of a multimodal interactional analytical approach, the analysis at hand also aims to illuminate the excerpts of pretend play from both a Vygotskyan and a Piagetian perspective, based on children's talk and imagination and with a particular focus on children's egocentric talk and socialization work.

The transcripts are informed by conversation analysis and work on talk-in-interaction (Jeffersson, 1984; Sacks et al., 1974), see transcription conventions in the Appendix. All transcripts are based on listening to the original Swedish recordings. The names of persons have been changed to preserve the participants' anonymity.

---

[1] The project *Preschool as children's language environment* (2009–2013) was funded by the Swedish Research Council, Dnr. 721-2008-5565, led by Professor Eva Björck, School of Education and Communication, Jönköping University; CHILD.

7.5 Preschooler's Pretend Play—Empiric Examples

I have chosen two different scenarios for the analysis to illustrate how pretend play can be differently designed depending on the context and number of participants, but also on the children's ages, which can be of special interest when it comes to Piaget's theory, since he relates children's development stages and abilities to their age.

The excerpts derive from a free-time play period at a Swedish preschool, and the first three scenarios are taken from a pretend play event in the block building room.[2] In focus are two boys, both four years old, playing with wooden blocks and plastic animals (Björk-Willén, 2021). The second play scenario (excerpts 4, 5 and 6) is taken from a family role-play staged by five girls, all in their sixth year (Björk-Willén, 2012). I have added some introductory ethnographic information to each play event to facilitate the understanding of the play context.

7.5.1 Pretend Play in the Block Room

The two boys, Viggo and Peter, have constructed two buildings with small wooden blocks in which they place the small plastic animals. Peter plays with a large and a small panther and Viggo with a "flying fish". One of the buildings represents a hospital built without a roof, and another building placed behind the hospital is a dwelling house named the "old house". The boys also use an empty set of shelves that is placed beside the block buildings and it also represents a house, named "the new house". When entering the first excerpt, the two boys' play has been going on for a while and the pretend reality is continuously being developed, as they verbalize the play narration out loud.

In the first excerpt, Viggo and Peter are sitting in front of the hospital building. Into this building they have put their three toy animals, of which the small panther is placed on a wooden block, lying down. The entire play event is very peaceful, with no loud voices or rapid actions. The two boys seem to be used to playing with each other, and their talk-in-interaction moves smoothly with few overlaps. To orient toward shared epistemic rights they use *proposals*, in order to make comments on events and objects in the play (Sidnell, 2011). The excerpt also shows how the boys use *past tense* to signal that they are within the pretend play frame.

---

[2] Note that this chapter, like Piaget's and Vygotsky's theories, derives from a monolingual view of children's talk and development. The target data is also taken from monolingual children's play activities. Had I considered multilingual children's play, the chapter would have had quite different content, focus and conclusions.

Excerpt 1—*The hospital*
Participants: Viggo and Peter, four years old

1	Peter:	nu va de natt (x) sovde på sjukhuset Now it was night sleeped ((slept)) at the hospital
2 3 4	Viggo:	nu va det <u>bra</u> nu var det morron oh ja öppnade jag Now it was good now it was morning and I opened I öppnade dörren och stängde opened the door and closed ((*brings the door down*))
5 6 7 8	Peter:	((*puts down the big panther between the small panther*)) och sen "*mår du bra*" "*jaha*"["*okej då åker vi hem*" And then "are you fine" "yes" "okay then we go home" ((using a high-pitched voice[*lifts up both panthers and walks toward the other block house where he squats*))
9 10	Viggo:	(x) [jag flög [hem I flew home ((*stands up and lifts the flying fish into the air*))

The boys contextualize their pretend scenario using the past tense (lines 1, 2, 3 and 9). Together with the past tense they also use the discourse marker "now" (lines 1 and 2). The combination of the discourse marker and tense use underlines that the pretend story is taking place here and now. It can further be noted that Peter in line 6, when giving voice to the panthers, also uses *reported speech* (Tannen, 1989), sometimes named *animated talk* (Goffman, 1979; Björk-Willén & Aronsson, 2014). The boys present themselves as being within the frame of pretense by "doing being animals", where Peter here has to stage two pretend characters, and this is accomplished through a played dialogue between the two panthers, characterized by Peter's use of a high-pitched voice.

When analyzing the boys' verbal interchange, their talk in this first excerpt has similarities with egocentric speech according to Piaget (1973), because no one seems to expect an answer from the other when verbalizing aloud what is going on in the play. Each turn of talk is based on the individual boy's imagination and storytelling. However, Piaget also points out that together with peers a child's talk is more social than with adults. When taking a closer look, it is obvious how the boys within their turn-taking are smoothly building up a joint narration of the pretend story, dealing with their ill animals that stay at the hospital until morning and then go home. In other words, the boys' individual talk is merged into a joint effort. Vygotsky (1978) would have added that the boys' speech and communication in the play worked as an independent melody that helped them to build their thinking and develop their cognitive skills.

The next excerpt shows how Viggo pushes the narration forwards, while he creatively incorporates and introduces a new topic and new concepts in the play.

Although the boys contribute different ideas, Viggo appears to be the crucial story-teller, displaying narrative competence in building cohesive and intertextual ties (Björk-Willén, 2021).

Excerpt 2—*Meal time*
Participants: Viggo and Peter, four years old.

1 2	Viggo:	ja har bara rött kött (.) som jag sparat n n nu I only have red meat that I have saved n n now va det nu va det måltid = it was now it was meal
3 4 5	Peter:	= ja Yes ((the boys stand close to the set of shelves and have put their animals on the upper shelf))
6	Viggo:	nu ska vi äta mat (x) Now we are going to eat food
7	Peter:	(x) pytte Tiny
8	Viggo:	de va giftigt It was poisonous
9 10	Peter:	ja Yea. ((*moves closer to Viggo lifting the panther*))
11	Viggo:	dom åt giftmat (x)den där store den blev också sjuk They ate poisonous food that big one it also got ill

The boys have moved from the hospital to the "new house", which is placed on a set of shelves, when Viggo introduces a new topic—mealtime. He opens up the new topic talking in the present tense, which gives Peter opportunities to make bids for upcoming events (Björk-Willén, 2012). Viggo, however, doesn't really give any room for comments, because he changes tense very quickly and declares "Now it was meal" (line 2) and Peter latches on and immediately agrees. The Swedish word "måltid" is not an everyday expression and is seldom used by children, thus it gives a ceremonious touch to the invitation and also a glimpse of Viggo's rich vocabulary. In the new framework of make-believe, he also introduces other concepts like "red meat" (line 1), "poisonous" (line 8), and "poisonous food" (line 11). Cekaite, Blum-Kulka, Grover, and Teubal (2014) suggest that peer relations and peer talk serve as the locus for co-construction of children's social world, and through interactional displays this forms peer cultures. It is also an arena for the development of pragmatic language skills. This is exactly what the target play event displays, as the narrated mealtime exposes a culturally specific content since Viggo inserted earlier experiences from the "outside world" into their pretend play, mixing fantasy and reality (Corsaro, 2018). He also "raises the bar" for their verbal interchange when introducing new concepts and being the verbally more capable peer (Vygotsky, 1978).

The last excerpt taken from Viggo and Peter's pretend play is a direct continuation of the mealtime above. Still, it is Viggo who is the active storyteller, but Peter's short interjections are as important to tie up their joint pretend world, and in the following their talk is more dialogical and socially interactive (Vygotsky, 1999; Piaget, 1973). The excerpt shows how the boys' joint storytelling is further developed and how their interjections clearly build a cohesive storyline.

Excerpt 3—*Poisoned animals*
Participants: Viggo and Peter, four years old

1	Viggo:	n nu var allt kött slut (x) nu fick vi gå in i vårt gamla
		N now all meat was gone now we had to go into our old
2		*((moves and sits down on the floor between the old*
3		*house and the hospital))*
4		det så skönare vårt gamla (x) och varmare
		that's nicer our old and warmer
5		*((puts the flying fish into the house))*
6	Peter:	*((moves to the hospital building))* han äh sjuk jag
		He is ill I
7		ska bygga
		will build.
8		*((sits with his back to the camera puts a new block*
9		*into hospital on which he lays the big panther))*
10	Viggo:	var den stora också sjuk
11		Was the big one also ill? *((takes out the flying fish turns*
12		*around looks into the hospital building))*
13	Peter:	ja
		Yea
14	Viggo:	men då måste du ha mer
		But then you need more
15		(1)
16	Viggo:	den här också så den lilla får va där
17		This one too so the small one can be there
		((puts another block into the hospital))
18	Peter:	*((lays the small panther on the new block))* båda va sjuka
		both were ill
19	Viggo:	men ja var inte sjuk ja ja ja tål gift det var inte
20		But I was not ill I I I can stand poison don't feel
		synd om mig jag öppnade dörren ja gick ᵉin i husetᵉ
21		sorry for me I opened the door I went into the house
		((opens the door to the hospital and puts the
22		*flying fish into the house))*
23	Viggo:	de va synd om er
		I felt sorry for you

Viggo ends the mealtime session in a sophisticated way when he declares that the meat is finished and makes a proposal that they have to go to their old house because it is nicer and warmer (lines 1–4). Peter does not protest but instead walks to the hospital building declaring that the big panther "is ill", and therefore he needs to build another bed (lines 6–7). The change of tense to present time allows for a discussion about the story line. Viggo shows his interest by asking if the big panther was also ill, while he moves with his flying fish from the old house to the hospital. Peter's interjection works successfully and engages Viggo, who suggests that there is a need for more beds, so the small panther also gets one, and Peter agrees and confirms that "both were ill" (line 18). Viggo further declares that he (the flying fish) was fine because he could stand the poison, and he adds … "don't feel sorry for me" … (lines 19–20) leaving the hospital and going back to the old house. Recycling his own expression, Viggo concludes his talk in an empathetic way, addressing the panthers, saying "I felt sorry for you" (line 23). Here, he displays an ability to gain insight into another person's situation, showing a non-egocentric behavior at an earlier age than Piaget (1973) presumed (Johansson, 2000). The excerpt also shows how the children, inside the pretend framework, give the opportunity to test and develop different scenarios and also test and use social expressions like "I feel sorry for". Piaget (1945) would have explained Viggo's vocabulary testing as an equilibration between the known and the unknown, as a way to recombine and experiment with what he had not yet quite mastered. Vygotsky takes a step further, as he suggests that imagination leads children's development to a de-contextual level of abstract thinking (Reyes & Ebbeck, 2010).

In sum, despite diverging theoretical explanations, both Vygotsky and Piaget emphasize the importance that play and imagination have for children's cognitive development. The in-depth analysis of the two boys' pretend play takes this to another level, as it displays the complexity of the boys' pretend narration, which includes both egocentric speech and dialogues. It also shows how the boys use propositions, introducing new topics and concepts, that orient them to shared epistemic rights (Sidnell, 2011) but also opens the way for further experiences and learning. Leaving the play dyad above, the next empirical part deals with older children who have set up a family role-play.

7.5.2 Family Role-Play

The following three excerpts derive from a role-play activity at preschool during the free play period (Björk-Willén, 2012). Five girls—Sue, Valery, Emma, Agatha, and Mary—all in their sixth year, are playing a family role-play. In the excerpts below, Valery and Agatha don't have any prominent roles. The play scenario is a hut (koja in Swedish) that four of the girls have built using two big mattresses and two plinths and a bench, accommodating two rooms. The extract below has been preceded by preparation talk, comprising the role of the participants, but also the use of different spaces that their hut offers. As we enter the play, it is already clear that the right part of the hut belongs to Sue and Valery and the left part to Emma and Agatha. Mary, the fifth girl, enters the play arena at a later stage. Since the casting of the play is already finished, she, as a newcomer, is assigned the subordinate role of being the dog in the play (cf. Cromdal, 2001; Scheldon,1996). The excerpt shows how Emma's talk, when addressing Mary, is based on the earlier role distribution within the pretend play framework, which in turn has created a hierarchical order between the girls.

Excerpt 4—*Being doggy*
Participants: Emma and Mary, almost 6 years

1	Emma:	Mary jag satte dig i koppel
		Mary I put you on the leash
2		[takes down a pretend leash((from the outside of the hut
3		(sv. koja)))
4	Mary:	[crawls towards the bench
5	Emma:	så du så du kunde inte gå längre än här
		So you so you couldn't walk further than here
6		[(.) du kunde bara sitta på bänken
		you could only sit on the bench
7	Mary:	[lays down ((under the bench))

Earlier, during the four girls' preparation talk in the play, Emma got the role of being the mother. This gives her a leading position. In family role-play, the mother and father are often treated as superior to children and older siblings as superior to younger. The most inferior are babies, pets, and unborn babies (Aronsson & Thorell, 1999; Goodwin, M. H., 1990; Sheldon, 1996).

Hence, in the target excerpt Emma is the one who decides the framework of Mary's participation, establishing the dog's freedom of movement. As a contextualization cue, she uses the past tense, which signals the pretend reality (in frame) but also that this is a matter that cannot be altered. That means that the terms of Mary's participation are not negotiable. However, the frame is blended (Sawyer, 1997) because Emma initially uses Mary's name, which signals out-of-frame, and then uses the past tense in "I put you on a leach" (line 1), which signals in frame. Mary seems in any case to accept her assigned role, as she responds nonverbally by crawling away and placing herself under the bench, in a doggy way. According to Piaget (1945), fantasy play or role-play is primarily an aspect of <u>young</u> children's development. In the target excerpt, the children are in their sixth year, hence still preschoolers from a Swedish perspective and still engaged in pretend role-play but compared to Viggo's and Peter's play, the girls' play talk is more socially oriented and culturally advanced, revealing a social hierarchy between the girls, and there is no kind of egocentric and parallel talk. The girls' language use mediates their shared experiences and according to Vygotsky (1978) this process is necessary for building thinking and cognitive skills, but also social skills, as the analysis points out.

In the next excerpt Mary, the doggy, opposes her limited room for maneuver, but Emma ignores her protest. It is also shown how their negotiation about the social order of the play is an out-of-frame business. In contrast to Viggo's and Peter's play, the girls' role-play shows how the pretend reality is built on a clear *dialogue* between the participants, which means their talk is less egocentric and more interactionally oriented (Bachtin, 1981; Vygotsky, 1999).

Excerpt 5—*Putting up resistance*
Participants: Mary, Agatha and Emma, almost 6 years.

1	Mary:	Emma kan inte jag få (.) jag kunde skära bort kopplet
		Emma couldn't you let me I could cut off the leash
2		så jag kom än dit
3		so I came there
4		((*climbs up and hangs over the plinth* in the direction towards Emma and Agatha))
5	Agatha:	*looks* ((at Mary))
6	Emma:	nä:
		No
7	Mary:	m men snä:lla
		B but ple:ase
8	Emma:	neje vi vill inte det för det är vi som har hittat på
		Noe we don't want that because it is us that made up the
9		leken
		play
10		(1)
11	Mary:	men det betyder inte att ni bestämmer allt
		But that doesn't mean that you decide everything

In this excerpt, Mary wishes to renegotiate the conditions for her doggy role, by cutting off the leash. Her suggestion is, however, refused by Emma (line 6). When Mary in the next turn very nicely appeals with a prolonged and marked "plea:se", Emma responds with an account that implies both her and the other girls' right to deny Mary influence, because <u>they</u> have made up the play (lines 8–9) (Cromdal, 2001; Sheldon, 1996). After a short silence, Mary produces a protest, however this time in a rather quiet voice, saying: "but that doesn't mean that you decide everything" (line 11). This controversy shows how Mary tries to renegotiate the play frames by stretching the limits of being the dog in this family role-play. Although she fails, her counteraction displays resistance, as she declares that even though they made up the play it does not justify their right to make <u>all</u> the decisions. According to Piaget (1973), peer play is socializing as the play gives children greater possibilities to negotiate and discuss various things. This excerpt really shows how the girls discuss the social order within the framework of their play. It is notable, when discussing Mary's position, that this is done out-of-frame, using the present tense (lines 6–11). In sum, the family role-play and the pretend reality give the participants possibilities to test social norms while stretching the frames of what can be legal or not (Sacks, 1992).

As the play continues, Mary's terms don't change. In the following excerpt, it has become morning and the four girls have slept inside the hut, but the doggy had to lie outside the entrance. The doggy has literally been locked outside the house, verbally, and physically excluded. Play can be joyful but also very serious (Danby, 2000) and the pretend reality can be as cruel as the real outside world.

Excerpt 6—*"It is just pretending"*
Participants: Sue and Mary, almost 6 years

1 2 3 4	Sue:	((sits on a small box and Mary sits below her on the floor)) °hundis ° *points* ((with one finger)) Doggy Mary de ä bara på låtsas eller hur Mary it is just pretending isn't it
5		(1)
6 7	Sue:	allså ja allså jag tycker du är °så himla° x hundis But yea but I believe you are so great doggy fy på dig *points* ((disciplinary with her finger)) shame on you
8	Mary:	*jumps up* ((on the bench)) *scratches* ((the mattress side)
9	Sue:	FY PÅ DIG *points with her finger* ((disciplinary)) Shame on you
10		(1)
11	Sue:	*looks* ((at Mary)) hi[ha ha Hi ha ha
12	Mary:	[ha ha HA fy på dig Ha ha ha shame on you

The last excerpt shows how Sue, who like Emma holds a high hierarchical position in the play, opens the way for a mitigation with Mary. Sue has placed herself on a small box and Mary, the doggy, is sitting below her. Sue addresses Mary first with "doggy" but then moves on to address Mary with her real name saying quite seriously: "Mary it is pretending isn't it" (lines 3–4). She doesn't get any answer from Mary and continues, after a short pause, in a playful way to talk to the doggy in a mix of pretend play talk and "real talk" (lines 6–7). Mary physically responds to Sue's playful addressing as, in a doggy way, she jumps up on the bench and scratches on the side of the mattress (line 8). Their social interaction culminates in joint laughter (lines 12–13). Sue's empathetic action has broken the exclusion of Mary, and this is done both seriously and in a humorous way, which seems to become a relief for both girls. According to Vygotsky (1981), children's play derives from the child's emotional and everyday experiences, and in their social play they can stretch and test the social everyday order, and this is exactly what takes place in the girls' interaction above.

7.6 Discussion

7.6.1 Egocentric Speech

The aim of this chapter is to examine how Piaget's and Vygotsky's ideas could be applied and understood *empirically*, along with the use of a multimodal interactional approach, highlighting children's pretend play as a breeding ground for socialization. Specifically, the analytical focus has been on children's *talk* and *social interaction*, which took place in two different pretend play scenarios in a Swedish preschool of today. The first three excerpts give a glimpse of two boys' pretend play trajectory. The four-year-old boys built a joint story out loud during their play, taking turns in a smooth way, and their talk and physical acting was closely connected (Söderbergh, 1988). Most of the time they were playing in the pretend world and this was signaled by their use of the past tense (Björk-Willén, 2012, 2021; Strömqvist, 1984). Their talking aloud had traits of *egocentric speech* (Piaget, 1973), and each single boy's talk can be understood as two parallel stories that hook together. However, as their play advanced, their talk developed to become more like a *dialogue*. Vygotsky (1999) suggests that social dialogue is central for the development of the child's thinking. Piaget claims the opposite, namely that the child's cognitive development is a prerequisite for their language development, although he emphasizes that children's talk together with peers is less egocentric and more social. I believe that Piaget was on to something here, because the analysis here shows that Viggo and Peter's talk out loud was above all social, even if their talk has traits of egocentrism. The analysis further shows that talking out loud in joint play not only represents a play script or a way of thinking aloud (Vygotsky, 1999), but also works as a necessity to give the co-participant information that he/she can further build on. It also gives the participants possibilities to act on its legality and feasibility (Bateman & Butler, 2014; Sacks, 1992). Consequently, the talk in Viggo's and Peter's pretend play was primarily the glue in building their trajectory of joint narration.

In the girls' play, there were no traces of egocentric talk at all, because their social talk dominated. Piaget (1973) would have argued that their talk has developed into fully mature and effective speech, *social speech*. In the girls' framework of the family role-play, a sophisticated power battle was going on, and the analysis shows how Emma in particular tested the limits of social order and norms, not without protest from Mary, playing the doggy role. However, Emma's acting toward Mary didn't show any empathy, rather an egocentric attitude. Sue, on the other hand, tried to balance the tension between the two other girls by being humoristic and highlighting that "it is just pretending". Her comment, which raised their play activity to a meta-level, also had a bearing toward empathy. To sum up, the pretend family play framed the girls' social interaction and served as a vehicle for communication and for building cognitive and, above all, social skills (Vygotsky, 1978), for better or worse.

7.6.2   Pretend Play at Various Ages and Social Levels

Both play scenarios show in fine detail how the children's talk is social and interactive. The scenarios have in common that the children transformed previous experiences from the "real world" into their play. Viggo's and Peter's pretend narration brought up themes concerning hospital, illness and home, and their play was, in Vygotsky's words, *culturally specific*. The girls' family role-play formed the framework for a social trial of strength between the girls, where the doggy ended up at the bottom. Family role-play is in itself a culturally related form of play, and without evidence I will presume it is a universal one, which takes on different expressions in various cultural settings. There is, however, a clear difference between the two play scenarios and the way the children accomplished their pretend play. Vygotsky (1995) argues that fantasy play develops children's thinking and understanding of the outside world, and that creativity increases with age and experience. Both examples point to this, though the children in the two play events display different skills. Viggo and Peter literally animate their play, "doing being animals", while the girls engage in social positioning work, negotiating the hierarchical order, where the family play is given a subordinate role. The boys' and the girls' different ways of pretending can be understood as age related and illuminate their amount and diversity of experiences, interests, and needs, so far in line with both Piaget's and Vygotsky's theories. In other words—age matters. This is, however, far from stage theories' limitations and shows that a child, depending on the context, can act egocentrically and be social at the same time, regardless of age.

Finally, without Piaget's and Vygotsky's theoretical work, preschool practice would without doubt have looked different. Their interest in children's development and learning has in many ways affected the theoretical framework of the Swedish preschool curriculum of today, especially Vygotsky's view of development and learning as an interactional device. Piaget's theory has a more hidden place in education nowadays, or as mentioned above, it is there but rather incorporated. However, although his theory has been criticized and to some extent discarded, his sincere interest in listening to and observing children's reasoning and taking the individual child's perspective can still be a model (Piaget, 1945). Hence, I will claim that preschool teachers can gain new insights into and understanding of children's development and skills from just *listening to and observing* children's pretend play and social interaction and will get a better understanding of how children incorporate social norms and values into their play and peer culture (Corsaro, 2018; see also Chapter 6). By extension, this knowledge can help teachers to build on children's experiences and further challenge their development and learning (Vygotsky, 1978). As the analyses have shown, pretend play offers a rich treasure that displays children's understanding of the real context (actual reality) and its transformation into their pretend world (alternate reality), and as such it is an important platform for learning and socialization. Finally, it has also been shown that children's play and social interaction in real life is often more intricate and multifaceted than the theories tell us.

Appendix

[ ]	square brackets mark the start and end of overlapping speech
word	underlining indicates emphasis
WORD	capitals mark speech that is audibly louder than surrounding speech
º º	degree signs surround talk in quieter speech (sotto voce)
(2)	pauses measured in seconds
(.)	micro-pause
(( ))	investigator's comments within double parentheses
:	prolongation of preceding vowel
↓ ↑	falling or rising intonation
> <	more rapid than surrounding speech
< >	slower than surrounding speech
=	immediate 'latching' of successive talk
( )	uncertain interpretation within parentheses
(x) (xx)	inaudible word or words
svenska	talk in Swedish
English	English translations.
points	nonverbal action transcribed in italics

References

Aronsson, K. (2010). Learning through play. In E. Baker, P. Peterson, & B. McGaw (Eds.), *International encyclopedia of education*. Elsevier.

Aronsson, K., & Thorell, M. (1999). Family politics in children's play directives. *Journal of Pragmatics, 31*, 23–47.

Bachtin, M. (1981). *The dialogic imagination*. (C. Holquist, Ed.). University of Texas Press.

Bateman & Butler. (2014). The lore and law of the playground. *International Journal of Play, 3*(3), 235–250.

Babakr, Z. H., Mohamedamin, P., & Kakamad, K. (2019). Piaget's cognitive developmental theory: Critical review. *Education Quarterly Reviews, 2*(3), 517–524.

Bevemyr, M., & Björk-Willén, P. (2016). Potential learning events at the computer during free play periods at Swedish preschools. *Nordisk Barnehageforskning, 12*(8), 1–16.

Björk-Willén, P. (2021). "Now it was meal": Use of tense work as an important social organizational device in preschoolers' pretend play. *Research on Children and Social Interaction, 5*, 2.

Björk-Willén, P. (2012). Being doggy: Disputes embedded in preschooler's family role-play. In S. Danby & M. Theobald (Eds.), *Disputes in everyday life* (pp. 119–140). Special Volume. Emerald.

Björk-Willén & Aronsson, K. (2014). Preschoolers' "animation" of computer games. *Mind, Culture and Activity: An International Journal, 21*, 318–316.

Björk-Willén, P., & Cromdal, J. (2009). When education seeps into 'free play': How preschool children accomplish multilingual education. *Journal of Pragmatics, 41*, 1493–1518.

Butler, W. C. (2008). *Talk and social interaction in the playground*. Ashgate.

Cekaite, A., Blum-Kulka, S., Grøver, V., & Teubal, E. (Eds.). (2014). *Children's peer talk: Learning from each other*. Cambridge University Press.

Corsaro, W. (2018). *The sociology of childhood* (5th ed.). Sage.

Cromdal, J. (2001). Can I be with?: Negotiating play entry in a bilingual school. *Journal of Pragmatics, 33*, 515–543.

Danby, S. (2000). The serious business of play. In J. Mason & M. Wilkinson (Eds.), *Taking children seriously* (pp. 208–236). University of Western Sydney.

Garfinkel, H. (1967). *Studies in ethnomethodology*. Prentice-Hall Inc.

Goffman, E. (1979). Footing. *Semiotica, 25*, 1–29.

Goodwin, M. H. (1990). *He-Said-She-Said: Talk as social organization among black children*. Indiana University Press.

Goodwin, C. (2000). Action and embodiment within situated human interaction. *Journal of Pragmatics, 32*, 1489–1522.

Gumperz, J. J. (1982). *Discourse strategies*. Cambridge University Press.

Guldal, T. M. (1997). *Three children, two languages. The role of code selection in organizing conversation*. Diss. Trondheim: NTNU.

Halmari, H., & Smith, W. (1994). Code-switching and register shift: Evidence from Finnish-English child bilingual conversation. *Journal of Pragmatics, 21*, 427–445.

Ivarsson, P-M. (2003). *Barns gemenskap i förskolan* [Children's communities in preschool]. Diss., Uppsala Studies in Education, Uppsala University.

Jefferson, G. (1984). Transcription notations. In J. M. Atkinson & J. Heritage (Eds.), *Structures of social action. Studies in conversations* (pp. ix–xvi). Cambridge University Press.

Johansson, E. (2000). *Etik i små barns värld: om värden och normer bland de yngsta barnen i förskolan.* [Ethics in young children's world: about values and norms among toddlers in preschool]. Gothenburg Studies in Educational Sciences, 0436–1121; 141. Gothenburg: University of Gothenburg. Diss.

Kyratzis, A. (2014). Peer interaction, framing, and literacy in preschool bilingual pretend play. In A. Cekaite Thunqvist, S. Blum-Kulka, V. Grøver Aukrust & E. Teubal (Eds.), *Children's peer talk: learning from each other* (pp. 214–234). Cambridge University Press.

Piaget, J. (1932/1973). *Språk och tanke hos barnet [Language and thinking in children]*. Gleerups.

Piaget, J. (1945). *Play, dreams, and imitation in childhood*. Norton.

Piaget, J. (1951). *Play, dreams and Imitation in childhood*. Norton.

Piaget, J. (2008). *Barns själsliga utveckling [Children's mental development]* (2nd ed.). Nordstedts.

Reyes, D. S., & Ebbeck, M. (2010). Children redefining learning in science through play. In M. Ebbeck & M. Waniganayake (Eds.),*Play in early childhood education. Learning in diverse contexts* (pp 197–212). Oxford University Press.

Rommetveit, R. (1974). *On message structure: A framework for the study of language and communication*. Wiley.

Sacks, H. (1992). *Lectures on conversation* (Vol. 2., G. Jefferson, Ed.). Blackwell.

Sacks, H., Schegloff, A. E., & Jefferson, G. (1974). A simplest systematics for the organization of turn-taking for conversation. *Language, 4*, 696–735.

Sawyer, R. K. (1997). *Pretend play as improvisation: Conversation in the preschool classroom*. Lawrence Erlbaum.

Sheldon, A. (1996). You can be the baby brother, but you aren't born yet: Preschool girls' negotiation for power and access in pretend play. *Research on Language and Social Interaction, 29*(1), 57–80.

Sidnell, J. (2011). The epistemics of make-believe. In T. Stievers, L. Mondada, & J. Steensig (Eds.), *The morality of knowledge in conversation* (pp. 131–155). University Press.

Strömqvist, S. (1984). *Make believe through words. A linguistic study of children's play with a doll's house*. Diss., Gothenburg monographs in linguistics, 4, Gothenburg: University of Gothenburg.

Söderbergh, R. (1988). *Barns tidiga språkutveckling [Children's early language development]*. Gleerups.

Tannen, D. (1989). *Talking voices*. Cambridge University Press.

The National Agency for Education. (2018). *Curriculum for Preschool, Lpfö 18*. Fritzes.

The National Board of Health and Welfare. (1987). *Pedagogiskt program för förskolan [Pedagogical program for preschool]*. National Board of Health and Welfare.

Vygotsky, L. (1999/1934). *Tänkande och språk* (Myšlenie i reč, 1934). Gothenburg: Daidalos.

Vygotsky, L. (1995). *Fantasi och kreativitet i barndomen* [*Imagination and creativity in childhood*]. Gothenburg: Daidalos.

Vygotsky, L. (1981). *Psykologi och dialektik* [*Psychology and dialectics*]. Nordstedts.

Vygotsky, L. (1978). *Mind and society: The development of higher psychological processes*. Harvard University Press.

Polly Björk-Willén is an assistant professor emerita in Educational Practice at Linköping University, Sweden. She has a background as preschool teacher and has educated preschool teacher students for many years. Her research interest is in interactional studies in preschool, investigating (bilingual) children's language use, ethnicity and religion at preschool, language policy in families and preschool, as well as the moral and emotional socialization of children. Based on ethnomethodology and conversation analysis her studies focus on multimodal interaction in mundane activities at preschool. She has published her research in international journals and contributed with chapters in various Swedish as well as international anthologies.

Chapter 8
Piaget and Vygotsky: Powerful Inspirators for Today's Students in Early Education and Developmental Psychology

Elly Singer

Abstract The writings of Piaget and Vygotsky are like great works of art and philosophy—the Shakespearean dramas or dialogues of Socrates. Every generation can be touched in another way and make its own interpretations of these works to reflect on the vital issues of their own time. This chapter invites students to study original work of Piaget and Vygotsky and focuses on two questions: (1) What are the benefits of studying the actual words of Piaget and Vygotsky (or translations thereof) rather than summaries, second-hand interpretations, and ready-made practical applications of their seminal works now available in overwhelming abundance to today's EC students?; (2) How can the experiences of the older generation of early childhood scholars and educators help today's students to find their way in the Piagetian and Vygotskian heritage in the context of their own academic and practical work? Today's students are confronted with modern issues, such as ecological crisis, digital revolution, that were unknown in the time of Piaget and Vygotsky. Students should be supported to develop their imagination and theories on how education can find answers to new challenges and contribute to a better society. In this respect, Piaget and Vygotsky are excellent models. They believed in the student's creativity and provided theoretical and empirical tools and methods for ongoing research. They stimulated to cross the borders between scientific disciplines and art and to discuss with colleagues from divers countries and cultures.

8.1 Introduction

Jan, a 5-year-old boy, is playing in our garden. He wants to make a parachute for his Pooh bear. I suggest light paper to let the parachute float. But Jan wants to make the parachute out of tree leaves and glues them with a thick glue suitable for paper sheets. Then he ties his Pooh bear to the parachute with a rope around his waist. Jan climbs the stairs and with a beaming face he lets go off Pooh bear. Plump! Pooh bear falls straight down on the floor

E. Singer (✉)
Utrecht University (retired), Utrecht, The Netherlands
e-mail: singer.elly@gmail.com

below. I feel sorry, his parachute does not float. But Jan is completely happy and satisfied, his parachute works!

Who of us is right? I love to discuss this kind of experiences with students in early education and child psychology. In this respect, I owe a great deal to Piaget and Vygotsky. I have learnt from Piaget, for instance, that children can find it difficult to combine different perspectives: the visual appearance—the parachute had the form of a parachute—and the function of the parachute, to float or fall down. From Vygotsky, I learnt to think about the child's motivation. We should not enforce the child to follow our activity plans when they are outside the child's imagination. Piaget and Vygotsky taught me the value of ongoing learning, of detailed observations and critical reflection on theoretical concepts to understand children's construction of reality.

Most of my students in developmental psychology and education are interested in young children, because of children's playfulness, spontaneity and curiosity. Nevertheless, I do not always succeed to convey my enthusiasm for theoretical reflection on children's development and for the study of Piaget and Vygotsky. This apparent disinterest is in sharp contrast to my own experience as a student in developmental psychology and education. I studied in the 1970s. Me and my fellow students were eager to read the books of Piaget and Vygotsky; the first translations from the originals in French and Russian became available at that time. Our attitude towards their work was so different from what I observe in today's students. Why? I decided to have a closer look at what caused the deep interest of my generation. Maybe this would provide clues for how to give young students a fresh look at Piaget and Vygotsky?

Recently, Sandie Wong and I interviewed prominent early childhood researchers and advocates that had started their studies in the 1970s and 1980s, in the context of an oral history project on early education. See for more information about the project: Singer and Wong (2018, 2021a, 2021b). Our interviewees are from Europe, Canada and the United States, South America, and Australia and New Zealand. They were selected based on recognition as leading advocates and/or having contributed significant research in a national context and internationally. They belong to the first generation of professors and academics specialized in early childhood education related to the increase of early education provisions since the 1970s. In the interviews, we followed a biographic timeline and asked open questions about the interviewees' childhood, education and professional career. We also asked about theories that had influenced their work. Piaget and Vygotsky were most often mentioned by 34 of the 44 interviewees that we interviewed up to now. Eighteen interviewees elaborated on why they had been attracted by Piaget and Vygotsky. From these 18 interviewees, I distilled four reasons to love the work of Piaget and Vygotsky. These reasons clarify the differences between studying the original work of Piaget and Vygotsky by the older generation in the 1970s and 1980s and studying summaries and second-hand interpretations of Piaget and Vygotsky, which is often the case for today's students. All academics named in this chapter's gave informed consent to be named.

In the conclusions, we discuss how the experiences of the older generation of early childhood scholars and educators might help today's students to find their way in the Piagetian and Vygotskian heritage in the context of their own academic and practical work: to meet these powerful Inspirators.

8.2 Commitment, Imagination and Freedom to Explore

Piaget and Vygotsky gave interviewees a 'light-bulb moment' or a 'never-to-forget experience'. That was what happened with Joy Goodfellow. Later in her career Goodfellow became an influential academic in Australia, because of her expanded thinking about professional practices in early childhood education and the integration of children with additional needs (Sumsion & Goodfellow, 2012). Reflecting on the 1960s, the time she worked as preschool teacher, she notices: "Preschool teaching was about providing activities for children to be engaged. I don't recall having conversations about children's thinking". Piaget and Vygotsky radically changed Joy Goodfellow's view on children's learning. Education was not about pouring knowledge into children's heads. For children to understand something, they have to construct the knowledge for themselves, to (re)invent it. Learning can be fun, playful and self-reinforcing. In addition to guidance by the teacher, children need freedom to experiment and to use their imagination. The values of experiments and imagination not only apply to children, but also to their teachers.

The interviewees were ambitious and had ideals to improve early education. They pioneered to set up a new kind of child centres and preschools to make a better world: to liberate the child from an authoritarian upbringing, to liberate women from a home-bound life and to provide equal opportunities in education for children from disadvantaged families (Singer & Wong, 2021b). Nowadays, there are hundreds of books that interpret or just summarize the main ideas of Piaget and Vygotsky. That wasn't the case when our interviewees encountered their work. Nowadays curricula for early education without references to these two giants are hardly found. Our interviewees did not have these summaries and had to find their own way to implement their innovative theories. They had to make connections between what was needed in their pedagogical practice and their imagination of new practices based on the approaches of Piaget and Vygotsky. Exactly, the lack of examples of implementation in practice appealed to their creativity and gave them freedom to experiment and excitement to be engaged in something new (Burman, J. T., 2008; Lindqvist, 2003; Singer & Wong, 2018, 2021b).

The creativity of the interviewees is mirrored in the great diversity of interpretations and implementations of the theories of Piaget and Vygotsky. Some examples: Ingrid Pramling Samuelsson was inspired by Piaget's clinical interview. She was the first professor early childhood education in Sweden; in that position she supervised the first generation of 15 PhD doctorates in Sweden and was involved in (inter)national research projects, journals and organizations for education policy. Pramling Samuelsson saw that Piaget's clinical interview method could be implemented in the so-called dialogic pedagogy as pedagogical tool for teachers: 'to listen to children, to dialogue and to analyse how a child structures the world'. The 'dialogic pedagogy' was part of the social-democratic philosophy which formed the basis of the Swedish preschools set up since the 1970s. Swedish teachers were trained to interview children and to connect to their interests and thoughts (Pramling Samuelsson & Pramling, 2009).

In France Sylvie Rayna, a former student of Piaget found ways to apply Piagetian ideas in group settings for babies and toddlers and beyond. At the National Institute of Pedagogical Research (INRP) in Paris, Sylvie Rayna did ground-breaking research in crèches with Mira Stambak (advocate and pioneer with Irene Lézine, of early childhood education and development in crèches in France) and Hermine Sinclair (a close co-operator and colleague of Piaget in Genève) (Rayna, 2001; Sinclair et al., 1989). The focus was on how young children construct cognitive schemes at nonverbal level and how they co-construct meanings with their peers. The research group Sylvie Rayna participated in was inspired by the French socialist-communist philosophy of Henri Wallon about the value of community life for children and parents (Van der Veer, 1996). That group cooperated with Tulia Musatti, who did research in crèches in northern Italy, also inspired by socialist-communist ideals of Malaguzzi and the famous early education of the Reggio Emilia area (Cagliari et al., 2016; Musatti & Picchio, 2010). Mainstream at that time was the believe that babies and toddlers cannot communicate and cannot play together. Rayna and colleagues (Sinclair et al., 1989; Stambak & Sinclair, 1993), however, observed that very young children positively influence each other, both cognitively and socially. They studied the 'origins of logic' in babies, and symbolic play at nonverbal level in 3-year olds. Sylvie Rayna notes: 'We observed peer relationships in babies and toddlers in group settings while they are discovering and inventing among themselves'. They warned teachers not to be too dominant and not to obstruct children's thinking.

In the USA, Alice Sterling Honig focused on Piaget's description of the developmental stages in early childhood to test infant's cognitive development. At the beginning of her career, she was co-worker of Bettye Caldwell in one of the first experimental infant-day care groups that led to the establishment of the 'Head Start Project' in 1965 (Zigler & Valentine, 1979); Head Start was aimed to stimulate the cognitive development of babies and toddlers from disadvantaged families. Later on, Honig became a leading early childhood researcher in the USA, with a particular focus on quality infant and toddler care, supporting parenting and cultural diversity. Talking about her work at the experimental infant-day care group Alice Honig Sterling states: 'I had to assess the infants in our centre. We wanted to find out whether the infants and pre-schoolers would have higher cognitive scores than (carefully matched) contrast youngsters' (Lally et al., 1988). She used Piaget's detailed description of the sequence of stages of development to construct a method to score the progress in cognitive development: birth—2 years: small steps in sensorimotor stage, experiences the word through senses and actions, object permanence and stranger anxiety; 2–6 years: preoperational stage, representing things with words and images, pretend play, egocentrism and language development; 7–11 years: operational stage, et cetera. Alice Sterling Honig and colleagues needed quantitative data conforming to the norms of the American positivist view on science to convince policymakers that their investment in early education paid off. This use of Piaget's theory on successive stages of development in tests to measure cognitive progress often led to an understanding of the 'stages' as the description of educational goals that had to be obtained (Burman, E. 2008).

Vygotsky inspired interviewees who were interested in improving the quality of early education of pre-schoolers (3–7 years old). According to Vygotsky (1978), all specifically human mental processes, the so-called higher mental processes, are mediated by cultural tools such as language, signs and symbols. These tools have been invented by human society, and they are acquired by children during interpersonal communication with adults and more experienced peers, and through education. The Vygotskyan approach offers theoretical tools to analyse the teacher's active role in children's learning activities (e.g. Fleer & Van Oers, 2018). In the Netherlands, Bert van Oers was the first Dutch professor in the Cultural-Historical Activity Theory (CHAT) -approach in education and applied the Vygotskyan theories on cultural tools and on play as leading activity in young children's learning. Van Oers and his colleagues elaborated the so-called Developmental Education approach in the 1980 and 1990, initially for younger children (until the age of 8 years, see Van Oers, 2012). Van Oers experimented, for example, with the introduction of 'schemes' in the play of 4-year olds: the children had built a beautiful train track; then the teacher warned them that in the evening the cleaners will come and break down their train track. What to do to rebuild the track? The children were suggested to make a drawing (cultural tool) for remembering and re-laying the construction of their train track. Later on, they also discover the usefulness of 'schemes' in other situations (Van Oers, 1994). Co-workers of Van Oers and the founders the Dutch CHAT-based Institute for professional development and training, Niko Fijma and Bea Pompert explain the merits of this approach: 'Of course children are active learners. But if teachers don't provide "scaffolds" to broaden their views and skills, they stay behind. That's disastrous for children who do not receive much at home. Vygotsky's theory gave us a solid basis to work on practical improvement in primary schools in a theoretically sound manner' (Pompert & Dobber, 2018).

Marilyn Fleer (Australia) described her excitement when she came across Vygotsky in the early 1980s. At that time, Piaget was already well-known in Australia, but Vygotsky wasn't. Fleer made Vygotsky's theories known as a professor in early childhood education and development and as President of the International Society for Cultural Activity Research (ISCAR) (Fleer & Van Oers, 2018). In the early 1980s, Marilyn Fleer worked to design a science education programme for young children and felt uncomfortable with the traditional theories that underpinned early education. 'The child development theory of Piaget was all-over dominant. That was about how children construct knowledge along a continuum: first you think this way, then you think like that, etc.'. But according to Marilyn Fleer, that approach missed the point that mathematics is cultural knowledge that has been built up by many generations. 'I asked myself the question: what's the essence of mathematics? What should pre-schoolers really need to have an understanding of?' Children do not spontaneously invent the logico-mathematic system by playing with objects and peers. For acquiring cultural tools, mathematical concepts and theories about laws of nature, they need the support of more experienced peers or adults (Fleer, 2019;

Fleer & Pramling, 2014). Marilyn Fleer: 'Vygotsky showed that, where children are together with the adult, the carrier of cultural heritage, they are able to do so much more. For me, that was transformative. I suddenly learned there is another way to think about curriculum'.

In Russia, in the time of communist Soviet Union, there was a huge array of pedagogical and educational experiments based on Vygotskyan theories. At that time, Nikolay Veraksa worked at the Moscow State University on the education programme for 3–7-year olds. Veraksa became a leading expert of the Federal Institute of Education Development of Russia. In the Soviet time, the focus was on the idea of Vygotsky and followers that the child learns by imitating an expert model. 'Based on Leontiev's theory of activity: the teacher, the expert model, initiates an occupation (drawing, construction) and shows the child the expert model as an example of the cultural and ideal form'. They developed an evidence-based structured programme that was tried-out by many teachers in practice before it was implemented on a large scale. Following the Soviet period, after 1991, Veraksa developed the most widespread programme in the Russian Federation 'The key to learning curriculum' (Veraksa & Dolya, 2018). In that programme' 'the teacher supports a child's interest in the play activity and forms skills to do several actions with one object, to transfer the known actions from one object to another and to use substitutes for the object' (Salmina & Veraksa, 2018, p. 453).

8.3   Intellectual Creativity in Social–Historical Context

Theories do not arise from a vacuum; they are embedded and influenced by the historical momentum in which they arise (Burman, J. T., 2008; Hedegaard, 2014). Cognitive activities are driven by values and emotions (Piaget & Inhelder, 1969; Vygotsky, 1993). Piaget was not only motivated by scientific interests, but also by his moral concern to establish a foundation for the reconstruction of the individual and society after World War 1 (Vidal, 1997, p. 7). Vygotsky was inspired by Marxist theories and his ambition to contribute to education after the communist revolution in Russia in the 1920s and 1930s. Van der Veer and Valsiner (1991, p. 13): 'Vygotsky and his group formed an almost quasi-religious movement, so overwhelming was the conviction that they were on the right track towards the development of the new science'. While I wouldn't call it quasi-religion, our interviewees were also driven by their social ideals (Singer & Wong, 2021b). The above examples of their interpretations of Piaget and Vygotsky show that scientific research goes through the lens of questions and concerns of the researcher in their social context. The interviewees of our oral history study, who started their careers in the 1970s and 1980s, studied Piaget and Vygotsky because they wanted to innovate early education; they were engaged in social-political issues about the liberation of children and mothers and equal chances for disadvantaged children. They used only parts of these theories that were relevant for what was possible and needed in *their* social context. We can conclude for recent students: to become passionately involved in the work of

Piaget, Vygotsky—or any theoretical approach—students need 'a cause' to pursue: an engagement and commitment to educational innovations, and the aspiration to contribute to their realization.

The questions of the generation that started their career in the 1970s and 1980s remain relevant. But the social conditions have changed. Today students are confronted with new pedagogical issues related to, for example, the ecological crisis, digital revolution, ethnic and racial diversity and changes in gender and authority relationships. That mothers have the right to work outside the family has become self-evident. But now parents can be overburdened because of too long working hours to earn a living or to survive in the rat race of their career. Because of the ecological crisis we must rethink the leading values in education; to redirect the focus on individual rights and freedom in favour of an emphasis on mutual responsibility, sharing prosperity and self-discipline. The cultural heritage of Piaget and Vygotsky, including all their followers, is resources for inspiration and knowledge to research unexplored issues. Their empirical and conceptual methods to explore new questions and phenomena in child development and early education are vital, also for new generations.

8.4 Researching the Unknown: Observing and Constructing Theoretical Tools

The merit of Piaget and Vygotsky is their method of inquiring, of studying, of theoretical discussions. Their books and papers show their commitment to study and to understanding how children learn and how they construct knowledge. The interviewees admire Piaget because of his descriptions of young children in everyday situations and his theoretical reflections in which he explains children's activities to relation to the construction of schemes and structures to understand reality.

According to Alice Sterling Honig (USA), Piaget was a superb describer. His daughter Jacqueline is one of his main characters in his early books written in the 1930s and 1940s. Even after 50 years Alice Sterling Honig remembers her favourites: 'When he describes how his little 3-year-old daughter Jacqueline came into the kitchen where the maid was preparing to cook a goose (slitting its throat and draining the blood). The next day the little girl laid down on a bench and went "Argh" with her tongue hanging out, just like the dead goose. That's adorable'. The 'dead goose' is described in *Play, dreams and imitation in childhood* (Piaget, 1972). He interpretates Jacqueline's imitation of the dead goose in light of his theory that young children's thinking manifests itself in action, the 'logic-in-action' in young children. The dead goose had impressed Jacqueline and she represents that incident by acting out in pretend play.

Piaget had the talent to give meaning to ordinary behaviour and to change that into an example of something extraordinary. Behaviour that was previously dismissed as childlike and unimportant suddenly turns out to be essential for development. In this regard, one of my favourite books is 'The moral judgement of the child' (Piaget, 1977). His book reads as a quest driven by the will to understand, not following a pre-determined research plan; this in sharp contrast to the academic demands on modern students whose research is squeezed into a pre-determined 3-year plan. In his books, we see Piaget as an ethnographer of children's worlds through his use of participant observation (Duveen, 2000). He starts by observing children playing marbles and hide-and-seek, and analyses how the 'rules of the game' are handed down from older to younger children. He carefully describes how children learn, and the moral pressure of the group upon the younger child. For instance, his 5-year-old daughter Jacqueline who is playing hide-and-seek with 8 to 12-year-old friends (Piaget, 1977, pp. 72–79). The older girls follow the rules. Piaget observes that Jacqueline happily runs after the others and enjoys the togetherness. But she does not follow the rules. When she is the seeker, she openly looks through her fingers and hardly tries to hide herself.

Piaget relates this observation to his theoretical understanding of the construction of reality in the child. He observes that the younger child imitates the older ones, but only succeeds as far as she understands the behaviour of the older girls. In his theoretical concepts: the younger child 'assimilates' what she observes into the cognitive schemes she has already constructed. Imitative play is not passively copying the original, but an active construction of what is observed and understood. He speaks about 'the cognitive egocentrism' of the child; that is not yet able to understand the rules of the game from the perspective of the other players. Piaget also observes the tolerance of the older children towards Jacqueline. But when Jacqueline gets older, the older children become less tolerant and conflicts arise. The young child comes in, what Piaget calls, a situation of 'disequilibrium'. The 'disequilibrium' motivates the child to accommodate her cognitive schemes and to construct schemes better adapted to the reality.

Piaget also uses his 'clinical interview' method. He asks children to teach him to play a game so he can join in, and discusses incidents of lying, cheating, punishment, adult authority and responsibility. Through carefully crafted questions he is probing the children's representations of the rules. He also uses vignettes. For instance, the vignette about two boys: a boy who broke several cups accidentally and a boy who broke one cup while doing something he should not have been doing. Which boy is the naughtiest? He always used a form of counter questioning in which he presented the child with a contrary case of the original argument.

Piaget used a variety of qualitative methods to analyse and evaluate the changing attitudes of children towards moral rules; from the early egocentric positions, to understanding the rules as 'absolute' and 'having to be followed', to understanding that rules are based on mutual agreements and can be changed. Rules are social constructions. Piaget is a great model for making detailed and repeated observations and theoretical interpretations (Burman, J. T., 2008; Deveen, 2000).

Piaget shows that it takes many years for each individual to construct concepts of moral judgement, time and place, causality in physics and logic in mathematics. Depending on the stage of development of cognitive structures, the child can live in a different reality than older peers and adults. Thus, he gave adults a new way to look at children.

Piaget highly valued that students got opportunities to do their own experiments and their own research (Burman, J. T., 2008). According to Sylvie Rayna, one of our interviewees and former student of Piaget in Geneva in the 1960s: 'Piaget did not like people to imitate him. He challenged his co-workers and students to study new issues'. Of course, teachers must guide students by providing appropriate materials, theoretical tools and inspiring examples of research and researchers. In this respect, Piaget and his theories and approach are very much alive, also for today's students in their exploration and study of new questions that did not exist in the time of Piaget.

8.5 Reconceptualization of the Mind and Society Relationships

Vygotsky, just as Piaget, inspired the interviewees to change their view on young children's learning. Key in Vygotsky's methodology is his theoretical analyses of the relationships between individual and culture; of the way the use of symbols and tools leads to more complex social interactions and to the development of human consciousness; of what it means to be human and what education is about. His work challenges to rethink the influence of cultural heritage on the human mind. His approach became known as the 'social constructivist approach', 'activity theory' and 'cultural-historical approach'.

Marilyn Fleer (Australia) was inspired by the Vygotskyan theoretical analysis of the relationship between play, imagination, creativity and the development of the higher mental functions. According to Vygotsky's play theory, children play by using their imagination (Vygotsky, 1976). For instance, in role play, children play out their ideas about roles and rules and create an imaginary situation. Vygotsky sees role play as an early form of abstraction; the use of imagination increases the child's cognitive skills to reflect on problems and situations. In role play and early forms of abstract thinking, children are not restricted to the here and now. Marilyn Fleer applies these theories in her approach for knowledge construction in early childhood science education, the so-called Conceptual PlayWorld (https://www.monash.edu/conceptual-playworld/about#). Teachers and parents are invited to create an imaginary scenario by telling stories and the children are invited to explore the imaginary world where they meet all kinds of problems. So, their imagination and creativity to find solutions are evoked, and children are stimulated to construct early forms of conceptual thinking in science and mathematics.

Inspired by the Vygotskyan approach, educators developed methods to assess children's learning potential: the *Zone of proximal development (ZPD)*. The zone of proximal development refers to the difference between what a student can do without help and what he or she can achieve with guidance and encouragement from a skilled partner. The term 'proximal' refers to the skills that the student is 'close' to mastering. The ZPD turned out to be a fruitful tool for micro-analysis of teacher–child interactions. Maritta Hännikäinen, one of the first professors in early childhood education in Finland explains: 'The educational process, the joint building of the zone of proximal development for learning, results in development. For me this was, and is, one of the fascinating viewpoints in the cultural-historical approach'. The teacher is not following the spontaneous development of the child, but education provokes and proceeds development (Hännikäinen & Rasku-Puttonen, 2010).

Vygotsky challenges us to rethink fundamental philosophical questions about being human and about learning. I still remember the time and place of my first reading of Vygotsky's 'Thought and language' (1965); he showed the development and social origins of my most private inner thoughts. First, there are the social dialogues with parents and caregivers that regulate the child's actions; then the child guides her actions by talking aloud; and then the inner dialogue comes. Until then I had never wondered about the origins of inner thoughts; how I internalized the voices of my culture. Human beings are relational beings, cultural beings and biological beings. Vygotsky only lived 38 years. His heritage contains many essays on theory, politics, philosophy and education; he did not have time to work out all these themes. About the relationships between art and science, creativity and imagination, language and thought and much more. Marilyn Fleer calls his work a treasure box: when she is struggling with a problem, she always finds new leads somewhere in his work. Many of the questions put forward—not solved—by Vygotsky are highly relevant today.

8.6   Pleasure in Crossing Borders

The last reason for the interviewees for loving to study the work of Piaget and Vygotsky were the discussions with great scientists and crossing the borders of scientific disciplines and international travelling. Piaget surrounded himself with scientists from diverse countries and backgrounds at the *Centre d'Epistémologie Génétique* in Geneva. They stayed there for shorter or longer periods to work on their own research projects: biologists, linguists, psychologists, sociologists and philosophers in epistemology and evolution theory. The *Centre d'Epistémologie Génétique* was a stimulating intellectual environment. Sylvie Rayna (France), a former student of Piaget: 'Every year he and his assistants had a new theme of research, and each year I was participating by collecting empirical data in the schools of Geneva. It was like working in close companionship with the assistants, within a big staff coordinated by the 'Patron'. Nikolay Veraska (Russia) had comparable experiences at *Moscow State University, the Academy of Pedagogical Sciences of USSR*. During his education and work he met psychologists who had known Vygotsky and further developed his cultural-historical approach. Several of them also became well-known, also in western universities, e.g. Luria, Galperin, Elkonin, Poddiakov and Leontiev. "We discussed different problems and famous and interesting people visited us (philosophers, writers, artists, etc.). We really did not like to leave the Institute as we were discussing the problems until late at the night'.

The interviewees tell about the highly stimulating intellectual climate that went far beyond discussions on early education and child development. Lively discussions were held on philosophical, theoretical and social-political issues. Bert van Oers (the Netherlands) and fellow students studied and discussed the Vygotskian approach to improve the education of children from disadvantaged families. Several of them even learn Russian, because translations of the Russian texts were hardly available in the 1970s. Bert van Oers: 'The completeness of the cultural-historical approach attracted me. The combination of theories on education, epistemology, anthropology, the image of Man and that kind of stuff'. Moreover, the theories on learning provided tools for teaching. To give an example: 'When we assume that learning is basically about the transformation of human actions, then the question is: on which parameters do actions change? What is the starting point to help a student to pick up an action and start changing it, and why should they?' The Vygotskyan approach challenged Bert van Oers to reflect on the body-mind dualism of Descartes that was dominant in mainstream psychology. 'I felt the correctness of the Vygotskyan theses that thinking and feeling are never that isolated'.

The interviewees mention their scientific heroes, professors, lecturers and educators that were surrounded by gifted, creative and socially engaged colleagues and students. For instance, Kathy Sylva (UK) studied at Harvard with Jerome Bruner. 'I attended a reading group of five people at Harvard. With Kurt Fischer we discussed every single Piaget book. We must have read 12 books of Piaget'. The National Institute of Pedagogical Research (INRP) in Paris, the institute to which Sylvie Rayna was affiliated, attracted colleagues from Piaget (like Hermina Sinclair), Italy (like Tullia Mussatti) and South America (like Clotilde Rossetti-Ferreira). But they also worked together with Edward Mueller from Boston University, and Bert van Oers visited INRP. In Finland and Denmark, left-wing students and scholars organized visits and exchanges with colleagues from East Germany that worked on innovations based on the Vygotskyan approach.

These networks and exchanges were great sources of inspiration and pleasure in the science of developmental psychology and education. Interviewees loved crossing borders of countries, languages, disciplines and between philosophy, science, art and politics. The study of early education was a window for discussions to understand mankind and the social problems of the time.

8.7 In Conclusion

Over the years many summaries and ready-made applications of the works of Piaget and Vygotsky have become available for today's students. Maybe discouraging to read the original text of their seminal works: Who am I to add a new interpretation?

But the writings of Piaget and Vygotsky are like great works of art and philosophy—the Shakespearean dramas or dialogues of Socrates. Every generation can be touched in another way and make its own interpretations of these works to reflect on the vital issues of their own time. How can we help today's students to find their way in the Piagetian and Vygotskian heritage? The first lesson that I learnt from the interviewees and reflection on my own career is: the drive to study Piaget, Vygotsky or any theoretical work arises from a combination of interest in their theories and sociopolitical ideals to make a better world for children and parents. Young adulthood is the period in which students develop world views and ideas about their career and future (Eriksson, 1963; Mannheim, 1970). The work of the pioneers that participated in our oral history (Singer & Wong, 2021a, b) was rooted in the cultural and social movements of the 1970s and 1980s; that motivated them to reflect on the contribution of early education to liberate children from authoritarian pedagogies, to fight for equal chances for children and against discrimination (Marwick, 1998). These issues are still very relevant, but new issues have emerged. Today's young people are often concerned about climate change and ecological issues: what will be our future? In the 1970s and 1980s, the concept of 'freedom' in prosperous countries was associated with individual freedom and rights to develop and do what they longed for. Climate change enforces to think about the boundaries of individual freedom, sharing prosperity and social responsibility; about finding new perspectives for climate and economic refugees. Changes in values affect upbringing and the study of education. Students must enter into discussions about the role of their science and profession in contemporary social debates; and must become aware of the moral and philosophical visions and choices that frame their discipline (Kessen, 1979; Singer, 1993, 2018). Changes in moral values will lead to re-questioning of the works of Piaget and Vygotsky: what do they write about moral development, on 'free will', 'self-discipline', 'authority', 'autonomy', 'creativity', 'culture' and 'imagination'? Are the interpretations of their work still valid today?

The changing life conditions also ask for new empirical research. The digital revolution has provided humanity with a new kind of language that deeply influences our communication and our feelings of identity and belonging. Young children get much information from digital media and less by direct sensory experiences in nature. What will be the impact on what Piaget called the sensorimotor learning in early childhood? How can we conceptualize this new sign system from a Vygotskyan perspective? And what is the impact on the relationships between affects and cognition, and on the development of the higher mental functions?

The older generation can help today's students to find their way in the Piagetian and Vygotskyan heritage. Their methods of research are of utmost importance, maybe more than the common interpretations of their work! Let them be inspired by the detailed observations and ethnographic method and experiments of Piaget. Let them be inspired by Vygotsky's talent to formulate new theoretical questions. Moreover, let them explore without being restricted by tight research plans that rob them from the freedom to learn during the process and to explore. We need close observations and empirical data to design well founded theories on new phenomena. Let them be involved in theoretical discussions with colleagues with different disciplinary backgrounds. Theoretical concepts need to be reconsidered. Reading the original work of Piaget and Vygotsky gives plenty of examples in this respect. To sum up:

– Social-cultural ideals and values are fundamental in the science and profession of early education and child development.
– The older generation has must help students to find their way in the rich heritage of Piaget and Vygotsky and followers: their methodology and theoretical reflections.
– Students need time and opportunities to form learning communities to exchange experiences, data and theoretical analyses. They need discussions in diverse fora of colleagues and multidisciplinary teams, of parents and practitioners and of policy makers.

Acknowledgements Thanks to Sandie Wong, my co-worker in the oral history study of pioneers in early education in the second half of the twentieth century, for her help and support; to Poppe de Boer for his talent to think along about underlying issues; to the anonymous reviewer for the critical comments and most useful suggestions. And above all, thanks to the interviewees of the oral history study for their time and willingness to share their experiences and thoughts.

References

Burman, E. (2008). *Developments: Child, image, nation*. Routledge.

Burman, J. T. (2008). Experimenting in relation to Piaget: Education is a chaperoned process of adaptation. *Perspectives on Science, 16*(2), 160–195.

Cagliari, P., Castagnetti, M., Giudici, C., Rinaldi, C., Vecchi, V., & Moss, P. (Eds.). (2016). *Loris Malaguzzi and the schools of Reggio Emilia: A selection of his writings and speeches, 1945–1993*. Routledge.

Duveen, G. (2000). Piaget ethnographer. *Social Science Information, 39*(1), 79–97.

Eriksson, E. H. (1963). *Childhood and society*. Hogarth Press.

Fleer, M. (2019). Scientific playworlds: A model of teaching science in play-based settings. *Research in Science Education, 49*(5), 1257–1278.

Fleer, M., & Pramling, N. (2014). *A cultural-historical study of children learning Science*. Springer.

Fleer, M., & Van Oers, B. (Eds.). (2018). *International handbook of early childhood education*. Springer.

Hännikäinen, M., & Rasku-Puttonen, H. (2010). Promoting children's participation: The role of teachers in preschool and primary school learning sessions. *Early Years, 30*(2), 147–160.

Hedegaard, M. (2014). The significance of demands and motives across practices in children's learning and development: An analysis of learning in home and school. *Learning, Culture and Social Interaction, 3*(3), 188–194.

Kessen, W. (1979). The American child and other cultural inventions. *American Psychologist, 34*(10), 815.

Lally, J. R., Mangione, P. L., & Honig, A. S. (1988). *The Syracuse University Family Development Research Program: Long-range impact on an early intervention with low-income children and their families*. In D. R. Powell (Ed.), *Annual advances in applied developmental psychology, Vol. 3. Parent education as early childhood intervention: Emerging directions in theory, research and practice* (pp. 79–104). Ablex Publishing.

Lindqvist, G. (2003). Vygotsky's theory of creativity. *Creativity Research Journal, 15*(2–3), 245–251.

Mannheim, K. (1970). The problem of generations. *Psychoanalytic Review, 57*(3), 378–404.

Marwick, A. (1998). *The sixties: Cultural revolution in Britain, France, Italy, and the United States, c.1958–c.1974.* Oxford: Oxford University Press.

Musatti, T., & Picchio, M. (2010). Early education in Italy: Research and practice. *International Journal of Early Childhood, 42*(2), 141–153.

Piaget, J. (1972). *Play, dreams and imitation in childhood.* Routledge & Kegan Paul.

Piaget, J. (1977). *The moral judgement of the child.* Penguin Books.

Piaget, J., & Inhelder, B. (1969). *The psychology of the child.* Basic books.

Pompert, B., & Dobber, M. (2018). Developmental education for young children in the Netherlands: Basic development. In M. Fleer & B. van Oers (Eds.), *International handbook of early childhood education* (pp. 1113–1140). Springer.

Pramling Samuelsson, I., & Pramling, N. (2009). Children's perspectives as 'touch downs' in time: Assessing and developing children's understanding simultaneously. *Early Child Development and Care, 179*(2), 205–216.

Rayna, S. (2001). The very beginnings of togetherness in shared play among young children. *International Journal of Early Years Education, 9*(2), 109–115.

Salmina, N., & Veraksa, A. (2018). Symbolic means in the educational programs for preschool children in Russia. In M. Fleer & B. van Oers (Eds.), *International handbook of early childhood education* (pp. 449–459). Springer.

Sinclair, H., Stambak, M., Levine, I., Verba, M., & Rayna, S. (1989). *Infants and objects: The creativity of cognitive development.* Academic Press.

Singer, E. (1993). Shared care for children. *Theory & Psychology, 3*(4), 429–449.

Singer, E. (2018). *Child-care and the psychology of development.* Routledge, Psychology library editions: Child Development.

Singer, E., & Wong, S. (2018). Reflections of pioneers in early childhood education research on their collaboration with practitioners in the development of theories and innovative practices. *Early Years, 38*(2), 125–138.

Singer, E., & Wong, S. (2021a). Emotional security and daycare for babies and toddlers in social-political contexts: Reflections of early years pioneers since the 1970s. *Early Child Development and Care, 191*(3), 461–474. https://doi.org/10.1080/03004430.2019.1622539

Singer, E., & Wong, S. (2021b). Early childhood theories, ideals and political movements, an oral history study of pioneers in the second half of the twentieth century. *Early Child Development and Care,* 1–16. https://www.tandfonline.com/eprint/RGBWGJQAA4H88G4IWVYJ/full? target=https://doi.org/10.1080/03004430.2020.1850445

Stambak, M., & Sinclair, H. (Eds.). (1993). *Pretend play among 3-year-olds.* Lawrence Erlbaum Ass.

Sumsion, J., & Goodfellow, J. (2012). 'Looking and listening-in': A methodological approach to generating insights into infants' experiences of early childhood education and care settings. *European Early Childhood Education Research Journal, 20*(3), 313–327.

Van der Veer, R. (1996). Henri Wallon's theory of early child development: The role of emotions. *Developmental Review, 16*(4), 364–390.

Van der Veer, R., & Valsiner, J. (1991). *Understanding Vygotsky: A quest for synthesis.* Blackwell.

Van Oers, B. (1994). Semiotic activity of young children in play: The construction and use of schematic representations. *European Early Childhood Education Research Journal, 2*(1), 19–33.

Van Oers, B. (Ed.). (2012). *Developmental education for young children: Concept, practice and implementation* (Vol. 7). Springer.

Veraksa, N., & Dolya, G. (2018). The key to learning curriculum. In M. Fleer & B. van Oers (Eds.), *International handbook of early childhood education* (pp. 1059–1074). Springer.

Vidal, F. (1997). Towards re-reading Jean Piaget. *Human Development, 40*(2), 124–126.

Vygotsky, L. S. (1976). Play and its role in the mental development of the child. In J. S. Bruner, A. Jolly, & K. Sylva (Eds.), *Play—Its role in development and evolution* (pp. 537–554). Penguin Books.

Vygotsky, L. S. (1978). *Mind in society: The development of higher psychological processes.* Harvard University Press.

Vygotsky, L. S. (1965). *Thinking and language.* MIT Press.

Vygotsky, L.S. (1993). The problem of mental retardation. In R.W. Rieber, & A.S. Carton (Eds.), *The collected works of L.S. Vygotsky, vol. 2: The fundamentals of defectology* (p. 220).

Zigler, E., & Valentine, J. (1979). *Project Head Start: A legacy of the war on poverty.* The Free Press.

Dr. Elly Singer was associate professor at the University Utrecht and University of Amsterdam. She studied the history of early childhood development and care: Relationships between social policy, curriculum development and science. She is involved in studies of play curricula, young children's social life in group settings, and professionalization. She and her co-workers widely published on play engagement, social learning, humour, language development, friendship and group dynamics, and professional development. With Sandie Wong, she is studying the history of early childhood education and care since the 70th: Chronicling the development of early childhood education and care since the 1970s—pedagogies and practices: An oral history project.

Chapter 9
Constructivism and Social Constructivism in the Study of Relationship Between Early Childhood Education Quality and Executive Function at 5–6 years Old

Anastasia Belolutskaya⬤, Darya Bukhalenkova⬤,
Evgeniy Krasheninnikov-Khait⬤, Igor Shiyan⬤, Olga Shiyan⬤,
and Aleksander Veraksa⬤

Abstract The study is devoted to the analysis of the relationship between the qualitative characteristics of the educational environment and executive function of preschoolers. To assess the quality of the educational environment the ECERS-R was used, based on both constructivist and social-constructivist approaches. This study presents empirical research data on the relationship of the level of executive functions (EF) with the ECERS-R scores. The study involved 34 groups of preschool children from Moscow (706 children aged 5–6 years). The NEPSY-II battery (subtests Inhibition, Memory for Design, Sentence Repetition) (Korkman et al., NEPSY II. Administrative Manual, Psychological Corporation, 2007), Dimensional Change Card Sort (Zelazo, Nature Protocols 1:297–301, 2006) were used as measuring tools for EF. A number of significant correlations between EF and such ECERS-R items as "Space for gross motor play", "Gross motor equipment", «Music/movement», «Blocks», «Dramatic play», «Promoting acceptance of diversity», |General supervision of children», «Free play», «Space for privacy», «Child related display», «Art», «Blocks», and «Schedule» were found.

The conclusions were drawn about the importance of creating conditions for EF development of children.

Today, the attention of researchers dealing with the psychology of education is increasingly drawn to preschool age. Heckman's work confirmed the importance of investments in the development of the quality of kindergartens in terms of subsequent

A. Belolutskaya · E. Krasheninnikov-Khait · I. Shiyan (✉) · O. Shiyan
Moscow City University, Moscow, Russia
e-mail: igor.bogdanovich@gmail.com

D. Bukhalenkova · A. Veraksa
Lomonosov Moscow State University, Moscow, Russia

145
N. Veraksa and I. Pramling Samuelsson (eds.), *Piaget and Vygotsky in XXI century*,
Early Childhood Research and Education: An Inter-theoretical Focus 4,
https://doi.org/10.1007/978-3-031-05747-2_9

socio-economic impact (Heckman et al., 2006). Results of EPPSE (Effective Pre-School, Primary & Secondary Education) study showed that the quality of preschool education has a long-term impact on the level of school academic achievements: those teenagers, who at an early age attended kindergartens ranked high in quality of education for a long period, have passed the final exams significantly better than those who did not have such experience (Sylva et al., 2004). These data contributed to the emergence of works that emphasized the importance of the influence of educational environment on the psychological development of children (Hall et al., 2013; Manning et al., 2017; Sammons et al., 2014; Vandell et al., 2010).

The ECERS scales are used as a tool to assess the educational environment in kindergartens (Sheridan et al., 2018; Slot, 2018; Sylva et al., 2014; Vermeer et al., 2016). It is interesting to analyze how the methodological foundations of this tool relate to the concepts of J. Piaget and L. Vygotsky. Modern pre-school education is based on their ideas: practically, all ECEC programs contain references to these two authors, the creators of the theories of child development (Bredekamp & Copple, 1997; French, 2007; Taguma et al., 2013). At the same time, the theories themselves are quite different in their basic positions, which allowed J.Bruner even to declare that "the two perspectives under discussion represent two incomparable approaches to development" (Bruner, 2001).

Piaget's concept describes development as the gradual formation of logical structures that permeate all areas of the child's psyche—both his representation of reality and his/her interaction with other people. According to Piaget, the developmental vector is the overcoming of centrality that makes it possible to gradually coordinate different points of view and to see the world in its sustained wholeness, rather than to fix only one or the other side of an object, as is evident in Piaget's phenomena (Jean Piaget: Theory, Experiments, Discussion, 2001). It is important to note that Piaget understands development as a gradual transformation of initial schemata: in a discussion with behaviorists, he argues that the child is not a "blank slate"; a new understanding of reality is not the result of training, but is the result of adaptation, that is, in the transformation of initial schemata. The two sides of adaptation—assimilation and accommodation—are equally important in development, and while accommodation is the transformation of schemata under the influence of encounters with objects, assimilation, on the contrary, is a kind of adaptation of reality to the schemata at hand. Piaget's concept is distinguished by its view of development as an independent process unfolding according to its own laws. As for learning, it should take into account the available level of development and should be based on it (Jean Piaget: Theory, Experiments, Discussion, 2001).

From these theoretical positions, the following consequences for the pedagogical process are presented: it is important to create conditions for children's independent discovery, for their active exploration of the world around them, so that they can move at their own unique pace. The pedagogical process is focused on supporting children's independent construction of knowledge began to be called *constructivism* (Matthews, 2003). It is also important to emphasize conditions for assimilation of reality—expression of one's attitude through symbolic means—drawing, play, and word.

The concept of development as the emergence of new qualities is also key in L. Vygotsky's concept, but the idea of a correlation between development and learning is radically opposed. From Vygotsky's point of view, development is only partly a consequence of maturation; the key role in it is played by the cultural context and the mastery of symbolic systems. Learning sets the benchmark for development and leads it. Vygotsky introduces the concept of the zone of proximal development, which "defines the functions that are not yet mature, but are in the process of maturation, which will mature tomorrow, which are now still in their infancy; functions that can be called not fruits of development, but buds of development, flowers of development, that is, that which is just maturing". And the most important role in development is played by the adult: "The development of the internal individual properties of the child's personality has as its nearest source cooperation (understood in the broadest sense) with other people" (Vygotsky, 1984, p. 265). And the specification: "What the child today is able to do in cooperation…, tomorrow he or she becomes capable to do independently" (Vygotsky, 1984, p. 264). Hence the term '*social constructivism*', which emphasizes the social context in which mental change, occurs.

Here, the question arises whether the two theories are in conflict with each other: Is the orientation to child's own activity, on the one hand, and the view of the importance of learning for development compatible? However, such a contradiction would arise if cooperation was understood as direct guidance of child action, ignoring child activity and child intention. Indeed, there is a risk of interpreting the idea of a proximal developmental orientation as learning, emphasizing above all the role of the adult in the educational process. E. Berezhkovskaya, in particular, points out the danger of such an understanding, who says that a teacher is tempted "to give a way of action to a child before he or she has felt the need for it. This is especially true when the way lies in the zone of the proximal development and, therefore, will be easily taken and learned on the underdeveloped material, which is available at the moment" (Berezhkovskaya, 2015). Research evidence confirms that Vygotsky's "didactic" interpretation of the zone of proximal development is indeed often found in Russian kindergartens, where the educational process is often adult-centered (Remorenko et al., 2017).

However, an analysis of both Vygotsky's works and the representatives of the cultural-historical approach show that such an interpretation is completely unjustified. First, the study of Vygotsky's works allows us to conclude about his understanding of man as an active actor. The main vectors of human development outlined in his last fundamental monograph "Thinking and Speech" are arbitrariness and consciousness, the ability to control one's mental processes and emotions, not to be dependent on either the external field or one's own affects. "From his point of view, a person does not simply submit to affect, however noble, but constructs his own affects, personality, and destiny", writes Vygotsky researcher E. Zavershneva (Zavershneva, 2007, p. 15).

Russian followers of Vygotsky have made a number of specifications concerning understanding of the zone of proximal development and specifics of cooperation between the adult and the child. Thus, G. Tsukerman, based on the research of B. Elkonin and V. Slobodchikov, writes that "the zone of the proximal development is a place of meeting of the child and the adult where the process of coordination of two plans leads to the result interesting, unexpected and convincing from the point of view of each participant of interaction" (Tsukerman & Venger, 2015). J. Shopina in her study of the conditions of transformation of the zone of proximal development into the zone of actual development found that successful development depends on the flexibility of the adult in taking different types of positions in interaction with the child—the adult should be able to take both "equal" and "under" positions so that the child can act not only as one who learns patterns, but also as one who passes on the patterns, teaches the other (Shopina, 2002). V. Zaretsky in his work "Zone of the proximal development: What Vygotsky didn't have time to write about…" points out that in the course of development the child not only masters cultural experience, but also acts as a subject of overcoming of own difficulties and forming of own plan, and for this purpose the adult should be not "influencing", but the subject of equal rights. The presence of a difficulty is crucial here—it becomes a stimulus for development rather than an obstacle and is transformed into a task by the skillful actions of the adult (Zaretsky, 2007).

As Tsukerman notes, such "active-mutual cooperation" differs both from "adult-centered and from child-centered interaction" (Tsukerman & Venger, 2015, p. 26). In this interpretation, the positions of Piaget and Vygotsky are not contradictory but complementary.

Our analysis of the text of the ECERS-R scales allows to see that their developers drew on both Piaget's and Vygotsky's ideas. Thus, in accordance with Piaget's theory, the educational environment should be accessible, rich and transformable, leaving the child a large space for his or her own activity. Great attention is paid to children's freedom of choice, to their interests and preferences, to their needs—for this purpose materials should be diverse and child-facing—at children's eye level, and during the day there should be a balance between children's free activity and activities organized by adults.

While at minimum (3 points) and "good" (5 points) quality levels there are predominantly indicators assessing accessibility and richness of the environment, at "excellent quality" (7 points) (and sometimes at good quality level) there are indicators assessing "developmental interaction" (not developmental influence, which is important) of the adult, i.e., his actions oriented to the zone of children's proximal development. Note that these indicators by no means describe directive intervention and training, but the careful inclusion of the adult in activities that are meaningful for the child. For example, in indicator 24 ('Role-playing') indicator 7.4 sounds like "Pictures, stories and excursions are used to enrich role-playing with new content". In Indicator 18 (Everyday Use of Speech), Indicator 5.3 is "Teachers add information by developing children's ideas" and Indicator 7.2 is "Children are asked questions, encouraging them to give increasingly elaborate answers". Indicators of this kind are found in 22 of the 43 scale indicators.[1]

---

[1] It should be noted that in the ECERS-3 scales, the number of indicators assessing the developmental interaction of the adult has increased dramatically: this suggests that the new version of the quality assessment tool is more oriented toward working in the zone of children's proximal development (Harms et al., 2014).

Thus, at high levels of quality, the indicators assess not only the adaptability of the environment to children's actual development, but also the extent to which adults are oriented in their work toward the zone of children's proximal development—that is, are ready to create situations that empower children, but at the same time take into account children's interests and meanings.

The ability of the scale to assess the educational environment oriented both on the zone of actual development and on the zone of the proximal development allowed us to propose that preschool groups with a higher level of quality will show the higher level of the development of the executive functions, which can be considered as a major aspect of higher mental functions development according to Vygotsky (1982).

In the perspective of the relationship of preschoolers' psychological development and their future academic success executive functions (EF) are called as a key predictor (Best et al., 2009; Blair, 2002; Cadoret et al., 2018; Diamond, 2013; Hanson et al., 2014; Howes et al., 2008; Monette & Bigras, 2008; Raver & Blair, 2014; Rimm-Kaufman et al., 2009; Saracho & Spodek, 2007; Simpson & Riggs, 2007; Welsh et al., 2010; Williford et al., 2013) According to Miyake's model, EF are a group of cognitive skills that provide targeted problem solving and adaptive behavior in new situations (Miyake et al., 2000). EF are divided into the following main components: (1) working memory, both visual and verbal; (2) cognitive flexibility, which is related to the ability to switch from one rule to another; and (3) inhibitory control, which presupposes the inhibition of the dominant response in favor of what is required in the task. It is important to note, that according to Vygotsky theory self-regulation is considered as a feature of the developmental process of child, of the transformation of lower mental functions in the higher ones (Vygotsky, 1984). It becomes logical to see in executive functions acquisition development of the higher mental functions (Ardilla, 2013). That is why in our research we have used complex of well-established methods, aimed at EF development measurement.

Results of the studies aimed at investigating the influence of the educational environment on the EF stress importance of a comfortable emotional and psychological climate in a group as well as the primacy of group work over the frontal one, the extensive benevolent nature of feedback from an adult as relevant for EF development (Curby et al., 2013; Deville & Meynier, 2014; Duval et al., 2016; Hamre & Pianta, 2007; Hamre et al., 2007, 2013; Hatfield et al., 2013; Hestenes et al., 2015; Hughes & Kwok, 2007; Kaufman, 2010; Mashburn et al., 2008; Phillips et al., 2000; Pianta et al., 2002; Schoofs et al., 2008; Simpson & Riggs, 2007).

Discussing the situation in Russia it is important to note that due to the Federal Law of the Russian Federation "On Education" (2012) stating a preschool education as level of the educational system. It means that the state has committed itself to provide free education to children from the age of three.[2] This important step led to a necessity to find instruments for measurement of the educational environment, establishing continuity between kindergarten and school. Traditionally, starting from works of Vygotsky (1982), it was assumed that main educational task of the kindergarten in Russia is to help children acquire different cultural forms of knowledge and cultural

---

[2] Attending the kindergarten is not obligatory and depends on parent's decision.

tools of operating with them (symbols, models, schemes, etc.). Thus, adult as a key figure, bearer of the ideal forms of culture, examples of actions came into front in educational work with children. This is also the reason of the highly disciplined way of life in Russian kindergarten, oriented toward social norms and rules, frontal type of work in groups, where imitation of adults' actions was the main way of knowledge acquisition.

However, Vygotsky also stated that environment is a source of child's action as it provides opportunity for the activity, approved by an adult (Vygotsky 1982).

This study is the first Russian research where an attempt to compare the children results of EF and the quality of the educational environment in preschool childhood is made. The novelty of the research lies in the fact that we did not use the average score based on ECERS to establish the relationships. Within our study, each of the 43 parameters of the methodology was taken into account to identify key environmental factors that are the most significantly associated with one or another components of EF.

This study is based on the following hypotheses: the quality of the educational environment of the kindergarten group is significantly related to the level of EF of children.

9.1   Methods

The ECERS-R (Early Childhood Environment rating Scale - Revised) (Harms et al., 2005) was elaborated to evaluate the environment quality. The validity, reliability, and adequacy of the results obtained with its help are confirmed by series of studies (Harms et al., 2005; Sylva et al., 2010).

The scoring in ECERS-R is based on the principle of expert observation. Depending on the conditions presented in the environment, the expert decides on assigning a score from 1 to 7 to each of the 43 items divided into 7 subscales.

ECERS-R is officially translated and published in Russia.

The following methods were applied to evaluate the EF performance:

1. Inhibition is a subtest of NEPSY-II complex (Korkman et al., 2007). The stimuli included two pages depicting black and white squares and circles, alternating without any regularity. One page, used for practice, displayed 8 figures arranged in a line; the other page, used for test trials, displayed 40 figures arranged in 5 lines. It consisted of two parts: (a) Naming (the shape of each object depicted on the page) and (b) Inhibition (naming each object with the opposite name—i.e., saying "circle" when seeing a square). The child was instructed to complete the page as quickly as possible. The number of errors (both corrected by a child and not corrected) and time spent for the both task execution were recorded.
2. Dimensional Change Card Sort (DCCS) (Zelazo, 2006) is aimed at cognitive flexibility (the child's ability to follow the rule and respond to its changes). Children are required to sort a series of bivalent test cards (with pictures of

red rabbits and blue boats), first according to one dimension (color) and then according to another (shape). At the third try, a child has to sort cards according to the more complicated rule with the additional factor (cards with/without borders). The accuracy score was calculated (max = 24).

3. Memory for Designs (MfD) (NEPSY-II) to assess the level of visual working memory. This task included four trials. On each trial, the child was shown a grid with four to eight designs. The grid was displayed for 10s and then removed from view. Next, the child was provided with a blank grid and a set of cards, some of which depicted the same designs that were presented before. The child's task was to select the appropriate designs and place them on a grid in the same location as previously shown. In this test, the following total scores were recorded: (1) Content reflects the correctness of memorizing image details; (2) Spatial reflects the correctness of the child remembering the configuration, and (3) Bonus stands for the correct memorization and consideration of both parameters simultaneously. Finally, all three indicators are summarized in the total score (max = 120).

4. Sentences Repetition (SR) (NEPSY-II) to assess verbal working memory. The stimuli included 17 sentences of increasing length and complexity. The child was read one sentence at a time and asked to repeat it. When the child recalled the sentence correctly, the response was scored as 2; when there was one or two mistakes, the response was scored as 1; and when there were more than two mistakes, the response was scored as 0. If the child received 0 points on three consecutive trials, the procedure was stopped; otherwise, the child received all 17 sentences. The accuracy score was calculated (max = 34).

All analyses were performed with use of SPSS v.18.0.

9.2 Sample

The sample of this study consisted of 706 children aged 5–6 years (Me = 5.6 years), who attended 34 groups of Moscow kindergartens. Of these, 357 (50.6%) were boys and 349 (49.4%) were girls. This study was conducted in 2016–2018. The diagnostics was carried out in a quiet room on one-to-one basis.

All parents were informed about the aims of the study and gave written permissions for children involvement in research. Children were free to quit or refuse from research at any time and were explicitly asked about their desire to participate in the research. The research was approved by the Ethics Committee of the Russian Psychological Society.

9.3 Results

The means and standard deviations for ECERS-R and EF measures are presented in Annex 1 and Annex 2. As for EF measures scores, the normal distribution took place. The ECERS-R scores are mostly fluctuating around the level of middle quality (3–4 scores), some groups showed the level of low quality (1–2 scores), but none of them reached the high quality (5–7 scores).

9.4 The Relationship of ECERS-R Scores and EF Tasks

A number of statistically significant, both positive and negative, relationships (Spearman's criterion) between ECERS-R items and EF tasks was obtained (Table 9.1).

The most number of significant correlations was found with such EF component as **inhibition**.

In the Inhibition subtest, the points are given for the uncorrected by a child errors: the higher the score, the lower the inhibition level. Therefore, the inverse correlation with environmental indicators shows that the relationship between the level of inhibition and the quality of the environment is positive. The better conditions are offered based on such parameters as "Space for privacy", "children-related display", "art", "blocks" "safety practices", "promoting the acceptance of diversity", the less the child makes mistakes while performing the task. Thus, the important conditions for the formation of the inhibitory control are the following: the availability of places where a child can be alone and rest from the group; the saturation of the environment with products of children's activities performed according to one's own idea, and not according to the model; the availability of sufficient materials for drawing, modeling, clip art, and design, as well as of components that clearly demonstrate the cultural diversity of the world (dolls, pictures, costumes of different nations).

Besides we obtained two positive correlations: with items "Blocks" and "Free play". It means that the higher score on these parameters the lower the inhibition level. Note that the key points of the item "Blocks" are related to the number and availability: if there are enough blocks in the group (the number should be such that two people can simultaneously build a large structure). As for the item "Free play" within the observation, it is important to establish if free play occurs indoors and outdoors; supervision is provided to protect children's health and safety and facilitate children's play; toys, games, and equipment are accessible for children to use for free play.

The level of children's **verbal working memory** (measured by SR test) development positively correlates with a whole set of items that point out the proper organization of physical activity:

– space for gross motor games. The examples of indicators: some space outdoors or indoors used for gross motor play; gross motor space is generally safe; space is

Table 9.1 Correlations between ECERS-R items and EF tasks (Spearman's criterion)

ECERS-R items/EF	Verbal working memory (SR)	Visual working memory (MfD)	Cognitive flexibility (DCCS)	Inhibition	Uncorrected mistakes (naming)	Time (inhibition)	Time (naming)
				Uncorrected mistakes (inhibition)			
Space for gross motor play	$r = 0.322; p = 0.055$						
Gross motor equipment	$r = 0.367; p = 0.033$						
Music/movement	$r = 0.342; p = 0.048$						
Blocks					$r = -0.333; p = 0.054$	$r = 0.354; p = 0.040$	
Dramatic play			$r = 0.326; p = 0.060$				
Promoting acceptance of diversity	$r = 0.349; p = 0.043$						
General supervision of children							$r = 0.336; p = 0.052$
Free play						$0.354; p = 0.040$	$r = 0.336; p = 0.052$
Furnishing for routine care, play and learning		$r = -0.393; p = 0.022$	$r = -0.357; p = 0.038$				
Space for privacy				$r = -0.404; p = 0.018$			

(continued)

Table 9.1 (continued)

ECERS-R items/EF	Verbal working memory (SR)	Visual working memory (MfD)	Cognitive flexibility (DCCS)	Inhibition		Time (inhibition)	Time (naming)
				Uncorrected mistakes (inhibition)	Uncorrected mistakes (naming)		
Child related display				$r = -0.358; p = 0.038$			
Safety practices				$r = -0.403; p = 0.018$			
Art				$r = -0.369; p = 0.032$			
Promoting acceptance of diversity				$r = -0.482; p = 0.004$	$r = -0.380; p = 0.027$		
Schedule	$r = -0.421; p = 0.013$						

easily accessible for children; space is organized so that different types of activities do not interfere with one another.

– gross motor equipment. This item includes such indicators as: some gross motor equipment is accessible for children during at least one hour daily; it is in good condition and appropriate for age and ability of the children; the equipment stimulates a variety of skills, etc.

– music/movement. The examples of indicators: some music materials are accessible for children's use; stuff initiates at least one music activity daily; some movement/dance activity is done at least weekly; various types of music are used with the children.

Also the positive correlation with the item "Promoting acceptance of diversity" was obtained. This item includes such indicators as: racial and cultural diversity visible in materials; staff intervene appropriately to counteract prejudice shown by children or other adults, etc.

As well we found one negative correlation of verbal working memory and the item "Schedule". Within this item an observer establishes, for example, if basic daily schedule exists that is familiar to children; written schedule is posted in room and relates generally to what occurs; schedule provides balance of structure and flexibility; a variety of play activities occur each day, some teacher directed and some child initiated and so on.

As for **visual working memory** we found one negative correlation with the item "Furnishing for routine care, play and learning". The important indicators for an observer are: sufficient furniture in good repair, most furniture is child-sized and convenient to use, etc.

Concerning **cognitive flexibility** the correlation with this item appeared to be significantly negative. We obtained positive correlation with "dramatic play". The item includes such indicators as: dramatic play materials and furniture for at least two different themes are accessible for a substantial portion of the day; dramatic play area clearly defined, with space to play and organized storage.

9.5 Discussion

Concerning the relation between **inhibition** and «Space for privacy» it can be explained by the fact that the rule not to disturb another child, when he/she is in the special privacy place requires considerable effort from a preschooler. A child has to manage with his/her impulses to remember to stop in time not bothering those persons who want to stay alone.

The inhibition also correlates directly with such items as: "child related display" and "art". These parameters are connected to each other. The main idea is to figure out if a child has opportunity to create some art-works coming out of his/her own plan or all children have to follow teacher's sample. With regard to inhibition two aspects seem to be important: (a) the necessity to think up own idea and to make a plan requires child self-control and (b) the fact that there are a lot of children's individual craftworks and different traces of their projects that recently have been done makes the group psychological climate more comfortable and safe. Research devoted to the problem of relations of EF and educational environment show that one of the main obstructing factor is stress (Curby et al., 2013; Schoofs et al., 2008; Simpson & Riggs, 2007). Our results also confirm this position taking into account additionally that the correlations with such items as "Safety practices" and "Promoting acceptance of diversity" were also obtained. The sense of personal physical and psychological safety (children's ideas and feelings are accepted by a teacher and a group) is a fruitful ground which helps a child to learn how to manage with his/her natural impulses and to master cultural ways of behavior.

We also obtained the results which reveal negative relations between the inhibition and ECERS-R items: the higher score is for "General supervision of children" and «Free play» the more time children need to perform the EF tasks. These items are also connected to each other. The observer has to clarify: (a) if children have spare time to do what they want (without any special classes) and (b) if a teacher provides protection of children's health and safety. At first sight, these results contradict to the previous conclusion about the positive relation between inhibition and safety. But in fact, we should pay attention that psychological meanings of the concept of safety could be different. In one case the safety includes acceptance, in other case it means external control of children's behavior by an adult. It is necessary to underline that typical score for these items were fluctuating around the level "middle quality" (3 points). Unfortunately, our sample did not include groups with a high level of support for children's play (i.e., "supervision used as an educational interaction" or "a balance is maintained between the child's need to explore independently and staff input into learning", related to the "high" and "excellent" level). Our observations show that a spare time mostly means that children are not supported at all: an adult interferes only in case of obvious conflict. These interventions can be rather authoritarian: children feel control but not support or acceptance. We suppose that such way of supervision can have negative outcomes in term of inhibitory control.

The following obtained results are contradictive: negative correlation of item "Blocks" with Inhibition subtest (parameter "uncorrected mistakes") and positive connection between item "Blocks" and Inhibition subtest (parameter "time"). The main aspects of observation for this item is if there are many different blocks that are accessible daily. It is important to note that typically in Russian kindergartens very few blocks are accessible for children's play. One of the reasons why kindergartens prefer not to provide children with a lot of blocks is a fear of increased injury. Playing with blocks is supposed to be unsafe. The majority of groups get 1 or 2 points (means "low quality") and none of them exceed 4 points. Usually, the sticking point is the indicator that sounds like: "special block area is set aside out of traffic with storage and suitable building surface". One can see such space organization very rarely.

We argue that to explain the obtained data properly it is crucially important to take into account such variable as the teachers' competence to support children's free play in particular with blocks. Pedagogical support of such kind excludes authoritarian external control but teachers' influence nevertheless carried out through the special organization of space, suggesting some ideas or materials that help to enrich children's activity. Concerning the connection to inhibition we suppose that two different situations can be defined. The positive one is the following: there are quite a lot of blocks, there is a special place for building that is aside of other activities, a teacher has the professional competence to support children's free play. In this case, children get an experience of cooperation constructing together and resolving possible conflicts that can often take place when the situation requires to share some materials and come to common decisions. Such experience can help children to learn how to control their impulses. The negative situation takes place when there are quite a lot of blocks, but there is no special place and no pedagogical support. Such situation can provoke conflicts and accidents that cannot serve as a ground for learning self-control.

As for **verbal working memory,** we found positive significant correlations with such items as "space for gross motor play", "gross motor equipment", and "music/movement". According to a number of research verbal memory is the main predictor of the future academic achievement (Best et al., 2009; Blair, 2002; Cadoret et al., 2018; Williford et al., 2013). So we can resume that it is very important for children to have opportunity for active movement every day. Especially, it concerns active team games with rules that include both movement and communication (cooperation and competition).

As well verbal working memory correlates directly with the item "Promoting acceptance of diversity" that can be explained with inevitable extension of children vocabulary when different nationalities, cultures, and category of people are discussed.

We found the only negative correlation of verbal memory with the item "schedule". Scoring this item an observer has to clarify if there is a schedule that regulates the order of change of activities and if it is well known for children. Almost all of the observed groups don't have schedule that presuppose some slots that could be fulfilled in response to children's interests. Usually, groups have very repetitive order that is too predictable for children and adults as well. Such situation leads to the fact that children get a lot of identical teachers' replicas every day that cannot enrich verbal development in general and in particular verbal memory.

The relation of **cognitive flexibility** with the item "Dramatic play" can be logically explained with the fact that within the role-play games children invent the rules by themselves so they can change them if they want to make a fruitful ground for learning how to follow rules and react properly when the rule modifies.

Discussing visual working memory and cognitive flexibility we should note that both of them correlate negatively with the item "Furnishing for routine care, play and learning". In this case, an observer fixes if there is enough furniture of suitable size. We suppose that this relation needs an additional verification involving the contrast groups.

9.6 Future Research

The conducted study also provides grounds for planning the next stages of verification of the proposed hypotheses. In the future, from our point of view, the following should be considered. First, the strategy of identifying the correlations of various aspects of individual development with specific indicators of subscales proved to be reasonable: such data are more informative than the average score across the whole ECERS-R scale or even with average data in the context of seven subscales. In order to obtain more valid data, it is necessary to increase the sample (the number of groups of preschool children) and to make it more balanced so that cohort with a really high quality of educational environment could be defined.

When interpreting data it is necessary to consider the specifics of the ECERS-R scales construction, where as a rule an expert in the process of observation scores some environmental parameters with 3–4 points and others (more subtly related to mental development) with 5–7 points. For example, according to the "Schedule" parameter, the minimum acceptable level of quality is the presence of a schedule known to children that fixes the sequence of events during the day. And in order to give a high score, the expert must track the quality of this schedule: whether the balance between the structure and flexibility of the program is ensured, whether the games are diverse, whether there are activities initiated by children, how smooth are the transitions between different activities and whether the individual interests of children are taken into account. The evaluation procedure assumes that if the schedule is not displayed on the premises or does not coincide with the actual events in the group, then the expert does not proceed to assessing the listed quality parameters. All subscales are designed in a similar manner. Therefore, the lack in the sample of a representative cohort with a really high quality level makes it difficult to identify the relationships of any individual mental development characteristics with environmental parameters.

It is also necessary to include in the instructions for the observer (expert) the requirement to evaluate them regardless of how well the group complies with the previous parameters. For example, at the moment, when studying the relationship of emotional and personal development and parameters related to interaction, negative correlations have been obtained. However, the indicators that are really important for the formation of decentration and emotional intelligence appear only in the section related to the excellent quality (6–7 points): teachers listen attentively; they maintain eye contact; they treat children fairly, without harming anyone; teachers are waiting for the children to complete their question before beginning to answer it; they sympathize with children who are offended or angry; they teach to cooperate and to implement the common tasks together. The data on the relationships with the lower scores turn out to be uninformative and contradictory.

9.7 Conclusion

The study made it possible to establish that there is a relationship between the quality of the educational environment, which is assessed using the ECERS, and the executive functions of older preschoolers. Taking into account that the instrument is based on both the constructivist and socio-constructivist approaches, it can be concluded that the optimal combination of orientation toward both the zone of actual development and the zone of proximal development creates conditions for the amplification (Zaporozhets, 1978) of child development. The socio-constructivist approach is more emphasized in the new modification of the scales—in ECERS-3, so in the future it will be interesting to see how the same relationships will manifest themselves when researching with the help of a new instrument.

The optimal combination of the space organization, accessible equipment and professional pedagogical support makes good possibilities for children to develop. The national monitoring of the quality of preschool education conducted in Russia suggests that kindergartens in different regions rarely receive scores above the 4 points on the most of the ECERS-R subscales (Le-van et al., 2021). The results of this study show the need to revise the principles of organizing a broad practice of preschool education in Russia in the direction of addressing children's interests. We also have to mention that the Russian research studies based on the Vygotsky's theory were focused more on developing the idea of "cultural means" (i.e., sensory etalon, visual model for preschool age children (Zaporozhets, 1986, Venger, 1986) or scientific concept for elementary school children (Davydov, 1972), but the idea of focusing on child's interests was not sufficiently represented. From the other hand, the concept of amplification (Zaporozhets, 1978)—enrichment of the content of specifically children's forms of play, art, and practical activities, as well as communication of children with each other and with adults, is the way to balance different values of childhood and child development.

One more important notice is about the item "promoting the acceptance of diversity", which turns to be related to EF development. Pre-school education programs widely used in Russia do not pay enough attention to this aspect and, as a rule, some evidence of cultural diversity can be found only in those regions of Russia where a large percentage of different ethnic groups is presented and therefore the program records the so-called ethno-cultural component (for example, in Republic of Tatarstan or Buryatia). However, Moscow is a cosmopolitan city where you can meet representatives of a different nationalities, which undoubtedly should be reflected in the environment surrounding children in kindergarten.

Acknowledgements This work was supported by grant RSF № 17-78-20198-П.

References

Ardilla, A. (2013). Development of metacognitive and emotional executive functions in children. *Applied Neuropsychology: Child, 2*(2), 82–87.

Berezhkovskaya, E. (2015). Age periodization of the zone of the proximal development and sensitive periods. In V. Kudryavtsev (Ed.), *Learning and development: Modern theory and practice: Materials of XVI international readings in memory* (2 parts) (pp. 161–166). Lev.

Best, J. R., Miller, P. H., & Jones, L. L. (2009). Executive functions after age 5: Changes and correlates. *Developmental Review, 29*, 180–200. https://doi.org/10.1016/j.dr.2009.05.002

Blair, C. (2002). School readiness: Integrating cognition and emotion in a neurobiological conceptualization of children's functioning at school entry. *American Psychologist, 57*, 111–127.

Bredekamp, S., & Copple, C. (1997). *Developmentally appropriate practice in early childhood programs* (Rev ed.). National Association for the Education of Young Children.

Bruner, J. (2001). The triumph of diversity: Vygotsky and Piaget. *Voprosy Psychologii, 4*, 3–13.

Cadoret, G., Bigras, N., Duval, S., Lemay, L., Tremblay, T., & Lemire, J. (2018). The mediating role of cognitive ability on the relationship between motor proficiency and early academic achievement in children. *Human Movement Science, 57*, 149–157.

Curby, T. W., Rimm-Kaufman, S. E., & Abry, T. (2013). Do emotional support and classroom organization earlier in the year set the stage for higher quality instruction? *Journal of School Psychology, 51*, 557–569. https://doi.org/10.1016/j.jsp.2013.06.001

Davydov, V. (1972). *Types of generalization in education*. Pedagogica.

Deville, Z., & Meynier, J. (2014). *Inhibition et flexibilité langagières dans les gliomes de bas grade: évaluation pré- et postopératoire* [Inhibition and language flexibility in low grade gliomas: Pre- and postoperative evaluation]. UFR de Médecine Pierre et Marie Curie/Faculty of Medicine Pierre et Marie Curie.

Diamond, A. (2013). Executive functions. *Annual Review of Psychology, 64*, 135–168. https://doi.org/10.1146/annurev-psych-113011-143750

Duval, S., Bouchard, C., Pagé, P., & Hamel, C. (2016). Quality of classroom interactions in kindergarten and executive functions among five year-old children. *Cogent Education, 3*, 1207909. https://doi.org/10.1080/2331186X.2016.1207909

Federal Law of the Russian Federation "On Education". (2012, December 31). *Rossiyskaya gazeta*.

French, G. (2007). *Children's early learning and development. A research paper*. NCCA. https://ncca.ie/media/1112/how-aistear-was-developed-research-papers.pdf

Hall, J., Sylva, K., Sammons, P., Melhuish, E., Siraj-Blatchford, I., & Taggart, B. (2013). Can preschool protect young children's cognitive and social development? Variation by center quality and duration of attendance. *School Effectiveness and School Improvement: An International Journal of Research, Policy and Practice, 24*(2), 155–176.

Hamre, B. K., Downer, J. F. M., & Pianta, R. C. (2013). Enhancing teacher's intentional use of efective interactions with children: Designing and testing professional development interventions. In R. C. Pianta (Ed.), *Handbook of early childhood education* (pp. 507–532). The Guilford Press.

Hamre, B. K., & Pianta, R. C. (2007). Learning opportunities in preschool and early elementary classrooms. In R. Pianta, M. Cox, & K. Snow (Dir.), *School readiness & the transition to kindergarten in the era of accountability* (pp. 49–84). Brookes.

Hamre, B. K., Pianta, R. C., Mashburn, A. J., & Downer, J. (2007). *Building a science of classrooms: Three dimensions of child-teacher interactions in pk-3rd grade classrooms*. University of Virginia.

Hanson, L. K., Atance, C. M., & Paluck, S. W. (2014). Is thinking about the future related to theory of mind and executive function? Not in preschoolers. *Journal of Experimental Child Psychology, 128*, 120–137. https://doi.org/10.1016/j.jecp.2014.07.006

Harms, T., Clifford, R. M., & Cryer, D. (2005). *Early Childhood Environment Rating Scale (ECERS-R)* (Rev ed.). Columbia University Press.

Harms, T., Clifford, R. M., & Cryer, D. (2014). *Early Childhood Environment Rating Scale (ECERS-3)* (3rd ed.). Columbia University Press.

Hatfield, B. E., Hestenes, L. L., Kintner-Duffy, V., & O'Brien, M. (2013). Classroom emotional support predicts differences in preschool children's cortisol and alpha-amylase levels. *Early Childhood Research Quarterly, 28*, 347–356. https://doi.org/10.1016/j.ecresq.2012.08.001

Heckman, J., Cunha, F., Lochner, L., & Masterov, D. (2006). Interpreting the evidence on life cycle skill formation. *Handbook of the economics of education* (vol. 1). Elsevier.

Hestenes, L. L., Kintner-Duffy, V. L., Wang, Y. C., La Paro, K. M., Mims, S. U., Crosby, D. A., Scott-Little, C., & Cassidy, D. J. (2015). Comparisons among quality measures in child care settings: Understanding the use of multiple measures in North Carolina's QRIS and their links to social-emotional development in preschool children. *Early Childhood Research Quarterly, 30*, 199–214.

Howes, C., Burchinal, M., Pianta, R., Bryant, D., Early, D., Clifford, R., & Barbarin, O. (2008). Ready to learn? Children's pre-academic achievement in pre-Kindergarten programs. *Early Childhood Research Quarterly, 23*, 27–50. https://doi.org/10.1016/j.ecresq.2007.05.002

Hughes, J. N., & Kwok, O. (2007). Influence of student-teacher and parent-teacher relationships on lower achieving readers' engagement and achievement in the primary grades. *Journal of Educational Psychology, 99*, 39–51. https://doi.org/10.1037/0022-0663.99.1.39

Kaufman, C. (2010). *Executive function in the classroom: Practical strategies for improving performance and enhancing skills for all students.* Brookes Publishing.

Korkman, M., Kirk, U., & Kemp, S. L. (2007). *NEPSY II.* Psychological Corporation.

Le-van, T., Shiyan, I., Shiyan, O., & Zadadaev, S. (2021). Preschool education quality in Russia: Trends and relations. *International Research in Early Childhood Education, 10*(2), 61–82. https://doi.org/10.26180/14339003.v1

Manning, M., Garvis, S., Fleming, C., & Wong, G. T. W. (2017). *The relationship between teacher qualification and the quality of the early childhood education and care environment: A Campbell systematic review.* The Campbell Collaboration. www.campbellcollaboration.org

Mashburn, A. J., Pianta, R. C., Hamre, B. K., Downer, J. T., Barbarin, O. A., Bryant, D., Burchinal, M., Early, D. M., & Howes, C. (2008). Measures of classroom quality in prekindergarten and children's development of academic, language and social skills. *Child Development, 79*(3), 732–749. https://doi.org/10.1111/j.1467-8624.2008.01154.x

Matthews, W. (2003). Constructivism in the classroom: Epistemology, history, and empirical evidence. *Teacher Education Quarterly, 30*(3), 51–64.

Miyake, A., Friedman, N. P., Emerson, M. J., Witzki, A. H., Howerter, A., & Wager, T. (2000). The unity and diversity of executive functions and their contributions to complex "frontal lobe" tasks: A latent variable analysis. *Cognitive Psychology, 41*, 49–100.

Monette, S., & Bigras, M. (2008). La mesure des fonctions exécutives *chez* les enfants d'âge préscolaire [The measure of executive function in children of preschool age]. *Psychologie Canadienne/Canadian Psychology, 49*, 323–341. https://doi.org/10.1037/a0014000

Phillips, D., Mekos, D., Scarr, S., McCartney, K., & Abbott-Shim, M. (2000). Within and beyond the classroom door: Assessing quality in child care centers. *Early Childhood Research Quarterly, 15*, 475–496.

Piaget, J. (2001). *Theory, experiments, discussion* (L. Obukhova, & G. Burmenskaya, Eds.). Gardariki.

Pianta, R. C., La Paro, K. M., Payne, C., Cox, M. J., & Bradley, R. (2002). The relation of kindergarten classroom environment to teacher, family, school characteristics, and child outcomes. *The Elementary School Journal, 102*(3), 225–238.

Raver, C. C., & Blair, C. (2014). *At the crossroads of education and developmental neuroscience: Perspectives on executive function.* Perspective on language [Enligne]. http://www.onlinedigeditions.com/article/At_the_Crossroads_of_Education_and_Developmental_Neuroscience%3A_Perspectives_on_Executive_Function/1714076/210099/article.html

Remorenko, I. M., Shiyan, O. A., Shiyan, I. B., Shmis, T. G., Le-van, T. N., Kozmina, Y., & Sivak, E. V. (2017). Key problems in the implementation of the federal standard on the ground of a research using Early Childhood Environmental Rating Scale (ECERS-R): "Moscow 36." *Preschool Education Today, 2,* 16–31.

Rimm-Kaufman, S. E., Curby, T. W., Grimm, K. J., Nathanson, L., & Brock, L. L. (2009). The contribution of children's self-regulation and classroom quality to children's adaptive behaviors in the kindergarten classroom. *Developmental Psychology, 45*(4), 958–972.

Sammons, P., Sylva, K., Melhuish, E. C., Siraj, I., Taggart, B., Smees, R., Toth, K., & Welcomme, W. (2014). *Effective Pre-school, Primary and Secondary Education 3–16 Project (EPPSE 3–16) Influences on students' socialbehavioural development at age 16.* Department for Education Research Report RR351. http://www.ioe.ac.uk/Research_Home/16-Influences-Students-Social-BehaviouralDevelopment-RR.pdf

Saracho, O. N., & Spodek, B. (2007). Early childhood teachers' preparation and the quality of program outcomes. *Early Child Development and Care, 177,* 71–91.

Schoofs, D., Preuss, D., & Wolf, O. T. (2008). Psychosocial stress induces working memory impairments in an n-back paradigm. *Psychoneuroendocrinology, 33,* 643–653. https://doi.org/10.1016/j.psyneuen.2008.02

Sheridan, S., Shiyan, O., & Shiyan, I. (2018). Preschool quality and conditions for children's learning in preschool in Russia and Sweden. In N. Veraksa & S. Sheridan (Eds.), *Vygotsky's theory in early childhood education and research* (pp. 193–205). Routledge.

Shopina, J. (2002). *Psychological regularities of formation and actualization of the zone of the nearest development* [Autoref] (Dissertation, candidate of Psychological Sciences: 19.00.070). Moscow.

Simpson, A., & Riggs, K. J. (2007). Under what conditions do young children have diffculty inhibiting manual actions? *Developmental Psychology, 43,* 417–428. https://doi.org/10.1037/0012-1649.43.2.417

Slot, P. L. (2018). *Structural characteristics and process quality in early childhood education and care: A literature review* (OECD Education Working Paper No. 176). http://www.oecd.org/officialdocuments/publicdisplaydocumentpdf/?cote=EDU/WKP(2018)12&docLanguage=En

Sylva, K., Melhuish, E. C., Sammons, P., Siraj, I., & Taggart, B. (2004). *The Effective Provision of Pre-School Education (EPPE) Project.* Technical Paper 12: The Final Report: Effective pre-school education. DfES/Institute of Education, University of London. http://www.ioe.ac.uk/EPPE_TechnicalPaper_12_2004.pdf

Sylva, K., Melhuish, E. C., Sammons, P., Siraj, I., Taggart, B. with Smees, R., Toth, K., & Welcomme, W. (2014). *Effective Pre-school, Primary and Secondary Education 3–16 Project (EPPSE 3–16), Students' educational and developmental outcomes at age 16.* Department for Education Research Report RR354. http://www.ioe.ac.uk/Research_Home/16-Influences-StudentsGCSE-Attainment-Progress-RR.pdf

Sylva, K., Siraj-Blatchford, E., & Taggart, B. (2010, November 14). *Ecers E: The four curricular subscales extension to the early childhood environment rating scale (Ecers).* Fourth Edition with Planning Notes Spiral-bound.

Taguma, M., Litjens, I., & Makowiecki, K. (2013). *Quality matters in early childhood education and care.* OECD.

Tsukerman, G., & Venger, A. (2015). *Development of learning independence.* Author's Club.

Vandell, D. L., Belsky, J., Burchinal, M. R., Steinberg, L., Vandergrift, N., & NICHD Early Child Care Research. (2010). Do effects of early child care extend to age 15 years? Results from the NICHD study of early child care and youth development. *Child Development, 81*(3), 737–756. https://doi.org/10.1111/j.1467-8624.2010.01431.x

Venger, L. A. (Ed.). (1986). *Development of cognitive abilities in the process of preschool education.* Pedagogics.

Vermeer, H. J., van IJzendoorn, M. H., Cárcamo, R. A., & Harrison, L. J. (2016). Quality of child care using the environmental rating scales: A meta-analysis of international studies. *International Journal of Early Childhood, 48,* 33–60.

Vygotsky, L. (1982). *Thinking and speech: Collected works* (in 6 vol., vol. 2). Pedagogics.

Vygotsky, L. (1984). *Problems of child (age) psychology: Collected works* (in 6 vol., vol. 4). Pedagogics.

Welsh, J. A., Nix, R. L., Blair, C., Bierman, K. L., & Nelson, K. E. (2010). The development of cognitive skills and gains in academic school readiness for children from low-income families. *Journal of Educational Psychology, 102*, 43–53. https://doi.org/10.1037/a0016738

Williford, A. P., Vick Whittaker, J. E., Vitiello, V. E., & Downer, J. T. (2013, January 1). Children's engagement within the preschool classroom and their development of self-regulation. *Early Education Development, 24*(2), 162–187.

Zaporozhets, A. (1978). *The importance of early periods of childhood for formation of child personality. Principle of development in psychology* (pp. 243–267). Science.

Zaporozhets, A. (1986). *Mental development of the child: Selected psychological works* (in 2 vol., vol. 1). Pedagogics.

Zaretsky, V. (2007). Zone of the nearest development: About what Vygotsky hasn't had time to write... *Cultural-Historical Psychology, 3*(3), 96–104.

Zavershneva, E. (2007). The way to freedom: To the publication of materials from the family archive of L. S. Vygotsky. *NLO, 3*(85). https://magazines.gorky.media/nlo/2007/3

Zelazo, P. D. (2006). The Dimensional Change Card Sort (DCCS): A method of assessing executive function in children. *Nature Protocols, 1*, 297–301.

Anastasia Belolutskaya is a PhD in Psychology and a Head of Laboratory of Assessment of Professional Competencies and Adult Development at the Research Institute of Urban Science and Global Education Studies (Moscow City University). At the same time she works as a Associate Professor at the Department of Psychology (Lomonosov Moscow State University). The main scientific interests are: psychology of education, psychology of creative thinking. A.Belolutskaya is a certified expert of Early Childhood Environment Rating Scales (ECERS-3) for Russia. She works with preschool assessment and conducts in-service training about the developmental management in kindergartens regularly. The main professional belief is the following: organizing collaborative thinking and horizontal communication is the key to improving the quality of life.

Darya Bukhalenkova is a PhD in Psychology, Assistant Professor at the Faculty of Psychology, Lomonosov Moscow State University. Much of her work is related to investigating children's executive functions, language, math and social skills development at preschool age, as well as children gadgets usage. She has extensive experience in organizing research and in teaching in preschooler's cognitive and social development assessment. In addition, her research interest is in the quality of preschool education and its impact on child development. She is an expert and trainer in the CLASS (Pre-K level) method that assesses teacher–child interaction in kindergarten groups.

Evgeniy Krasheninnikov-Khait is a Junior Researcher at the Laboratory of Child Development in the Research Institute of Urban Science and Global Education Studies of Moscow City University. He has conducted individual and group research work with pre-school children, evaluated the quality of pre-school education as national certified expert ECERS-3 for Russia, and developed the other methodological tools for that purpose. His main interests are cognitive and emotional development of children and analyzing their abilities of creativity.

Igor Shiyan is a PhD in Psychology, Chairperson of the Laboratory of Child Development, Deputy Director of the Research Institute of Urban Science and Global Education Studies of Moscow City University. His main research interests are: development of creative dialectical thinking of children and adults, developmental education from ECE to University, preschool education quality. He was the leader of the Russian national research on the quality of early childhood education using ECERS-R (more than 1300 kindergartens participated in the study). I.Shiyan is a head of the Master program "Design and assessment of preschool education (cultural-historical approach by L.Vygotsky)" in Moscow City University. His teaching experience includes several universities in Moscow and University of Central Arkansas (USA).

Olga Shiyan is a PhD in Education and a Leading Researcher of Laboratory of Child Development at the Research Institute of Urban Science and Global Education Studies of Moscow City University. The main scientific interests are: psychology of creative thinking, psychology of preschool education, preschool education assessment. O. Shiyan is an international expert of Early Childhood Environment Rating Scales (ECERS-3) certified by Environment Rating Scales Institute (USA). She conducts research in the development of children's creative abilities, education quality assessment and development of professional competencies of preschool teachers. The main professional belief is the following: in educational practice both with children and adults it is important to work in the zone of proximal development and to look for cultural means that inspire and help to move.

Aleksander Veraksa is head of the Chair Psychology of Education and Pedagogy, Faculty of Psychology, Lomonosov Moscow State University and vice-direct of of the Psychological Institute, Russian Academy of Education. His sphere of interest is research in child development from a cultural-historical perspective. He is a principal investigator of the first all-Russian longitudinal study "Growing Together", which involves children from different regions, starting from 4 years old. As a vice-president of the Russian Psychological Society he has succeeded in organizing cross-cultural studies as well as possibilities for their results dissemination all over the world.

Chapter 10
Piaget and Vygotsky's Play Theories: The Profile of Twenty-First-Century Evidence

Nikolay Veraksa⊕, **Yeshe Colliver**⊕, **and Vera Sukhikh**⊕

Abstract Young children's play has been the object of hundreds of educational and psychological studies over the last half-century, an interest predominantly owed to two theories about its importance for learning: those of Jean Piaget (1896–1980) and Lev Semenovich Vygotsky (1896–1934) (Siraj-Blatchford et al., in Education and Child Psychology, 26(2):77–89, 2002; Thomas et al., in Australasian Journal of Early Childhood 36(4):69–75, 2011). While countless papers have examined the differences in the theories, none have sought to examine each in relation to the profile of the recently proliferating high-quality, experimental, and longitudinal research on the topic, including adult-led play as well as child-initiated, child-led play. To do so, we examine the theories in detail and how they have been applied in early childhood education and care (ECEC) settings and curricula. From this analysis, we find limited evidence for the efficacy of play to lead to academic learning outcomes, but higher quality evidence mounting that "soft skills," such as social, emotional, and intrapersonal abilities, are associated with free play in homes and ECEC settings. In light of Vygotsky's emphasis on the role of the more knowledgeable other in learning through play, we also examine the growing evidence that adult-led play can achieve "hard" skills such as reading and mathematical skills. We examine this profile of evidence in relation to the two theories and suggest that historical assumptions about what play is, informed strongly by Piaget's theory, can be reconfigured to include the adults and peers in play research.

N. Veraksa · V. Sukhikh (✉)
Faculty of Psychology, Lomonosov Moscow State University, Moscow, Russia
e-mail: msu.edupsy@gmail.com

N. Veraksa
Psychological Institute, Russian Academy of Education, Moscow, Russia

Y. Colliver
School of Education, Macquarie University, Sydney, Australia
e-mail: yeshe.colliver@mq.edu.au

© The Author(s), under exclusive license to Springer Nature Switzerland AG 2022
N. Veraksa and I. Pramling Samuelsson (eds.), *Piaget and Vygotsky in XXI century*,
Early Childhood Research and Education: An Inter-theoretical Focus 4,
https://doi.org/10.1007/978-3-031-05747-2_10

10.1 Piaget and Vygotsky's Play Theories: The Profile of Twenty-First-Century Evidence

The first half of the twentieth century saw the emergence of two models that have shaped the theoretical foundations of most recent research on play and learning: Piaget's theory of cognitive development, which considers importance of play among other things, and Vygotsky's cultural-historical approach, which considers play crucial in child's development. Both approaches have been subject to comparative analysis (e.g., DeVries, 2000; Gaskins & Göncü, 1988; Glassman, 1995; Vianna & Stetsenko, 2006), but they have not been viewed in the context of recent empirical data on development in and learning through play since 2013 (Lillard et al., 2013). Critical reviews of the evidence for play leading to learning and development such as Zosh et al. (2018) and Lillard et al. (2013) (including responses to it) have shown that the weight of evidence falls on the acquisition of "soft" skills (socio-emotional and open-ended cognitive flexibility skills) rather than "hard" skills (Slot et al., 2016, p. 7). However, a growing body of research indicates adult-led play may provide superior conditions for learning (Pyle et al., 2021), particularly of hard skills (Zosh et al., 2018). Different aspects of Piaget's and Vygotsky's theories appear to be supported by this profile of evidence.

In this chapter, we will look at Piaget's views on learning through play and the uptake of his ideas in practice and research. While Piaget himself did not consider play to be crucial for the development of the logical thinking he studied, his influence on researchers advocating the importance of play for development has proved to be enormous. Despite considering play as an epiphenomenon, the practice of Early Childhood Education and Care (ECEC) was strongly influenced by Piaget's image of the child as a lone scientist (Sanders & Farago, 2017), and led to the promotion of a particularly passive role for the educator, particularly from the 1980s to early 2000s in many Western-heritage contexts around the world (Cannella, 1997; Colliver, 2019; Epstein, 2007). Next, we will consider Vygotsky's views on how learning and development occurs in play. We will then compare the two approaches to play, not only from the perspective of classical theories, but also from that of their modern followers. We describe how, while Piaget's theory of cognitive development charts the so-called structure of age changes, the cultural-historical approach emphasizes the important role of the social context in which development occurs. Whereas Vygotsky's cultural-historical approach deems play to be a driving force of development, during which multiple processes of new knowledge and skills acquisition are realized, Piaget considered play to be more of a measure of development, as the complexity of play marked the cognitive development of the child.

In the next two sections, we elaborate the main differences between the two theories as we describe how they have been enacted in curricula within Western-heritage contexts. This then allows us, in the final sections of the chapter, to review the current research on play and learning, comparing the patterns of findings with the two theories and their enactment in practice.

Despite the differences in approach, both theories have had a great impact on current thinking about how play can be used in early childhood education. To conclude this chapter, we highlight several key principles of effective play-based learning from Piaget and Vygotsky and how they compare with the emerging profile of evidence on learning through play.

10.2   Learning Through Play According to Piaget

Piaget's theory of play is presented in his classic work "Play, Dreams, and Imitation" (Piaget, 1962), which predominantly focusses on play in the context of children's cognitive development. Play serves as a preparatory stage for possible forms of behavior, and through play the child learns to navigate and overcome difficulties existing in reality.

Piaget viewed play as a natural child activity that emerges spontaneously in step with the child's cognitive development. Piaget's general thesis that the child is innately egocentric but through natural development, moves toward greater understanding of the outside world and therefore moves from a subjective to objective lens. Likewise, the content of the child's play progresses from purely subjective constructions and progresses toward an adequate reflection of reality (Piaget, 1945, 1962; Nicolopoulou, 1993). Piaget considered types of play along a predictable developmental continuum also, which begins as functional practice, then acquires the use of symbols, and finally takes on the notion of rules in play (Piaget, 1948). As such, Piaget distinguished sensorimotor play, symbolic play and play with rules (Korotkova, 1985; Piaget, 1964). Piaget (1962) proposed six stages of play in the sensorimotor period of cognitive development (birth to two years), followed by five stages (with four sub-stages) of symbolic play, then two stages of rule-based play.

During what Piaget called the "sensorimotor" period of development, play was considered "functional," usually consisting of repeating various previously learned behaviors (Garwood, 1982). Piaget saw these as having no external purpose or goal other than simply the enjoyment the child would gain from the predictability of repeated actions, and the child's sense of mastery over her environment as a result of creating predictable reactions. For example, Piaget (1962, p. 169) recorded a 2-month-old "adopting the habit" of throwing his head back to see the world upside-down, repeating so many times that it could not be in any way serious. What is notable was that Piaget considered this play as "no longer an effort to learn, it is only a happy display of known actions" (p. 171), betraying his underlying premise that play only ever served one of the two core actions necessary for learning: assimilation but not accommodation. In assimilation, the individual integrates events, objects, or situations into existing mental structures, whereas accommodation is characterized by the opposite process: the existing mental structures are reorganized to incorporate new aspects of external reality (Piaget, 1964). Piaget also believed that functional play, which occurred in the sensorimotor period of cognitive development, was relegated to the context from which it was taken; in other words, the use of symbols (e.g., pretending to sleep) were not yet freed from contexts where one sleeps, and not yet able to be used as a tool for thinking.

Piaget believed the child begins to engage in symbolic play as soon as she applies ritualized practices (e.g., cooking, cleaning) to new objects and contexts (between the ages of four and seven), as these practices have become symbolic. Such symbolism shows a separation of the "signifier" (e.g., a banana) from the "signified" (e.g., a gun) (Piaget, 1962, p. 120), paralleling the larger cognitive development that occurs where the child develops semiotic function—an ability to represent an absent object or an event not directly perceived through symbols or signs. Symbolic play represents the child's ability to link concrete experience with abstract thinking as she connects the signified with the signifier (Avdulova, 2018). In this process, the child develops representations, a product of cognitive activity that allows categorization of various objects, properties and situations, creating opportunities for orientation in situations of uncertainty (Veraksa, 2015). The development of representations is an important link in intellectual development. Piaget differentiates between two types of mental representations: playful (subjective, egocentric and unrealistic) and serious, real (progressively objective, balanced, and realistic) (1964). It is at this stage that pretend play and role-playing emerge. Symbolic play requires the child not only to begin to take the role of another (either animate or inanimate) but also to recall past experiences for present use and both of these are cognitively based (Garwood, 1982). Symbolic play, according to Piaget, is a form of assimilation that interferes with accommodation and is thus a maladaptive process that children are bound to outgrow over time as they develop further (Kavanaugh, 2012).

Finally, play with rules is the self-initiated application of rules from outside, "interiorizing a social behavior" (Piaget, 1962, p. 143), particularly as children increasingly play with peers, and Piaget noted its rarity in the preceding age bracket (four to seven) and frequency in the third (from seven to eleven years) (p. 142). For Piaget, there is a greater amount of accommodation than before, as the child's ego gives way to reality, and she interacts with others more. This stage of play is characterized by competition and cooperation, limited by the framework of collective discipline and rules. The emergence of play with rules (i.e., games) was seen by Piaget as an indicator that the child was moving from subjective egocentrism to a wider and more objective conception of the world. In other words, the development of play tracks that of the child's cognitive abilities, in both its content and type (Nicolopoulou, 1993; Piaget, 1945); For Piaget (1964), play is an *indicator* rather than driver of development.

There is one central reason for this distinction between indicators and drivers. In analyzing Piaget's work, Garwood (1982) drew attention to the role of *imitation* as well as play in learning and more generally in the development of intelligence. Imitation requires the child not only to observe others' behavior and her own, but also to represent these observations through internal symbolic processes or through explicitly mediated behavior. Play, in turn, represents a context where children practice certain skills and apply prior knowledge about how to solve various problems effectively, so becomes an important mediator of intellectual development (Garwood, 1982). As Piaget (1962) noted, "imitation is a continuation of accommodation, play is a continuation of assimilation, and intelligence is a harmonious combination of the two" (p. 104). New mental models that the child builds through imitation of others are consolidated and practiced in her play.

Piaget himself did not consider play to be crucial for the development of the logical thinking he studied. Despite Piaget's deliberate bifurcation of accommodation and assimilation (and, correspondingly, of imitation and play), Piaget's influence on researchers advocating the importance of play for development has proved to be enormous (Butler et al., 1978; Ebbeck, 1996; Guldberg, 2009; Kamii, 1974; Walkerdine, 1984), although many have argued his work was misinterpreted (Burman, 1994; Smith, 1988; Trawick-Smith, 1989; Walsh, 1991). For example, Fein (1978) studied symbolic play as an expression of the child's capacity for symbolic action and a measure of intellectual development, she also justified the importance of play for cognitive development, and by doing so she advocated play-based educational programs. Countless other advocates for Piaget's supposed promotion of play have followed (Burman, 1994; Goffin & Wilson, 2001; Walsh, 1991).

Further, the importance of Piaget's theory for the current pre-eminent status of play in today's ECEC practice and research is also likely a product of how amenable his "ages and stages" were to quantification for research purposes (Walsh et al., 2010, p. 55). The systematization of developmental milestones opened the way for the study of play and the collection of empirical data using his theory. The understanding of behavioral manifestations and their development in play described in the theory of cognitive development served particularly as a guide for diagnosing and treating developmental disorders. For example, on the basis of the theory Nicolich (1977) developed a five-point scale to assess the level of development of play (the scale covers sensorimotor and symbolic levels). These five levels describe the transition from the child's fusion of meaning and action to the point at which action is internally directed. The Test of Pretend Play (ToPP; Lewis & Boucher, 1997), formerly known as the Warwick Symbolic Play Test (WSPT) is also based on Piaget's theory and focuses on the symbolic aspects of play. The test offers verbal and nonverbal versions of tasks for children from Grades 1 to 6: with objects from everyday life, with toys and unstructured materials, only with a toy and without toys and materials. Three types of symbolic play can be assessed: object substitution (e.g., a napkin as a blanket), referring to a missing object as if it were there (e.g., drinking imaginary tea) and endowing an object with imaginary properties (e.g., saying the doll is sick). In addition, ToPP assesses the child's ability to link several symbolic actions into a meaningful (i.e., realistic) sequence.

Piaget emphasized the cognitive activity of the individual child, carefully considering what discoveries the child makes in her development and what skills she acquires. Piaget understood the development of thinking as a central process of development, in which the child acts as an active participant, an inquisitive researcher, making experiments in her interaction with the world around her. In this way, Piaget's stages describe play as an epiphenomenon of cognitive development, as only assisting one part of a two-part process. In the course of this exploration, the child consolidates her cognitive abilities and practices valuable skills in making sense of the world and phenomena.

10.3 Curricular Applications of (Various Interpretations of) Piaget's Theory

While there are no predominant curricular approaches explicitly designed with only Piaget's play theory as their basis, the influence of Piaget on educational theory cannot be understated (Birns & Golden, 1974; Burman, 1994; Kamii, 1974; Lee & Johnson, 2007; Murray, 1979; Walsh, 1991). The Developmentally Appropriate Practice (DAP; Copple et al., 2009) was developed with Piaget's theories as a principal rationale (Sanders & Farago, 2017). Yet, a more active adult role in play-based learning conflicted with the predominant view from psychological research on children's learning (often in laboratory conditions in which the child is most frequently isolated from her everyday social context), wherein adult interference would impair the quality of the learning. For example, a principal feature of the 1987 edition of DAP was its insistence that play is spontaneous and should not be "interfered" with by adults (Goodley & Runswick-Cole, 2010, p. 502; Walsh, 1991):

> *The correct way to teach young children is not to lecture or verbally instruct them. Teachers of young children are more like guides or facilitators.* (Bredekamp, 1987, p. 52. italics added)

Inspired by Piaget's ideas of individual learning and constructivism, many educationalists sympathetic to DAP believed "certain concepts should not be presented to children until they reach the appropriate level of cognitive development necessary to understand them" (Ranz-Smith, 2007; Spodek & Saracho, 1999, p. 8). Developmental psychologists also adopted the Piagetian (and constructivist) notion that the child learned about the world through self-guided discovery (Burman, 1994; Goffin & Wilson, 2001; Walsh, 1991). Within this paradigm, the educator would merely *provide* play to aid the child's discoveries (Burman, 2008; Ryan & Goffin, 2008). The psychological perspective on ECEC continued to emphasize the child's autonomous psychological processes involved in learning through play rather than the content to be taught by the educator (Gibbons, 2007; Krieg, 2011). This approach aligned with the belief that "the play world belongs to the child" and that teachers must not impinge on play's inherent freedom (O'Gorman & Ailwood, 2012, p. 267). A similar sentiment of the time appears to be reflected in the spirit of the United Nations (UN) Convention on the Rights of the Child (UN, 1989), which is known for its framing of play as a representation of children's free choice (Colliver & Doel-Mackaway, 2021) in accordance with their developmental level:

> States Parties recognize the right of the child to rest and leisure, to engage in play and recreational activities *appropriate to the age of the child* and to participate freely in cultural life and the arts. (Article 31(1), p. 9, italics added)

After much controversy over "the teacher's role [being] relegated to 'following the child's lead'" (Bodrova, 2008, p. 358) (Walsh et al., 2010), the DAP guidelines were amended (Bredekamp et al., 1997) to account for educators "failing to challenge children adequately" in learning through play (Dickinson, 2002, p. 28) and the role of the child's social context, including the educator, in her learning (Sanders & Farago, 2017). These changes show the popularization of Piaget's (1962; 1972) theories of a universal process of cognitive development, and their adaptation to accommodate an increasing appreciation of the social lives of young children.

Influenced by the developmental process Piaget dubbed *equilibration*, dominant ECEC practice in the 1980s–2000s advocated that educators should focus on the "processes" of learning rather than its "products" (Cullen, 1999, p. 23; Edwards & Cutter-Mackenzie, 2011, p. 51; Gibbons, 2007, p. 301; Krieg, 2011, p. 47; Wood & Paolo, 2007, p. 123). This influence has persisted globally and has only in the last couple of decades begun to be challenged by emphasis on a more intentional and active role of teachers in children's learning through play (Colliver, 2019). Such emphasis has resulted from the increasing popularization of Vygotsky's play theory and its acknowledgment of the important role of the teacher in play, coupled with uptake of research verifying this importance (e.g., Siraj-Blatchford, 2009).

10.4 Development of Play According to Vygotsky

This section turns now to Vygotsky, for whom authentic play began around the age of three (Karpov, 2005), although the imaginary situation (which characterizes play for Vygotsky) has been shown in children as young as two (e.g., Colliver & Veraksa, 2019; Quiñones et al., 2020). Whether at two or three years of age, it emerges for Vygotsky later than Piaget because Piaget's sensorimotor, functional play does not have this imaginary or symbolic situation. Moreover, in contrast to Piaget's relatively individualistic consideration of learning through play, all components of play, according to Vygotsky's cultural-historical approach, are sociocultural in character, including roles, plots, and narratives. Even solitary play (wherein the presence of the adult can even be merely conceptual or imagined) is considered as social—in it the child uses tools, context, and representations of what he sees in everyday life (Vygotsky, 1966/2016).

Vygotsky posited that development in play occurs primarily through interaction with an empathetic adult or another, more experienced child: a more knowledgeable other (MKO). As someone with experience and knowledge, the MKO scaffolds the child's inferior knowledge and skills to achieve their goals. It is the MKO, being a carrier of the culturally ideal forms (e.g., how to be considerate of others' feelings or sensitive around taboo subjects), who sets the zone of proximal development (ZPD) in play—the area of skills and knowledge which lie beyond the child's reach when alone. Vygotsky defined ZPD as a distance between the current level of development as measured by independent behavior or skills and the level of potential development when accompanied by a MKO (Vygotsky, 2004). The ZPD acts as a meeting place of the primary form (a genetically determined initial mental formations, such as depth perception or instinctual reflexes like flinching when an object moves rapidly toward us) and the ideal form (that mental formation which, on the one hand, is due to appear at the end of development and, on the other hand, it already exists in culture and is a cultural model, like behavioral inhibition) (Veraksa & Dolya, 2018). In play, children need to suppress certain aspects of the primary form in order to enact the ideal form, such as seeing a water bottle but playing as if it is a rocket, or wanting to escape a dog catcher but forcing herself to run away in the more cumbersome manner that a dog would (i.e., on all fours). So the existence of ZPD in play represents the myriad ways in which a child is prompted to develop further (whether via abstraction, emotional restraint, or otherwise).

Within Vygotsky's view, children's play development occurs "from the outside" because concepts that children use in play (e.g., how to enact a pirate or Geisha) are derived from the social world (Van Oers, 1998). Said in another way, ethnographers do not find children in remote areas of the Solomon Islands playing with Spiderman™, expressly because the children are not exposed to such cultural ideas. Thus, according to the cultural-historical approach, development during play occurs from the outside. Since children can imagine something only due to their existing experience, role-playing is predetermined by culture. Trying out different forms of behavior in play promotes the transition of knowledge from the outside (the external world and the environment) into the inside (the child's own first-hand experience, even if only in the imagination, as this is understood conceptually in abstract form). This transition takes place through interiorization, a process Vygotsky famously explained as:

> *We can formulate the general genetic law of cultural development in the following way: every function in the child's cultural development appears on the stage twice, in two planes: first socially, then psychologically, first between people as an interpsychic category, then within the child as an intrapsychic category. It equally applies to voluntary attention, logical memory, formation of concepts and the development of will.* (Vygotsky, 1983, p. 145)

In the preschool years (three to seven years of age), play is not merely an index of development, but *leads* it (Vygotsky, 1966/2016). Vygotsky's general theory of play sees the culture as the source of all development, and play as the context for accelerated learning because primary forms begin to take on the ideal during play. Thus, whether directly or indirectly, adults are crucial for learning through play. Play begins via basic symbolism (e.g., a stick becoming a spoon), but increasingly take on more rules of behavior, as the symbolized begins to amass greater cultural context (e.g., how a witch should behave—what she should do, how she should interact with others, forming implicit rules that could even be extended to hypothetical situations like how she would interact with a robot). Similar to Piaget, Vygotksy saw symbolism as important for the conceptual development of abstraction, but the acquisition and utilization of rules associated with the ideal forms begin to become more explicit, as they come to in rules for chess or soccer (Winther-Lindqvist, 2021). In this way, the ideal form of playing elaborate games with explicit rules, like the adult card game Poker, is present in the earliest forms of play, such as a the toddler's gesture of cuddling a cushion as she would a baby because it contains the faintest traces of rules of behavior (Vygotsky, 1997, p. 135).

10.5 Curricular Applications of Vygotsky's Theory

Many play-based ECEC curricula follow Vygotsky's cultural-historical approach to play. Play-based learning combines play, child-initiated elements with adult intervention to achieve specific educational goals (Pyle & Danniels, 2017). One of the most well-known approaches, the *Tools of Mind* program (Bodrova & Leong, 2001), focuses on the development of self-regulation, along with the development of math skills and literacy in the form of play-based interactions between children and teachers. The program includes 40 Vygotsky-inspired activities designed to promote "mature" (complex) sociodramatic play, encourage the use of self-regulatory private speech (colloquially known as "talking to oneself"), and teach the use of external aids to scaffold attention and memory. The Tools of Mind program does not just allow children to play, but provides a nurturing environment for developing "mature" play by incorporating complex, planned, and sustained play scenarios with different roles.

Another approach to the use of play in the educational process in the cultural-historical tradition is based on Lindqvist's *Playworlds* approach (Lindqvist, 2001). This is collective role-play involves larger groups of children and teachers alike as they play out complex plots (i.e., involving multiple events) with problematic situations taken from fairy tales and other imaginary stories. The playworlds become a context for educational interventions (i.e., where adults provide prompts to scaffold more complex ways of thinking and problem-solving). It is also important that the teacher is fully involved as a character in the play. This allows him to set educational tasks in the context of an imaginary situation (e.g., writing letters to Martians or imagining how to bore a well in the desert), thereby not only achieving pedagogical goals (e.g., literacy skill development, abstract reasoning), but also developing the play (e.g., increasing its complexity or introducing information relevant to the real world). An example is detailed in Fleer et al. (2019), wherein playworlds were used by teachers to target EF development in children. Activities that encouraged EF training were woven into daily practices by teachers, and within the play, meaningful tasks were set for children to solve by engaging their EF (e.g., introducing a password to enter a "pirate ship," walking a map backwards to find treasure).

Another application of the cultural-historical approach is the *Golden Key program* for preschool and elementary school-age children (Kravtsov & Kravtsova, 2018). The program is designed to create a space for tapping children's potential and to promote harmonious and comprehensive development of the child's personality. To achieve these goals, the program includes several principles: multi-age groups (in contrast to the dominant same-age grouping) where children aged 3 to 6 are grouped and play together, the formation of a family atmosphere by including the children's parents and close friends in each group, the naming of each group protagonized by an emblem and even its own traditions, and an "event" relevant to the children's lives as a meaningful experience experienced and enacted together with group. The final principle of the program is a plot component engaging all the children as much as possible. For example, during the first year of primary school, the children spend a lot of time building a house from cardboard and paper for a certain character that is dear to them.

The children devise an architectural plan, design the interior, mark and draw windows and doors, create and arrange furniture, and much more as a way of elaborating the complexity of the imaginary situation. They plan, measure, and glue objects together to integrate important curriculum areas such as mathematics, planning and engineering. The use of the program in different regions of Russia has shown its high potential for overcoming solving children's physical and psychological difficulties (Kravtsov & Kravtsova, 2018). Children appear to develop self-regulation skills, attentiveness, and curiosity. Perhaps the most important aspect of the program is the opportunity for teachers and parents to develop skills to communicate with children. Many adults who start to work with the program report substantial improvements in their relationships: parents with their family members; teachers, with colleagues.

The Key to Learning Curriculum is also created in line with the cultural-historical thesis that cultural tools that determine cultural development of a child are the result of socially determined process (Veraksa & Dolya, 2018). The child cannot acquire those tools by himself—he needs an adult who transfers cultural tools to a child. So the goal of the program is to develop general cognitive, communicative, and regulatory skills with a focus on the potential of the ZPD. The program has module organization and thus makes it possible to develop abilities systematically. *The Key to Learning* curriculum based on Vygotsky's and his followers Zaporozhets' and Venger's ideas has two stages: an initial stage referred to as "caterpillars" and the second one referred to as "butterflies." The main focus is directed to a broad and maximally appropriate child development, rather than to the acceleration of children's development—the amplification strategy. The skills developed under the program include general skills (those needed in any activity: self-regulation, cognitive, and communicative functions); and specific skills (those needed in certain types of activities: literacy, math, music, physical skills, etc.). The Key to Learning approach recognizes three types of learning and teaching process: it includes teacher-organized activities, collaborative work, where teachers and children interact and possibly create something together, and free play (where the teacher can regulate the degree of his participation).

The above applications of Vygotksy's play theories show the importance of peers and adults in learning through play, the importance of imagination as a context for learning real-world skills, particularly through abstraction and maintaining multiple "realities" and their associated (at times conflicting) rules, and adults scaffolding increasing complexity in play narratives. Having explored applications of both Piaget's and Vygotsky's theories, this chapter can compare the two in the following section.

10.6 Comparison of Approaches to Play: Piaget and Vygotsky

This section begins with a comparison of Vygotsky's to Piaget's theory, via a summary of four main ways Vygotsky saw play leading to learning. We then review two main differences between the theories when taking Piaget's views on the adult's role in play as a starting point. These six points of difference provide a framework to begin an analysis of the contemporary research evidence on play.

In their review of Vygotsky's writing on learning through play, Colliver and Veraksa (2019) suggest four main ways play can lead to learning. First, all imagination in play finds its origins in the real world, and what children have experienced, which is not dissimilar to the assimilation function that Piaget ascribed to play, where "playing with" ideas and concepts the child has experienced (and accommodated) can be more fully assimilated through trial-and-error exploration of ideas. Unlike, Piaget, however, Vygotsky (2004, as cited in Colliver & Veraksa, 2019, p. 297) made an important note that imagination has a "distorting action" wherein certain components of reality are exaggerated or minimalized, in a way that can lead to creative, new ideas that may be considered part of the accommodation process that Piaget thought impossible in play.

The second main way Vygotsky saw play leading to learning was the use of imagination in order to understand other's experiences of reality, another way in which children may accommodate others' alternate perspectives via play that Piaget's (1962) theory appears to omit. Thus, skills like Theory of Mind (ToM) should be uniquely correlated even when predictor covariates are partialled out (Lillard et al., 2013) if Vygotsky's theory were correct and Piaget's incorrect. Experiments should yield consistent ToM improvements if Vygotsky was correct.

A third way is one in which play provides real-world emotional experiences, providing the child the opportunity to meter out the emotionality in the safety of a play context of which she is in control. Such emotional development is similar to the emotional assimilation Piaget theorized, except that Vygotsky saw the child as capable of generating new emotional experiences and perspectives in play that Piaget's focus on assimilation would have omitted. It will be difficult to find strong quantitative evidence for either position, as anything but proxy measures of emotional development such as externalizing behaviors are difficult to quantify.

The fourth and final way Vygotsky saw play leading to learning was via imaginary play providing internal cognitive or emotional resources to face real-life circumstances. Examples might include imaginary companions that allow a child to feel braver in facing challenging situations, or imaginary narratives providing cognitive tools like a "moral of the story" or a simple mnemonic device to remember the order of the planets' distance from the sun. While Piaget posited no such cognitive tools from play, the descriptions of Vygotsky's theory in ECEC curricula such as the Golden Key or Keys to Learning approaches provide some examples of the learning children might acquire during guided play experiences in the previous section.

This section now examines two key differences of Vygotsky's theory when compared with Piaget's. In the principal tenets of constructivism, Piaget believed the child to be the creator of her own cognition. The adult's role in this system was to give the child enough freedom without limiting her through strict didactic frameworks or adult beliefs about learning. For Piaget, if the adult takes on a role of much greater authority, she risks the child assimilating knowledge and skills without challenging or questioning them, precluding their inclusion in her development (Piaget, 1948). For Piaget, emphases on adult authority, child subordination to it, adult restriction of children's autonomy and lack of mutual respect all prevent the development of concepts such as that of reversibility and mutual moral behavior. Instead, intellectual development is enhanced in equal relationships with one's peers, with cooperation and mutual respect. For example, according to Piaget, the development of self-regulation is promoted by the adult offering the child opportunities to make independent choices, decisions and set rules both personally and collectively (e.g., in a play situation). Piaget saw external regulation as an obstacle to the development of autonomy and self-regulation (DeVries, 2000). Vygotsky, on the other hand, considered the only possible way of learning in play through the child's relationship with someone who exceeds his level of development (MKO). According to Vygotsky, while the child is born with certain psychological functions and mechanisms (impulses, biases, etc.; the child is not a *tabula rasa*), these functions are largely formed by the sociocultural context (Nicolopoulou, 1993); the MKO is the child's primary conduit to the external world for her development. It is the MKO who sets ZPD in play. By being together with the MKO (usually an adult), the child is able to achieve more than when left alone or even in the company of peers. According to the view of Vygotsky, a child sharing a play situation with an adult would gain more in terms of learning and development compared to the play situation experienced with peers only. But if Piaget's position were correct, we would expect that a limited role of an adult in children's play would promote children development and learning as opposed to the case where an adult regulates and determines essential features of the play.

The second set of differences between Piaget and Vygotsky's theories concerns the specific conditions that contribute to the child's development in play: it often occurs spontaneously, which, in part, also relates to the adult's role in play. After analyzing the existing empirical data, Hirsh-Pasek et al. (2009) concludes that adult-directed play does promote development, but what precisely constitutes play-based learning is still not quite clear. Zosh and colleagues (2018) elaborate this further, making a strong case for adult-initiated, playful games that are led by children, but following adult rules, at least until the children are old enough to regulate the group's adherence to the rules. The empirical support for guided play would seem to support Vygotsky's theory of play leading development in concert with the social environment (Weisberg & Zosh, 2013; Zosh et al., 2018). The challenge of doing so well, particularly in light of increased development and use of technological games that can provide this guidance seems particularly relevant in the current context (children's widespread exposure to, and use of, digital, augmented and/or virtual reality applications that are rapidly developing; Colliver et al., 2020). Many digital games which are colloquially known as play may not involve Vygotsky's original criterion of a child-developed imaginary situation, nor arguably Piaget's emphasis on child autonomy or the moral development required to establish socially indexed rules for games, as children as young as one year old are regularly engaged in such supposed digital "play." Reviews to date suggest that guidance of even simple processes like instruction of literacy and numeracy in apps is uncommon (Callaghan & Reich, 2018), so it seems unlikely that the apps young children are most likely to used mimic the expert adult guidance required to lead to learning outcomes like those described in the previous section and in Zosh et al. (2018). It is *-this the intention of the chapter's next section to review current research on play and compare the patterns found with Piaget and Vygotsky's theories.

10.7 Play and Learning: Empirical Evidence

Since the time Vygotsky and Piaget elaborated their theories, a large body of empirical data has been accumulated about the role of play in the development and learning of preschool children. That the bulk of play studies have examined child-initiated, child-led play (henceforth "free play"), rather than adult-initiated or adult-led play, may also be considered testimony to the legacy of the individualist and autonomous image of the playing child in Piaget's play theory.

Empirical evidence on the first point of difference between Piaget and Vygotsky outlined above—play as a context for imagination development—has yet failed to show causal or even equifinal relationship between creativity and play (Lillard et al., 2013). Correlational studies show that engagement in pretend play is associated with higher measures of creativity (Mottweiler & Taylor, 2014; Wallace & Russ, 2015). However, until the study conducted by Hoffmann and Russ (2016), it was not clear if there is causality—if it is pretend play that causes increase in creativity. In the Hoffmann and Russ study (2016), 50 eight-years girls participated in an intervention group twice a week—they were asked to tell the stories using the toys provided. It was found that only for the children with initially low level of creativity the intervention turned out to be effective. For the other girls in the experiment, there were no significant results. This study shows that pretend play might be beneficial for the development of creativity that is closely related to imagination, however, the underlying mechanisms remain unknown (Hoffmann & Russ, 2016).

The second difference above, the view of Vygotsky on play as an opportunity to develop sense of what other people are thinking or feeling (ToM), seems to be supported by limited research. Again, empirical results on this aspect of development in play remains unclear and inconsistent, pointing toward epiphenomenalism rather than equifinality (Lillard et al., 2013). Lillard et al. (2013) mention the need for another variable included in the research in order to explain the correlation of more advanced ToM skills and participation in more advanced pretend play (i.e., parents who interact with children). A subsequent study conducted by Qu et al. (2015) showed that the role of a teacher mediates (as well as initial level of EFs) the association between participation in sociodramatic play and ToM scores. The study included 71 preschoolers (M = 60.2 months, SD = 5.7) who were assigned to three groups: free play, sociodramatic play, and sociodramatic play and ToM coaching. The experimental intervention lasted four weeks and included weekly 45-min play sessions. Thus, the assumption brought by Vygotsky needs more consistent and full empirical verification in order to confirm the idea of play being the space for understanding other people better.

Regarding the third way of learning through play introduced by Vygotsky, there are many studies which focus on the relationship between role-play and the emotional development (e.g., Colwell & Lindsey, 2005; Gilpin et al., 2015; Lindsey & Colwell, 2013; Russ et al., 1999). Empirically, the association between emotion regulation skills and features of pretend play (e.g., fantasy orientation) has been widely confirmed (Galyer & Evans, 2001; Gilpin et al., 2015; Goldstein & Lerner, 2018; Kelly et al., 2011; Slot et al., 2017; Thibodeau-Nielsen & Gilpin, 2020). Goldstein and Lerner (2018) conducted a randomized, component control trial of dramatic pretend play games with a low-SES group of 4-year-old children (n = 97) to test whether such practice yields generalized improvements in multiple social and emotional outcomes. Specific effects of dramatic play games on emotional self-control were found. Results suggest that dramatic pretend play games involving physicalizing emotional states and traits, pretending to be animals and human characters, and engaging in pretend scenarios in small groups may improve children's emotional control. A study conducted by Fung and Cheng (2017) included preschool children (M = 5.44, 34.44% girls) participating in two types of play sessions for one month: with and without an element of pretend play. The results showed that for girls, the training with the pretend component was more effective in terms of emotional regulation—they had lower rates of destructive behavior in play. For the boys' emotional regulation skills, both types of training were equally effective (also according to the indicator of destructive behavior). However, studies in which researchers have tried to understand the mechanisms of social and emotional competence as they develop in pretend play are lacking. Thus, Piaget and Vygotsky's different understandings of play leading to emotional development cannot be discerned in the profile of current evidence, except to say that Piaget's view that play may be one of several routes for children to find emotional equilibration may be easier to evidence. The conclusion of Lillard et al. (2013) regarding the relationship between emotional development and play perhaps remain relevant today—it is still an open question whether pretend play leads to the development of emotional regulation. More experimental, longitudinal research is needed in order to clarify this aspect of development through play.

Several studies have investigated the potential role that play can have in preparation of children for facing real-life challenges, the fourth and final way in which Vygotsky saw play leading to learning—a function precluded from Piaget's view of play as incapable of stimulating accommodation of new concepts. For many children, school entry represents a formidable transition for which they must be emotionally and academically prepared (Blankson et al., 2017). Thus, it is possible to consider the preparatory function of play in relation to school. A longitudinal study by Wallace and Russ (2015) assessed girls' play characteristics (n = 31) and their academic learning outcomes 4 years later, their mean age being 11.1 years. The results of this study showed a relation between math computational skills and the following characteristics of play: imagination, degree of play organization, emotions (positive or negative), and frequency of their manifestation. However, none of the play characteristics were significantly related to math problem-solving and reading skills. Interestingly, early executive functions have been shown to be a key factor in predicting school adjustment and achievement at school entry (Blankson et al., 2017; Lan et al., 2011), and several studies find associations between play and EF (e.g., Barker et al., 2014; Berk & Meyers, 2013; Carlson et al., 2014; Lan et al., 2011; Pierucci et al., 2013; Thibodeau et al., 2016; Thibodeau-Nielsen & Gilpin, 2020; Thibodeau-Nielsen et al., 2020; Veraksa et al., 2019; White & Carlson, 2016; 2021).

On the matter of play as preparation for real life, Ivrendi's (2016) study also found a correlation between the play level and number sense. One possible explanation for this appears to be the following: in play children are engaged in many mathematical concepts such as counting, classifying, and adding, which are essential parts of number sense concept. Thus, an interactive play context may offer children opportunities to use counting, adding, and ordering. Because children are self-motivated in peer play contexts, they may take more risks in using newly learned mathematical skills. Also, the relationship between sociodramatic play and mathematics and reading ability was examined in a longitudinal study by Hanline et al. (2008), where "symbolic substitution" was associated with and levels of mathematical ability (number comparison, mastery of number facts, calculation skills, and understanding concepts) and reading at age 8. The "symbolic substitution" that both Piaget and Vygotsky saw in play reflects children's ability to move farther away from actual objects in their sociodramatic play, providing evidence of the child's ability to think more abstractly. The obtained results show that the child's ability to think symbolically in preschool relates positively to both math and reading abilities and rate of growth, as both academic areas involve abstract thinking and the use of symbols. However, more ambiguous results were found for Hanline et al.' (2008) "symbolic agent" indicator: it correlated positively with math skills, but negatively with reading. As in the two theories, the authors concluded that the use of transformations and representations in pretend play may facilitate the shift from concrete to symbolic thinking that is necessary to understand written symbols in reading and mathematics, so both theories find support in this study.

The relationship between role-playing and academic learning outcomes can also be indirect. For example, participation in role-play requires a certain level of self-regulation, which, in turn, is associated with future academic performance (Braza et al., 2007; Vieillevoye & Nader-Grosbois, 2008). Developing self-regulation through play enables children to focus on classroom tasks (McClelland et al., 2007) and on peer acceptance (Johnson et al., 2004). As an example, in Ivrendi's study (2016), significantly higher levels of self-regulation were observed in children engaging in challenging role-play with other children. Children who were able to concentrate on the story and act appropriately in a social context were more likely to engage in play, experiencing positive social-emotional experiences while interacting with others (Ivrendi, 2016). Children with reduced self-regulation skills may be less likely to be perceived as desirable play partners, further reducing their chances of improving executive function (Fantuzzo et al., 1998). The effect of play on self-regulation was also described in a study by Walker and colleagues (2020), which involved integrating play situations into the educational process for 227 preschoolers for 10 weeks. Before and after the intervention, their EF levels—consisting of: working memory, cognitive flexibility and inhibitory control—were assessed. The study outcomes indicated that there was a significant improvement in EF from pre-test to post-test on all EF measures. A recent longitudinal study of 2,213 toddlers and preschoolers' play showed every extra hour of free play they engaged in predicted a very modest 3% of a standard deviation increase in their self-regulation skills two years later (Colliver et al., 2022), so longitudinal designs need to be sensitive to the difficulties in defining play if they are to show stronger effects.

Limited evidence exists for the association between free play and academic learning outcomes, or "hard skills" (Slot et al., 2016, p. 7). Empirical studies show that this relation is perhaps mediated by other cognitive functions (e.g., EFs) that are subject to development during play. However, again, it seems to be too early to make adequate conclusions—pretend play itself does not show effects on problem-solving or reasoning that are required for school and later life generally (Lillard et al., 2013).

The next discrepancy between Piaget's and Vygotsky's views is how they considered the role of an adult in play. In kindergarten settings, the role of an adult in play can be divided to free play and guided play (Pyle & Danniels, 2017; Weisberg & Hirsh-Pasek, 2013). The term "playful learning" includes both types of play, however, excessive adult control can mean children cease to consider the activity to be play (Breathnach et al., 2017; Colliver & Doel-Mackaway, 2021) and may deprive it of certain benefits (van Oers, 2013). In other words, the role of an adult in play needs to balance between children's playful autonomy and needs (which is related to the Piaget's position) and the directedness of play toward a learning purpose (which is associated with Vygotsky) (Pyle & Danniels, 2017).

The majority of research of the adult's role in play is aimed to specify the conditions that promote learning (Pyle & Bigelow, 2015; Weisberg, Hirsh-Pasek et al., 2013; Weisberg, Zosh et al., 2013). Zosh et al. (2018) reviewed play research for evidence that adult-led play (henceforth "guided play") might result in improvements in learning and argued that explicit learning goals (such as learning particular hard skills, like reading) are best met through guided, rather than free play. Subsequent research has shown guided play is superior for hard skills like reading (Dickinson et al., 2019) or mathematics (Bower et al., 2020; Eason & Ramani, 2020; Ramani & Scalise, 2020; Thomson et al., 2020; Weber et al., 2020). A recent meta-analysis of 22 studies comparing the effects on literacy of adult-led, child-led, and balanced curricula found the latter most effective, suggesting that neither free play nor direct instruction yield the best literacy outcomes (Chambers et al., 2016). Findings where child-initiated activities lead to superior literacy outcomes may be explained *not* by the lack of adult involvement in play, but rather that adult-initiated activities may be too easy or difficult for the child to learn maximally from them (Lerkkanen et al., 2016; Montie et al., 2006). Typically, small group interactions where adults and children balance their autonomy are most efficacious for learning (Kangas et al., 2015;

Montie et al., 2006; Timmons et al., 2016), which broadly support Vygotsky's theory of play more than they do Piaget's.

A recent study including training experiment was conducted to evaluate adult involvement in play on EF (Sukhikh et al., 2021). Two experimental conditions were contrasted on the level of adult participation: for one group of preschool children (*n* = 28, 42.8% of females) adult acted as a director of the plot, whereas for the other (n*n*= 39, 43.5% of females) adult assumed a supportive, facilitative role. Results of this study did not directly test assumptions of Piaget and Vygotsky but showed that different processes occurred when an adult is actively or passively involved in the play. Following both quantitative and qualitative data (play sessions were video-taped), adult-directed play showed more creative performance of their play roles by adding new or atypical features of their character, and child-directed play was characterized by greater emotional play engagement and more vivid expression of emotions. These observations were examined through the prism of Vygotsky's conception of *perezhivanie*: when children "live through" play, the largely individual executive functions appear to mediate development, consistent with Vygotsky's rather than Piaget's writing.

Thus, a number of studies indicate an association between play, academic performance, and soft skills. However, research findings do not always allow for unequivocal conclusions. In 2013, Lillard et al., reviewing the studies that had been accumulated over 40 years, were forced to state that if play had anything to do with child development, it was not clear how or how critical this connection was: there is considerable evidence in favor of equifinality (play helps development, but it is only one possible developmental route—other activities may work as well or even better) and epiphenomenalism (play is an epiphenomenon or a byproduct of another activity or condition that indeed contributes to development) (Lillard et al, 2013; Veraksa et al., 2020). It is thus important to evaluate the emerging profile of evidence in support of Piaget and Vygotsky's theories bearing in mind the methodological challenges these studies have faced, not least the experimental control of free play, which is by its nature controlled by the child.

10.8 Conclusion

This chapter has reviewed the main aspects of Piaget's and Vygotsky's theories on learning and development through play. We described four commonalities between them and three points of discrepancy. First, the origin of imagination expressed in play—Vygotsky stated that it derives from the real world, which is closely related to Piaget's assimilation phenomena. Also, according to Vygotsky, imagination in play promotes better understanding of others, and play represents a safe space for emotion expression. The last way of the learning through play according to Vygotsky relates to the cognitive and emotional resources derived from play in order to face real-world challenges, which Piaget did not overtly recognize in his writing. Two other differences between Piaget and Vygotsky included the role of an adult in play and conditions that promote learning. According to Piaget, adult's involvement in play is largely detrimental for development, while peer interaction is associated with enhanced development. In contrast, for Vygotsky, the adult holds a pivotal role in play by introducing the ideas from her more extensive understanding of the surrounding world and the ideal forms of culture, as well as by supporting the child's development through the ZPD. We then compared these differences to the profile of evidence in contemporary research using Lillard et al (2013) and Zosh et al. (2018), including more recent research on the topic, we found broad support for play as assimilation and practice, as Piaget theorized, but also for the important role of the adult in guided play, and for superior outcomes in hard skills such as reading and mathematics. We also noted that it is a much more difficult empirical task to design research which can show play has a causal role in development and learning, as Vygotsky theorized, than an equifinal role, as Piaget did. We noted that the empirical research is still not mature enough to fully support or discard either of the theories. However, it seems that the Vygotsky's view on learning through play is supported by the research to a greater extent. Specifically, in terms of developmental potential, play should involve adults, however, the degree of one's involvement should follow certain criteria and remains being a subject for investigation.

Acknowledgements The work was supported by the RSF grant #20-18-00423.

References

Avdulova, T. P. (2018). *Psihologiya igry: uchebnik dlya akademicheskogo bakalavriata* [The play psychology: A textbook for academic undergraduate studies] (Trans. N. E. Veraksa) Moscow: Urajt.

Barker, J. E., Semenov, A. D., Michaelson, L., Provan, L. S., Snyder, H. R., & Munakata, Y. (2014). *Less-structured time in children's daily lives predicts self-directed executive functioning.* Frontiers in Psychology, 5.https://doi.org/10.3389/fpsyg.2014.00593

Berk, L. E., & Meyers, A. B. (2013). The role of make-believe play in the development of executive function: Status of research and future directions. *American Journal of Play, 6*(1), 98–110. https://files.eric.ed.gov/fulltext/EJ1016170.pdf

Birns, B., & Golden, M. (1974). The implications of Piaget's theories for contemporary infancy research and education. In M. Schwebel & J. Raph (Eds.), *Piaget in the classroom* (pp. 114–131). Routledge & Kegan Paul.

Blankson, A. N., Weaver, J. M., Leerkes, E. M., O'Brien, M., Calkins, S. D., & Marcovitch, S. (2017). Cognitive and emotional processes as predictors of a successful transition into school. *Early Education and Development, 28*(1), 1–20. https://doi.org/10.1080/10409289.2016.1183434

Bodrova, E. V., & Leong, D. J. (2001). *Tools of the mind: A case study of implementing the Vygotskian approach in American early childhood and primary classrooms.* Innodata monographs 7. International Bureau of Education, P. https://eric.ed.gov/?id=ed455014

Bodrova, E. V. (2008). Make-believe play versus academic skills: A Vygotskian approach to today's dilemma of early childhood education. *European Early Childhood Education Research Journal, 16*(3), 357–369. https://doi.org/10.1080/13502930802291777

Bower, C., Odean, R., Verdine, B. N., Medford, J. R., Marzouk, M., Golinkoff, R. M., & Hirsh-Pasek, K. (2020). Associations of 3-year-olds' block-building complexity with Later spatial and mathematical skills. *Journal of Cognition and Development, 21*(3), 383–405. https://doi.org/10.1080/15248372.2020.1741363

Braza, F., Braza, P., Carreras, R. M., Munoz, J. M., Sanchez-Martin, J. R., Azurmendi, A., Sorozabal, A., Garcia, A., & Cardas, J. (2007). Behavioral profiles of different types of 904 A. IvrendiSocial status in preschool children: An observational approach. *Social Behavior and Personality: An International Journal, 35*(2), 195–212. https://doi.org/10.2224/sbp.2007.35.2.195

Breathnach, H., Danby, S., & O'Gorman, L. (2017). 'Are you working or playing?' Investigating young children's perspectives of classroom activities. *International Journal of Early Years Education, 25*(4), 439–454. https://doi.org/10.1080/09669760.2017.1316241

Bredekamp, S. (1987). *Developmentally appropriate practice in early childhood education programs: Serving children from birth through age 8*. National Association for the Education of Young Children.

Bredekamp, S., Copple, C., & National Association for the Education of Young Children (Eds.). (1997). *Developmentally appropriate practice in early childhood programs* (Rev. ed.). National Association for the Education of Young Children.

Burman, E. (1994). *Deconstructing developmental psychology* (1st ed.). Routledge.

Burman, E. (2008). *Developments: Child, image, nation*. Taylor & Francis. https://public.ebookcentral.proquest.com/choice/publicfullrecord.aspx?p=327303

Butler, A. L., Gotts, E. E., & Quisenberry, N. L. (1978). *Play as development*. Merrill.

Callaghan, M. N., & Reich, S. M. (2018, August 3). Are educational preschool apps designed to teach? An analysis of the app market. *Learning, Media and Technology, 43*(3), 280–293. https://doi.org/10.1080/17439884.2018.1498355

Cannella, G. S. (1997). *Deconstructing early childhood education: Social justice and revolution*. Peter Lang.

Carlson, S. M., White, R. E., & Davis-Unger, A. C. (2014). Evidence for a relation between executive function and pretense representation in preschool children. *Cognitive Development, 29*, 1–16. https://doi.org/10.1016/j.cogdev.2013.09.001

Chambers, B., Cheung, A. C. K., & Slavin, R. E. (2016). Literacy and language outcomes of comprehensive and developmental-constructivist approaches to early childhood education: A systematic review. *Educational Research Review, 18*, 88–111. http://dx.doi.org/10.1016/j.edurev.2016.03.003

Colliver, Y., & Veraksa, N. E. (2019). The aim of the game: A pedagogical tool to support young children's learning through play. *Learning, Culture and Social Interaction, 21*, 296–310. https://doi.org/10.1016/j.lcsi.2019.03.001

Colliver, Y. (2019). Intentional or incidental? Learning through play according to Australian educators' perspectives. *Early Years: An International Research Journal*. https://doi.org/10.1080/09575146.2019.1661976

Colliver, Y., Brown, J., & Harrison, L. (2022). Toddlers' and preschoolers' free play predicts their self-regulation two years later: Longitudinal evidence from a representative Australian sample. *Early Childhood Research Quarterly*.

Colliver, Y., & Doel-Mackaway, H. (2021). Article 31, 31 years on: Choice and autonomy as a framework for implementing children's right to play in early childhood services. *Human Rights Law Review*. https://doi.org/10.1093/hrlr/ngab011

Colliver, Y., Hatzigianni, M., & Davies, B. (2020). Why can't I find quality apps for my child? A model to understand all stakeholders' perspectives on quality learning through digital play. *Early Child Development and Care, 190*(16), 2612–2626. https://doi.org/10.1080/03004430.2019.1596901

Colwell, M. J., & Lindsey, E. W. (2005). Preschool children's pretend and physical play and sex of play partner: Connections to peer competence. *Sex Roles, 52*(7), 497–509. https://doi.org/10.1007/s11199-005-3716-8

Copple, C., Bredekamp, S., & National Association for the Education of Young Children (Eds.). (2009). *Developmentally appropriate practice in early childhood programs serving children from birth through age 8* (3rd ed.). National Association for the Education of Young Children.

Cullen, J. (1999). Children's knowledge, teachers' knowledge: Implications for early childhood teacher education. *Australian Journal of Teacher Education, 24*(2), 2. https://doi.org/10.14221/ajte.1999v24n2.2

DeVries, R. (2000). Vygotsky, Piaget, and education: A reciprocal assimilation of theories and educational practices. *New Ideas in Psychology, 18*(2–3), 187–213. https://doi.org/10.1016/S0732-118X(00)00008-8

Dickinson, D. K. (2002). Shifting images of developmentally appropriate practice as seen through different lenses. *Educational Researcher, 31*(1), 26–32. https://doi.org/10.3102/0013189X031001026

Dickinson, D. K., Collins, M. F., Nesbitt, K., Toub, T. S., Hassinger-Das, B., Hadley, E. B., Hirsh-Pasek, K., & Golinkoff, R. M. (2019). Effects of teacher-delivered book reading and play on vocabulary learning and self-regulation among low-income preschool children. *Journal of Cognition and Development, 20*(2), 136–164. https://doi.org/10.1080/15248372.2018.1483373

Fantuzzo, J., Coolahan, K. C., Mendez, J. L., McDermott, P. A., & Sutton-Smith, B. (1998). Contextually-relevant validation of peer play constructs with African American head start children: Penn interactive peer play scale. *Early Childhood Research Quarterly, 13*(3), 411–431. https://doi.org/10.1016/S0885-2006(99)80048-9

Eason, S. H., & Ramani, G. B. (2020). Parent-Child math talk about fractions during formal learning and guided play activities. *Child Development, 91*(2), 546–562. https://doi.org/10.1111/cdev.13199

Ebbeck, M. (1996). Children constructing their own knowledge. *International Journal of Early Years Education, 4*(2), 5–27. https://doi.org/10.1080/0966976960040202

Edwards, S., & Cutter-Mackenzie, A. (2011). Environmentalising early childhood education curriculum through pedagogies of play. *Australasian Journal of Early Childhood, 36*(1), 51–59. https://doi.org/10.1177/183693911103600109

Epstein, A. S. (2007). *The intentional teacher*. National Association for the Education of Young Children.

Fein, G. G. (1978). Play and the Acquisition of Symbols [PhD Thesis]. National Institute of Education. https://files.eric.ed.gov/fulltext/ED152431.pdf

Fung, W., & Cheng, R. W. (2017). Effect of school pretend play on preschoolers' social competence in peer interactions: Gender as a potential moderator. *Early Childhood Education Journal, 45*(1), 35–42. https://doi.org/10.1007/s10643-015-0760-z

Galyer, K. T., & Evans, I. M. (2001). Pretend play and the development of emotion regulation in preschool children. *Early Child Development and Care, 166*(1), 93–108. https://doi.org/10.1080/0300443011660108

Garwood, S. G. (1982). Piaget and play: Translating theory into practice. *Topics in Early Childhood Special Education, 2*(3), 1–13. https://doi.org/10.1177/027112148200200305

Gaskins, S., & Göncü, A. (1988). Children's play as representation and imagination: The case of Piaget and Vygotsky. *The Quarterly Newsletter of the Laboratory of Comparative Human Cognition, 10*(4), 104–107. http://home.uchicago.edu/~johnlucy/papersmaterials/1988%20vy&piaget-oc88v10n4-1.pdf

Gilpin, A. T., Brown, M. M., & Pierucci, J. M. (2015). Relations between fantasy orientation and emotion regulation in preschool. *Early Education and Development, 26*(7), 920–932. https://doi.org/10.1080/10409289.2015.1000716

Gibbons, A. (2007). The politics of processes and products in education: An early childhood metanarrative crisis? *Educational Philosophy and Theory, 39*(3), 300–311. https://doi.org/10.1111/j.1469-5812.2007.00323.x

Glassman, M. (1995). The difference between Piaget and Vygotsky: A response to Duncan. *Developmental Review, 15*(4), 473–482. https://doi.org/10.1006/drev.1995.1020

Goffin, S. G., & Wilson, C. (2001). *Curriculum models and early childhood education: Appraising the relationship* (2nd ed.). Prentice Hall.

Goldstein, T. R., & Lerner, M. D. (2018). Dramatic pretend play games uniquely improve emotional control in young children. *Developmental Science, 21*(4), 1–13. https://doi.org/10.1111/desc. 12603

Goodley, D., & Runswick-Cole, K. (2010). Emancipating play: Dis/abled children, development and deconstruction. *Disability & Society, 25*(4), 499–512. https://doi.org/10.1080/096875910037 55914

Guldberg, H. (2009). *Reclaiming childhood: Freedom and play in an age of fear*. Routledge.

Hanline, M. F., Milton, S., & Phelps, P. C. (2008). A longitudinal study exploring the relationship of representational levels of three aspects of preschool sociodramatic play and early academic skills. *Journal of Research in Childhood Education, 23*(1), 19–28. https://doi.org/10.1080/025 68540809594643

Hirsh-Pasek, K., Golinkoff, R., Berk, L., & Singer, D. G. (2009). *A mandate for playful learning in preschool: Presenting the evidence*. Oxford University Press.

Hoffmann, J. D., & Russ, S. W. (2016). Fostering pretend play skills and creativity in elementary school girls: A group play intervention. *Psychology of Aesthetics, Creativity, and the Arts, 10*(1), 114–125. https://doi.org/10.1037/aca0000039

Ivrendi, A. (2016). Choice-driven peer play, self-regulation and number sense. *European Early Childhood Education Research Journal, 24*(6), 895–906. https://doi.org/10.1080/1350293X. 2016.1239325

Johnson, J. E., Christie, J. F., & Wardle, F. (2004). *Play, Development and early education*. Pearson/A and B.

Karpov, Y. V. (2005). *The Neo-Vygotskian approach to child development*. Cambridge University Press.

Kamii, C. (1974). Pedagogical principles derived form Piaget's theory: Relevance for educational practice. In M. Schwebel & J. Raph (Eds.), *Piaget in the classroom* (pp. 199–215). Routledge and Kegan Paul.

Kangas, J., Ojala, M., & Venninen, T. (2015). Children's self-regulation in the context of participatory pedagogy in early childhood education. *Early Education and Development, 26*(5–6), 847–870. https://doi.org/10.1080/10409289.2015.1039434

Kavanaugh, R. D. (2012). Origins and consequences of social pretend play. *The Oxford Handbook of the Development of Play, May 2018*, 1–23. https://doi.org/10.1093/oxfordhb/9780195393002. 013.0022

Kelly, R., Hammond, S., Dissanayake, C., & Ihsen, E. (2011). The relationship between symbolic play and executive function in young children. *Australasian Journal of Early Childhood, 36*(2), 21–27. https://search.informit.org/doi/abs/10.3316/ielapa.052689338142076

Korotkova, N. A. (1985). Sovremennye issledovaniya detskoj igry [Contemporary research on children's play]. *Voprosy psihologii, 2*, 163–169. http://www.voppsy.ru/issues/1985/852/852163. htm

Kravtsov, G. G., & Kravtsova, E. E. (2018). The 'Golden Key' program and its cultural-historical basis. In M. Fleer & B. van Oers (Eds.), *International handbook of early childhood education* (pp. 1023–1039). Springer Netherlands. https://doi.org/10.1007/978-94-024-0927-7_52

Krieg, S. (2011). The Australian early years learning framework: Learning what? *Contemporary Issues in Early Childhood, 12*(1), 46–55. https://doi.org/10.2304/ciec.2011.12.1.46

Lan, X., Legare, C. H., Ponitz, C. C., Li, S., & Morrison, F. J. (2011). Investigating the links between the subcomponents of executive function and academic achievement: A cross-cultural analysis of Chinese and American preschoolers. *Journal of Experimental Child Psychology, 108*(3), 677–692. https://doi.org/10.1016/j.jecp.2010.11.001

Lee, K., & Johnson, A. S. (2007). Child development in cultural contexts: Implications of cultural psychology for early childhood teacher education. *Early Childhood Education Journal, 35*, 233–243. https://doi.org/10.1007/s10643-007-0202-7

Lerkkanen, M.-K., Kiuru, N., Pakarinen, E., Poikkeus, A.-M., Rasku-Puttonen, H., Siekkinen, M., & Nurmi, J.-E. (2016). Child-centered versus teacher-directed teaching practices: Associations with the development of academic skills in the first grade at school. *Early Childhood Research Quarterly, 36*, 145–156. https://doi.org/10.1016/j.ecresq.2015.12.023

Lewis, V., & Boucher, J. (1997). *The test of pretend play.* The Psychological Corporation.

Lillard, A. S., Lerner, M. D., Hopkins, E. J., Dore, R. A., Smith, E. D., & Palmquist, C. M. (2013). The impact of pretend play on children's development: A review of the evidence. *Psychological Bulletin, 139*(1), 1–34. https://doi.org/10.1037/a0029321

Lindqvist, G. (2001). When small children play: How adults dramatise and children create meaning. *Early Years, 21*(1), 7–14. https://doi.org/10.1080/09575140123593

Lindsey, E. W., & Colwell, M. J. (2013). Pretend and physical play: Links to preschoolers' affective social competence. *Merrill-Palmer Quarterly, 59*(3), 330–360. https://doi.org/10.13110/merrpalmquar1982.59.3.0330

McClelland, M. M., Cameron, C. E., Connor, C. M., Farris, C. L., Jewkes, A. M., & Morrison, F. J. (2007). Links between behavioral regulation and preschoolers' literacy, vocabulary, and math skills. *Developmental Psychology, 43*(4), 947–959. https://doi.org/10.1037/0012-1649.43.4.947

Montie, J. E., Xiang, Z., & Schweinhart, L. J. (2006). Preschool experience in 10 countries: Cognitive and language performance at age 7. *Early Childhood Research Quarterly, 21*(3), 313–331. https://doi.org/10.1016/j.ecresq.2006.07.007

Mottweiler, C. M., & Taylor, M. (2014). Elaborated role play and creativity in preschool age children. *Psychology of Aesthetics, Creativity, and the Arts, 8*(3), 277–286. https://doi.org/10.1037/a0036083

Murray, F. B. (1979). The generation of educational practice from developmental theory. *Educational Psychologist, 14*, 30–43. https://doi.org/10.1080/00461527909529205

Nicolich, L. M. (1977). Beyond sensorimotor intelligence: Assessment of symbolic-maturity through analysis of pretend play. *Merrill- Palmer Quarterly, 23*, 89–99.

Nicolopoulou, A. (1993). Play, cognitive development, and the social world: Piaget, Vygotsky, and beyond. *Human Development, 36*(1), 1–23. https://doi.org/10.1159/000277285

O'Gorman, L., & Ailwood, J. (2012). "They get fed up with playing": Parents' views on play–based learning in the preparatory year. *Contemporary Issues in Early Childhood, 13*(4), 266–275. https://doi.org/10.2304/ciec.2003.4.3.5

Piaget, J. (1945). *Play, Dreams, and Imitation in Childhood.* Norton.

Piaget, J. (1948). *The moral judgment of the child.* Free Press.

Piaget, J. (1962). *Play, dreams and imitation in childhood.* Norton.

Piaget, J. (1964). Part I: Cognitive development in children—Piaget development and learning. *Journal of Research in Science Teaching, 2*, 176–186. https://doi.org/10.1002/tea.3660020306

Pierucci, J. M., O'Brien, C. T., McInnis, M. A., Gilpin, A. T., & Barber, A. B. (2013). Fantasy orientation constructs and related executive function development in preschool: Developmental benefits to executive functions by being a fantasy-oriented child. *International Journal of Behavioral Development, 38*(1), 62–69. https://doi.org/10.1177/0165025413508512

Pyle, A., & Bigelow, A. (2015). Play in kindergarten: An interview and observational study in three canadian classrooms. *Early Childhood Education Journal, 43*(5), 385–393. https://doi.org/10.1007/s10643-014-0666-1

Pyle, A., & Danniels, E. (2017). A continuum of play-based learning: The role of the teacher in play-based pedagogy and the fear of hijacking play. *Early Education and Development, 28*(3), 274–289. https://doi.org/10.1080/10409289.2016.1220771

Pyle, A., Pyle, M. A., Prioletta, J., & Alaca, B. (2021). Portrayals of play-based learning. *American Journal of Play, 13*(1), 53–86. https://www.journalofplay.org/sites/www.journalofplay.org/files/pdf-articles/13-1-Article-4-Portrayals-of-Play-Based-Learning.pdf

Qu, L., Shen, P., Chee, Y. Y., & Chen, L. (2015). Teachers' Theory-of-mind coaching and children's executive function predict the training effect of sociodramatic play on children's Theory of Mind. *Social Development, 24*(4), 716–733. https://doi.org/10.1111/sode.12116

Quiñones, G., Ridgeway, A., & Li, L. (2020). Holding hands: Toddler's imaginary peer play. In A. Ridgeway, G. Quiñones, & L. Li (Eds.), *Peer play relationships: International early childhood research perspectives* (pp. 77–92). Springer. https://doi.org/10.1007/978-3-030-42331-5_6

Ramani, G. B., & Scalise, N. R. (2020). It's more than just fun and games: Play-based mathematics activities for Head Start families. *Early Childhood Research Quarterly, 50*, 78–89. https://doi.org/10.1016/j.ecresq.2018.07.011

Ranz-Smith, D. J. (2007). Teacher perception of play: In leaving no child behind are teachers leaving childhood behind? *Early Education & Development, 18*(2), 271–303. https://doi.org/10.1080/10409280701280425

Russ, S. W., Robins, A. L., & Christiano, B. A. (1999). Pretend play: Longitudinal prediction of creativity and affect in fantasy in children. *Creativity Research Journal, 12*(2), 129–139. https://doi.org/10.1207/s15326934crj1202_5

Ryan, S., & Goffin, S. G. (2008). Missing in action: Teaching in early care and education. *Early Education & Development, 19*(3), 385–395. https://doi.org/10.1080/10409280802068688

Sanders, K., & Farago, F. (2017). Developmentally appropriate practice in the twenty-first century. In M. Fleer & B. Van Oers (Eds.), *International handbook of early childhood education* (pp. 1379–1400). Springer. https://doi.org/10.1007/978-94-024-0927-7_71

Siraj-Blatchford, I. (2009). Conceptualising progression in the pedagogy of play and sustained shared thinking in early childhood education: A Vygotskian perspective. *Education and Child Psychology, 26*(2), 77–89. http://discovery.ucl.ac.uk/10006091/1/Siraj-Blatchford2009Conceptualising77.pdf

Siraj-Blatchford, I., Sylva, K., Muttock, S., Gilden, R., & Bell, D. (2002). *Researching effective pedagogy in the early years (Research report RR356).* Institute of Education, University of London.

Slot, P., Cadima, J., Salminen, J., Pastori, G., & Lerkkanen, M.-K. (2016). *Multiple case study in seven European countries regarding culture-sensitive classroom quality assessment.* EU CARE project. Urn:Nbn:Nl:Ui:10-1874-342309

Slot, P., Mulder, H., Verhagen, J., & Leseman, P. P. M. (2017). Preschoolers' cognitive and emotional self-regulation in pretend play: Relations with executive functions and quality of play. *Infant and Child Development, 26*(6), e2038. https://doi.org/10.1002/icd.2038

Smith, P. K. (1988). Children's play nad its role in early development: A re–evaluation of the 'play ethos'. In A. D. Pellegrini (Ed.), *Psychological bases for early education* (pp. 207–226). Wiley.

Spodek, B., & Saracho, O. N. (1999). *Issues in early childhood curriculum. Yearbook in Early Childhood Education* (Vol. 2). Educators International Press.

Sukhikh, V. L., Veresov N. N., & Veraksa N. E. (2021). *Role-play, dramatic Perezhivanie and executive functions' development in early childhood.* Submitted for publication.

Timmons, K., Pelletier, J., & Corter, C. (2016). Understanding children's self-regulation within different classroom contexts. *Early Child Development and Care, 186*(2), 249–267. https://doi.org/10.1080/03004430.2015.1027699

Thibodeau, R. B., Gilpin, A. T., Brown, M. M., & Meyer, B. A. (2016). The effects of fantastical pretend-play on the development of executive functions: An intervention study. *Journal of Experimental Child Psychology, 145*, 120–138. https://doi.org/10.1016/j.jecp.2016.01.001

Thibodeau-Nielsen, R. B., & Gilpin, A. T. (2020). The role of emotion regulation in the relationship between pretense and executive function in early childhood: For whom is the relationship strongest? *Infant and Child Development*, e2193. https://doi.org/10.1002/icd.2193

Thibodeau-Nielsen, R. B., Gilpin, A. T., Nancarrow, A. F., Pierucci, J. M., & Brown, M. M. (2020). Fantastical pretense's effects on executive function in a diverse sample of preschoolers. *Journal of Applied Developmental Psychology, 68*, 101137. https://doi.org/10.1016/j.appdev.2020.101137

Thomson, D., Casey, B. M., Lombardi, C. M., & Nguyen, H. N. (2020). Quality of fathers' spatial concept support during block building predicts their daughters' early math skills—But not their sons'. *Early Childhood Research Quarterly, 50*, 51–64. https://doi.org/10.1016/j.ecresq.2018.07.008

Thomas, L., Warren, E., & deVries, E. (2011). Play-based learning and intentional teaching in early childhood contexts. *Australasian Journal of Early Childhood, 36*(4), 69–75. https://doi.org/10.1177/183693911103600410

Trawick-Smith, J. (1989). Play is not learning: A critical review of the literature. *Child & Youth Care Quarterly, 18*(3), 161–170. https://doi.org/10.1007/BF01085654

UN. (1989). *Convention on the rights of the child*. http://www.unhcr.org/refworld/docid/3ae6b38f0.html

Van Oers, B. (1998). The fallacy of detextualization. *Mind, Culture, and Activity, 2*(2), 135–142. https://doi.org/10.1207/s15327884mca0502_7

Van Oers, B. (2013). Is it play? Towards a reconceptualisation of role play from an activity theory perspective. *European Early Childhood Education Research Journal, 21*(2), 185–198. https://doi.org/10.1080/1350293X.2013.789199

Veraksa, N. E. (2015). Representation of objective situations in preschool children. *Cultural-Historical Psychology, 11*(3), 110–119. https://doi.org/10.17759/chp.2015110310

Veraksa, A., Bukhalenkova, D., & Yakupova, V. (2018). Development of executive functions through play activities: A theoretical overview. *Russian Psychological Journal, 15*(4), 97–112. https://doi.org/10.21702/rpj.2018.4.5

Veraksa, N. E., & Dolya, G. N. (2018). The key to learning curriculum. In M. Fleer & B. van Oers (Eds.), *International handbook of early childhood education* (pp. 1059–1073). Springer Netherlands. https://doi.org/10.1007/978-94-024-0927-7_54

Veraksa, A. N., Gavrilova, M. N., Bukhalenkova, D. A., Olga, A. V., Veraksa, N. E., & Colliver, Y. (2019). Does Batman™ affect EF because he is benevolent or skilful? The effect of different pretend roles on pre-schoolers' executive functions. *Early Child Development and Care*. https://doi.org/10.1080/03004430.2019.1658091

Veraksa, N. E., Veresov, N. N., Veraksa, A. N., & Sukhikh, V. L. (2020). Modern problems of children's play: Cultural-historical context. *Cultural-Historical Psychology, 16*(3), 60–70. https://doi.org/10.17759/chp.2020160307

Vianna, E., & Stetsenko, A. (2006). Embracing history through transforming it: Contrasting Piagetian versus Vygotskian (activity) theories of learning and development to expand constructivism within a dialectical view of history. *Theory & Psychology, 16*(1), 81–108. https://doi.org/10.1177/0959354306060108

Vieillevoye, S., & Nader-Grosbois, N. (2008). Self-regulation during pretend play in children with intellectual disability and in normally developing children. *Research in Developmental Disabilities, 29*(3), 256–272. https://doi.org/10.1016/j.ridd.2007.05.003

Vygotsky, L. S. (1997). *The collected works of L. S. Vygotsky* (Vol. 3). Plenum Press.

Vygotsky, L. S. (1983). *The collected works of L.S. Vygotsky* (Vol. 4. Child Psychology). Pedagogika.

Vygotsky, L. S. (2004). *Psihologiya razvitiya rebenka* (T. 6). Smysl: Eksmo.

Vygotsky, L. S. (2016). Play and its role in the mental development of the child (with Introduction and Afterword by N. Veresov and M. Barrs, Trans.). *International Research in Early Childhood Education, 7*(2), 3–25.

Wallace, C. E., & Russ, S. W. (2015). Pretend play, divergent thinking, and math achievement in girls: A longitudinal study. *Psychology of Aesthetics, Creativity, and the Arts, 9*(3), 296–305. https://doi.org/10.1037/a0039006

Walker, S., Fleer, M., Veresov, N., & Duhn, I. (2020). Enhancing executive function through imaginary play: A promising new practice principle. *Australasian Journal of Early Childhood, 45*(2), 114–126. https://doi.org/10.1177/1836939120918502

Walkerdine, V. (1984). SomeDay my prince will come: Young girls and the preparation for adolescent sexuality. In A. McRobbie & M. Nava (Eds.), *Gender and generation.* Youth Questions. Palgrave Macmillan. https://doi.org/10.1007/978-1-349-17661-8_7

Walsh, D. J. (1991). Extending the discourse on developmental appropriateness: A developmental perspective. *Early Education & Development, 2*(2), 109–119. https://doi.org/10.1207/s15566935 eed0202_3

Walsh, G., Sproule, L., McGuinness, C., Trew, K., & Ingram, G. (2010). *Developmentally appropriate practice and play-based pedagogy in early year's education: A literature review of research and practice school of psychology.* Queen's University Belfast Stranmillis University College.

Weber, K., Dawkins, P., & Medina-Ramos, J. P. (2020). The relationship between mathematical practice and mathematics pedagogy in mathematics education research. *ZDM, 52,* 1063–1074. https://doi.org/10.1007/s11858-020-01173-7

Weisberg, D. S., Hirsh-Pasek, K., & Golinkoff, R. M. (2013). Guided play: Where curricular goals meet a playful pedagogy: Guided play. *Mind, Brain, and Education, 7*(2), 104–112. https://doi.org/10.1111/mbe.12015

Weisberg, D. S., Zosh, J. M., Hirsh-Pasek, K., & Golinkoff, R. M. (2013). Talking it up: Play, language development, and the role of adult support. *American Journal of Play, 6*(1), 39–54.

White, R. E., & Carlson, S. M. (2016). What would Batman do? Self-distancing improves executive function in young children. *Developmental Science, 19*(3), 419–426. https://doi.org/10.1111/desc. 12314

White, R. E., & Carlson, S. M. (2021). Pretending with realistic and fantastical stories facilitates executive function in 3-year-old children. *Journal of Experimental Child Psychology, 207,* 105090. https://doi.org/10.1016/j.jecp.2021.105090

Winther-Lindqvist, D. A. (2021). Caring well for children in ECEC from a wholeness approach—The role of moral imagination. *Learning, Culture and Social Interaction, 30,* 100452. https://doi.org/10.1016/j.lcsi.2020.100452

Wood, R., & Paolo, E. D. (2007). New Models for Old Questions: Evolutionary Robotics and the 'A Not B' Error. In F. Almeida e Costa, L. M. Rocha, E. Costa, I. Harvey, & A. Coutinho (Eds.), *Advances in artificial life. ECAL 2007.* Lecture Notes in Computer Science, vol. 4648. Springer. https://doi.org/10.1007/978-3-540-74913-4_114

Zosh, J. M., Hirsh-Pasek, K., Hopkins, E. J., Jensen, H., Liu, C., Neale, D., Solis, S. L., & Whitebread, D. (2018). Accessing the inaccessible: Redefining play as a spectrum. *Frontiers in Psychology, 9,* 1124. https://doi.org/10.3389/fpsyg.2018.01124

Prof. Nikolay Veraksa is a specialist in preschool education, works at Faculty of Psychology, Lomonosov Moscow State University, Moscow City University and Psychological Institute of the Russian Academy of Education, Head of UNESCO Chair in Early Childhood Care and Development, Honorary Doctor of the University of Gothenburg. He is a co-author of the most popular educational program in Russia for children in preschool "From Birth to School" as well as a program in English "Key to Learning". His main interests are development of child thinking and personality

Dr. Yeshe Colliver is an Honorary Lecturer at the Macquarie School of Education. He has worked in early childhood education and care (ECEC) settings for nearly a decade in multiple cities across the world including Osaka (Japan), Ulsan (South Korea), Wakayama (Japan), Concepcion (Chile), Granada (Spain) and Honiara (Solomon Islands). Through his work and life overseas, he has acquired an interest in natural learning that we have evolved with (e.g., the types we needed in Indigenous cultures). His career has reflected a belief in two premises: that all social problems can be addressed most effectively through education, and that early childhood is the most crucial period in life.

Vera Sukhikh is a researcher at the Faculty of Psychology, Lomonosov Moscow State University. Her research interests include psychology of education, play in early childhood, as well as learning and development through play. Her research approach is based on Cultural-historical theory. She is involved in research projects focused on different types of play and their developmental potential for cognitive and emotional development of children. Also has extensive experience in assessing the quality of preschool education and coaching kindergarten teachers. She is a co-author of a program "A kindergarten that everyone wants to go to" which aimed to develop professional community and competencies of preschool teachers in Russia.

Chapter 11
Vygotsky and Piaget as Twenty-First-Century Critics of Early Childhood Education Philosophizing

Niklas Pramling

Abstract Aligning with the topic of Piaget and Vygotsky in the twenty-first-century (Veraksa & Pramling Samuelsson in *Piaget and Vygotsky in XXI century: Dialogue on education*, Springer, 2022), in this chapter, I anachronistically let these developmental theorists come alive, as it were, to enter into critical debate with contemporary early childhood education and care (ECEC) philosophizing in the form of posthumanism/new materialism. Through this contemporary debate, I argue that Vygotsky precedes key features of the latter philosophizing *and* that his theorizing in fact takes us further in understanding children's development and particularly play. Piaget and Vygotsky are argued to be two theorists for whom matter matters, something that is frequently by posthumaist/new materialists claimed to be missing from the understanding of children's development and ECEC. Finally, the implications of a posthumanist/new materialist perspective on ECEC, and particularly the role of the preschool teacher (ECEC professional), are critically scrutinized, and contrasted with a Piagetian and a Vygotskian perspective. This chapter serves to illuminate Piaget and Vygotsky as scholars of great actualization and relevance to twenty-first-century debate on ECEC and the supporting of children's development.

11.1 Introduction

The topic of the present volume (Veraksa & Pramling Samuelsson, 2022) is "Piaget and Vygotsky in the XXIst century: Dialogue on education." In this final chapter, I will take a somewhat unusual approach to this topic: anachronistically, I will let the twentieth-century theoretical contributions of Piaget and Vygotsky serve as critical resources in discussing what at the time of writing (twenty-first century) is contemporary philosophizing common in and about early childhood education and care (ECEC) and related processes, such as children's development. The philosophizing to be critically discussed from a Piagetian and a Vygotskian point of view is what is

N. Pramling (✉)
University of Gothenburg, Gothenburg, Sweden
e-mail: Niklas.Pramling@ped.gu.se

alternatively referred to as posthumanism and new materialism. In this anachronistic critical debate, I will clarify (i) not only how the latter without recognition in the form of references build upon insights from Vygotsky, (ii) but do not incorporate other parts of his theorizing that are decisive for the understanding of children's learning and development, and (iii) that there are inherent and subsequent problems (implications) with a posthuman/new matieralist philosophy for understanding and organizing ECEC.

The texts in this volume testify to the rich contributions made to the understanding of children's learning and development by the theorizing of Jean Piaget and Lev Vygotsky, not only historically but also as contemporarily relevant and for posing new research questions (Säljö & Mäkitalo, 2022; Singer, 2022; Veraksa et al., 2022; see also, Bruner, 1997; Tryphon & Vonèche, 1996). Not only have these researchers made tremendous contributions to collective knowing, their theorizing are also remarkable in their longevity and continuous re-actualization. There are many lines of investigation in the texts of the present volume that could be commented upon in this epilogue. However, in this chapter, I will focus on one important feature of the theorizing of Piaget and Vygotsky: the importance of materiality in human development. I will do so in an unusual way, in that I will build upon Piaget's and Vygotsky's theorizing to critically scrutinize and discuss contemporary philosophizing on children's learning and development and early childhood education. That is, I will—anachronistically— position Piaget and Vygotsky as critics of twenty-first-century philosophy, which was not available to these theorists in their time. While this may appear peculiar an approach, it is motivated thus: The contemporary philosophizing I will critically discuss is what is alternatively referred to as new materialism and posthumanism. This line of philosophizing constitutes an example of the more overarching philosophical line of reasoning called postmodernism. Furthermore, postmodern philosophy—and as typified by new materialism/posthumanism—tends to be presented as critique of developmental theorizing, such as that stemming from the works of Piaget and Vygotsky. By reversing the relationship, that is, allowing us to use Piaget's and Vygotsky's theorizing to critically illuminate new materialism/posthumanism philosophizing, a rejoinder is made possible that will potentially contribute to further collective knowing, stemming from the premise that critical debate is imperative to such knowledge building (Säljö, 2009).

I will start by briefly presenting some key notions of postmodernism as an umbrella under which new materialism/posthumanism resides. Thereafter, I present some key notions of the latter line of philosophizing. This is followed by a more in-depth presentation of matters of materiality in human development and learning as investigated and theorized by Piaget and Vygotsky. Finally, based on this elaboration, I will discuss the implications for early childhood education and care (ECEC) of new materialism/posthumanism, on the one hand, and building on the theorizing of Piaget and Vygotsky, on the other.

11.2 Piaget and Vygotsky as Critics

The works of Piaget and Vygotsky were, of course, shaped as, and by their, critique of the state of the art of psychological research at their time. In Piaget's case, his critical reflection on the intelligence testing of Alfred Binet—for whom he early in his career worked and thus gave him a first-hand perspective on the work of—provided the incentive for his basic approach. In response to this critique, some premises formed the Piagetian approach to the study of children's development. The first was that studying whether or to what degree children of different ages can answer correctly particular kinds of questions constitutes no insight into the nature of their development. Rather, how children make sense of the questions they face is what needs to be clarified, regardless of them arriving at the expected answer. Following from this critical remark, the importance of studying the processes of development rather than their outcomes was emphasized (see also, Valsiner, 2005, on this distinction). With this followed a conceptualization of development as qualitative change, rather than as a quantitative one. Stemming from the first premise is what has since gained tremendous spread in developmental research in terms of studying learning and/or development from the child's perspective. Hence, Piaget's critique of the state of the art of psychological investigation laid the foundation for what is today generally referred to as "the child's or the learner's" (cf. in more sociologically informed research: "members' categories") perspective in research.

In Vygotsky's case, his work formed in response to him addressing and criticizing what he perceived as the crisis of psychology in the 1930s, where psychological study was divided into two distinct strands, one for what could be referred to as elementary functions, and as shared among animals, and one for what could be referred to as higher mental functions, as unique to humans. These were separate strands without any interdisciplinary dialogue or synthesizing ambition. In contrast, an ambition of Vygotsky's theorizing was to develop *one* psychology that could encompass both what humans share with other animals and what makes us distinct as a species in a psychological sense. Hence, like Piaget, Vygotsky's theorizing was clearly developed in critical response to perceived shortcomings of existing theories. These two cases serve as examples of a general principle of scientific knowledge building: critical scrutiny is decisive for scientific progress. It is through collectively critically scrutinizing knowledge claims and their grounding that the scientific community assures quality of knowledge progression.

In at least one sense, there is no expiry-date on critique in research, since the points previously made may be re-actualized in regards to future theorizing or empirical study that can be addressed with the same critical analysis, since many problems reoccur. For example, the Piagetian critical point that in order to better understand children's development, an important analytical principle is to study the logic of the child's answers (or responses in a more general sense) rather than simply measuring if or to what extent (or when, at what age) they are able to give the expected answer, could be reiterated in relation to much research conducted after he initially formulated this critique. In the present chapter, I go one step further, as it were, in using principles of Piagetian and Vygotskian theorizing to critically discuss a long-standing matter of early childhood education and development theorizing that has gained increased emphasis in recent years: the matter of matter in child development, learning and, per implication, for early childhood education and care practices and institutions.

11.3   Postmodernism and Posthumanism

Postmodernism denotes a more general mode of thinking that has gained traction in many fields of inquiry: philosophy, the arts/aesthetics, gender studies, literary studies, and early childhood education research, to name but a few. Such a mode of thinking tends to emphasize the deconstruction of so-called grand narratives (e.g., scientific progression), contradiction, and to promote dissensus and plurality (Docherty, 1993b). While presented as a radical reorientation of intellectual life, there is some irony already in the very term, postmodern:

> The word postmodernism sounds not only awkward, uncouth; it evokes what it wishes to surpass or suppress, modernism itself. The term thus contains its enemy within, as the terms romanticism and classicism, baroque and rococo, do not. Moreover, it denotes temporal linearity and connotes belatedness, even decadence, to which no postmodernist would admit. (Hassan, 1993, p. 148)

The term "postmodern" indicates how this mode of thinking is contingent on what it opposes: modernism. The quote is also noteworthy in that it exemplifies a recurring thought figure in posthuman (as subsumed under postmodernism) thinking: the displacement of agency. In the quote "postmodernism" is reified into someone (or something: "it") who has intention ("wishes"). This conflation of a perspective on something and that something is a recurring fallacy of posthuman thinking or the posthuman ideology. In the words of Docherty (1993a), with reference to the literary theorist, Paul de Man, "such a confusion [between 'sense' and 'reference'] is precisely what we know as 'ideology': 'What we call ideology is precisely the confusion of linguistic with natural reality, of reference with phenomenalism'" (Docherty, 1993a, p. 7).

11.4   Posthumanism/New Materialism

An oft-quoted phrase in posthuman (aka new materialism) is that "Discourse matters. Culture matters. There is an important sense in which the only thing that does not seem to matter anymore is matter" (Barad, 2003, p. 801). This claim—which as such is without grounding in a review of scientific literature—stands as something of the doxa of posthuman or new materialism thinking. Not only is this general claim groundless; in the case of developmental research and more specifically that of two of its most prominent and pioneering scholars, Jean Piaget and Lev Vygotsky, it is simply not true. On the contrary, the material (matter) is given ample importance in both these theorists' accounts of human learning and development.

In order to enter Piaget and Vygotsky into dialogue with twenty-first-century ECEC philosophizing, I will quote from some texts advocating or building on a posthuman/new materialism perspective. However, my intention is not to criticize those texts per se; rather, what I will raise critique against are premises and lines of reasoning that are commonplace and generally endorsed in the latter literature. Quoting texts here only serve as exemplification. None of the critical comments I raise are particular to any of the quoted texts.

Reflecting a key premise of posthuman/new materialism thinking, Charteris et al. (2017) clearly posits how agency is conceived in this tradition:

> [W]e adopt a new materialist ontology as our theoretical framework decentering the human and adopting a view of the agency of matter. This led us to wonder what sorts of relationalities are produced […] between entangled: objects, spaces, policy discourses, practices, students and teachers. (p. 809)

This constitutes a clear statement on the agency of materiality (matter, objects), according to which agency is not restricted to humans. Noteworthy is also that new materialism is referred to as a "theoretical framework" despite lacking empirical grounding and coordination imperative to theory in science. Without such grounding and coordination, posthumanism/new materialism, I argue, is more properly to be considered philosophizing in building on premises, without empirical basis and coordination, that are not as such critically scrutinized but taken as self-evident beyond questioning, within which further reasoning is conducted. Phrased differently, philosophy could be conceived as carried out in the world on paper, to borrow Olson's (1994) metaphor (cf. Luria, 1976), rather than in the world of lived experience. Another metaphor common in new materialism thinking, as employed in the quote, is "entangled." Arguably, this metaphor entails a case of black-boxing. What is here referred to as black-boxing denotes labeling something rather than explaining it, that is, it works in hiding from rational view precisely what needs to be explained: how this process happens and what its mechanism is (cf. Cole, 1996, on referring to "influence" as another example of black-boxing).

Closely related to the metaphor of "entanglement" is the metaphor of "assemblage," according to which, "An assemblage is the coming together of different kinds of entities, in order to produce something new" (Charteris et al., 2017, p. 811). This reasoning begs the question of "new" for whom: the participant(s) (children, teachers in ECEC, e.g.) and/or the analyst studying the processes of learning and development. Apparently, "assembling" is something that just happens, allegedly needing no explanation, merely labeling (cf. my previous critical remarks on black-boxing).

> Assemblages can be read as transversal connection of human and non-human objects. Objects themselves are influential and exert agency on other objects and on human as 'agential matter' [---] Agential matter […] special geography and material objects influence the kinds of social interactions that can occur in schooling spaces. (Charteris et al., 2017, p. 811)

Here, another common case of black-boxing (Cole, 1996), "influence," appears. In line with the previous reasoning about the agency of objects, objects are here constituted as "selves": "objects themselves," capable of "exert[ing] agency," per implication being ascribed intention as if they were psychological beings (cf. Bruner, 1990). Hence, the question of how to conceive of agency comes to the fore in relation to posthuman/new materialism writing. I will return to this issue.

Another common argument in posthuman/new materialism writing is the close relationship between architecture and education. This relationship is, of course, not new or unique to this tradition; rather, conceiving of the making of educational milieus and what they imply or afford in terms of actions and education have a long history. Already the difference between many ECEC settings (such as Swedish preschool) and a traditional classroom in school imply very different practices and relationships between participants (children/students and teachers). However, the take on the relationship between architecture and education is different and particularly emphasized in posthuman/new materialism philosophizing. Charteris et al. (2017) suggest, "there is the need for synergy between architects and educators" (p. 809) and, "Architectural designs for learning and emerging technologies influence the ubiquitous conception of anywhere/anytime learning" (p. 810). The first claim will be returned to and discussed later. The second claim, about learning is problematic from an education as well as from a learning and development point of view, in (i) black-boxing the learning process—and here more specifically the question of the relationship between institution and individual action or learning, a classic question in developmental research (see Olson, 2003, for an extensive discussion)—and in (ii) disregarding that learning is always the learning *of* something (see Marton & Säljö, 1976, for an early discussion of this). The latter question also has institutional implications; in ECEC (such as Swedish preschool and in most other countries around the world), there are generally guidelines, curricula and other documents that point out certain forms and domains of knowledge that children are to be supported in starting to appropriate. While there is a point that people learn "anywhere/anytime," that is, that learning is an outcome of participating in any cultural practice—speaking about "influence" on "anywhere/anytime learning" risks making *the what* of learning invisible and thus what children are supported in encountering and appropriating in ECEC. While a cultural-historical (aka sociocultural, Vygotskian) theory emphasizes that learning is an outcome of participating in any cultural practice, for research (and with implications for organizing ECEC) this begs the questions of *what* and *how* someone learns. Simply stating that learning happens "anywhere/anytime" by "influence" remains void and cannot serve in guiding ECEC personnel in supporting children's learning and development.

11.5 Materiality in Piaget's and Vygotsky's Theorizing

To Piaget, the child fundamentally develops through engaging, interacting, primarily with the physical world and secondarily with other children. It is interaction that results in the developmental processes of accommodation and assimilation (see also, Veraksa, 2022, for an analysis and discussion). Through exploring the physical world, the child comes to experience and re-experience how the world works. When observations made or her interacting with the physical world coheres with her understanding (schema), new information is assimilated; when observations do not make sense in terms of existing structure of thinking (schema), the latter begins to be re-organized to accommodate new information. Also in interaction with other people, primarily other children, the child encounters different perspectives, which also come to form her thinking skills.

In Vygotsktian theorizing, matter primarily in the form of the kind of cultural tools generally referred to as artifacts is integral to understanding human growth, on a sociohistorical and on a, and related, individual "level." As collectives and individuals, people learn through communication—mediated by cultural tools—and through "inscribing," as it were, human experience in artifacts, and through appropriating cultural tools (discursive and artifacts), that is, gradually taking over and being able to use these in contextually relevant and dynamic ways (Wertsch, 1998, 2007). What we as human know and can, we know and can with cultural tools. What cultural tools (encompassing discursive and physical: artifacts) we have appropriated (are in the midst of appropriating) is decisive for what we can and know.

Hence, from this point of view, human knowing and development are contingent on what is referred to as cultural tools, and which encompasses discursive as well as physical ones; it should here be emphasized that according to this theorizing, there is no clear-cut boundary between discursive and material: text serves as a classic example of illustrating this point: it is material (ink, print, visual pattern on a surface/screen) and discursive (a tool for thought, something we think and make sense with).

New tools afford new action, including new ways of thinking, and are thus critical to developing new insights and skills. This could be phrased as things "do" things with us; however, the inverted commas are important: objects are not ascribed agency (i.e., action and therefore intention, presuming a psychology). In contrast, in new materialist/posthumanist philosophizing, objects are ascribed agency, and thereby intention (psychology). While there may be a point as an *as-if* or *what-if* exploration to think in this way, failing to explicate this stance and instead make reality claims means to confuse epistemology with ontology (cf. de Man, on ideology, above). The perspective is conflated with what it is used to think about.

11.6   On Matter and Children's Play

A premise of posthuman/new materialism philosophy (and as seen above) is that the individual/the child cannot be separated from the physical environment (also, e.g., Lenz Taguchi, 2011). With this premise—presented not as a premise but as a knowledge claim—it is not possible to use this perspective to say anything of value regarding children's play and their development of play and playing. These are, arguably, central concerns both of developmental research, in Piaget (1951/1962) and in Vygotsky (1933/1966), and many others (see also, Björk-Willén, 2022; van

Oers, 2022) and for ECEC, where play tends to be a nexus of activity and a mode of learning and developing as a child (e.g., Fleer, 2010, 2011; van Oers & Duijkers, 2013). The idea that the physical environment in some sense "steers" the (young) child's actions (also in play) is no new idea. Already Vygotsky, building on gestalt psychologist Kurt Lewin's research, extensively writes on this observation. These precedencies tend to remain unrecognized (through referencing) in posthuman/new materialism writing; rather the idea is presented as if it was new. In the following text, I will use a number of quotes from Vygotsky's writing on this issue to comment on how he not only precedes posthuman/new materialism thinking in this sense, but also how his research and theoretical elaboration takes collective knowledge much further than these later thinkers, contributions that when remaining unrecognized in restating an earlier stage of knowledge building is rendered invisible.

As already mentioned, Vygotsky (1933/1966) puts forward his understanding of the relationship between the physical environment and children's play in dialogue with previous research in gestalt psychology:

> To a considerable extent the behavior of a very young child – and, to an absolute extent, that of an infant – is determined by the conditions in which the activity takes place, as experiments by Lewin and others have shown.
>
> [---]
>
> It is hard to imagine a greater contrast to Lewin's experiments showing the situational constraints on activity than what we observe in play. In the latter, the child acts in a mental and not a visible situation. I think this conveys accurately what occurs in play. It is here that the child learns to act in a cognitive, rather than an externally visible realm, relying on internal tendencies and motives, and not on incentives supplied by external things. I recall a study by Lewin on the motivating nature of things for a very young child; in it Lewin concludes that things dictate to the child what he must do: a door demands to be opened and closed, a staircase to be run up, a bell to be rung. In short, things have an inherent motivating force in respect to a very young child's actions and determine the child's behavior. (Vygotsky, 1933/1966, s. 11)

That there is, metaphorically speaking, "an inherent motivating force" in the material environment for how children act is thus clearly argued already in the 1930s on the basis of gestalt psychology research. However, what is more important than this historical precedence is that Vygotsky takes our knowledge further. He does so through asking how we can understand this observation, that is, he engages in going from *that* something is the case to *how* it is that it is so (how we can understand it, cf. above on this important distinction in research):

> What is the root of situational constraints upon a child? The answer lies in a central fact of consciousness which is characteristic of early childhood: the union of affect and perception. At this age perception is generally not an independent feature but an initial feature of motor-affective reaction; i.e., every perception is in this way a stimulus to activity. Since a situation is always communicated psychologically through perception, and perception is not separated from affective and motor activity, it is understandable that with his [her] consciousness so structured the child cannot act otherwise than as constrained by the situation – or the field – in which he [she] finds himself [herself]. (Vygotsky, 1933/1966, s. 11)

The explanation to the observation, according to Vygotsky, lies in an initial undifferentiated psychology of the child. For the young child, perception, affect, and motor activity constitute a whole. Unable to differentiate what she perceives from what she feels and how she acts, the child's actions become dependent on the physical environment. However, and this is decisive for the child's development as a psychological being and for her playing, as adults, we are able to resist opening a door simply because there is a handle, or push a button on an escalator because there is one whose color, placing and design "attract" our attention. These mundane examples testify to a development according to which the individual learns to differentiate between perception, affect, and action. This development takes place in early childhood and is particularly associated with play as a cultural activity:

> In play, things lose their motivating force. The child sees one thing but acts differently in relation to what he [or she] sees. Thus, a situation is reached in which the child begins to act independently of what he [or she] sees. (Vygotsky, 1933/1966, s. 11)

Being able to do so, that is, to act in difference (contrast) to what is actually visible in the physical environment is decisive for playing:

> It is at preschool age that we first find a divergence between the fields of meaning and vision. [---] [I]n play activity thought is separated from objects, and action arises from ideas rather than from things. Thought is separated from objects because a piece of wood begins to be a doll and a stick becomes a horse. Action according to rules begins to be determined by ideas and not by objects themselves. This is such a reversal of the child's relationship to the real, immediate, concrete situation that it is hard to evaluate its full significance. (Vygotsky, 1933/1966, s. 12)

According to this theorizing, it is during early childhood (the preschool years) that the child starts separating between perception and meaning. A well-known example of this in Vygotsky's writing is the stick that becomes a horse (Vygotsky, 1933/1966). By mediation of a pivot, the child develops the ability to separate the object from its reference and re-mediate it to give it a new meaning and function in play. With this development, the relationship between object (the physical environment) and meaning are reversed: from now on, the child will act in terms of the meaning she gives the object, rather than being "dictated" by it: "Word meanings replace objects, and thus an emancipation of word from object occurs" (p. 13).[1] This transformation occurs in play, and play "with an imaginary situation is something essentially new," a "form of behavior in which the child is liberated from situational constraints through his [or her] activity in an imaginary situation" (p. 11). It may be noted that there is even more to Vygotsky's theorizing of this important development, but in the context of the present discussion, what has been rendered should be ample to clarify how the inherent dependence of the child on her physical environment, as claimed by posthumanism/new materialism, and in generally failing to acknowledge preceding scholarly work in this regards, constitutes a form of historical revisionism, *and* the returning to a point in time where we knew less about children's play and development than what was known in the 1930s. What ensues is a form of scholarly regression. Remaining in claiming that the child's actions cannot be separated from the physical

---

[1] Distinguishing between word (and meaning) and reference is critical also to develop literacy skills (Olson, 1994).

environment means that posthuman/new materialism is unable to say anything about children's development, play, and creativity (perceiving something as something other than how it conventionally is perceived), as these require a separation of and a changed relationship between matter and the semantical.

11.7 Anthropocentrism, Anthropomorphism, and Animism

A common general critique from a posthuman/new materialism perspective is that theories of development and learning (and about other issues as well) represent an "anthropocentrism" (Charteris et al., 2017, p. 811), that is, they ascribe humans a particular position as agents and sense makers. Given the fact that these theories are about human development and that there is a long-standing interest in developmental science about what distinguishes humans from other animals (e.g., Tomasello, 1999), this premise is not surprising. However, the perspective could be reversed in the following manner: posthuman/new materialism philosophy constitutes a case of "anthropomorphism" and "animism," figures of thought that incidentally were much studied by Piaget in his work on children's development (see particularly, Piaget, 1926/1951). According to his analysis, these constitute immature (i.e., as contingent development) modes of thought. In contrast, later research and theorizing (Lakoff & Johnson, 1980; Pramling, 2006; Pramling & Säljö, 2015) have considered and shown such modes of thinking to be present also in adults' and even in specialized discourse, such as scientific ones. However, being able to take a meta-perspective on this, that is, to distinguish between this mode of speaking and making sense, on the one hand, and what is spoken about, on the other, is critical, in order not to displace one's perspective in the world as such. The claim about developmental theories being cases of anthropocentrism could also be countered with the Vygotskian premise that to understand human development implies attending to this process as a biological, cultural, and social process, and as encompassing artifacts (discursive and material, with the two not always being distinguishable). Hence, human development is not restricted to "the human being" as such.

The matter of the relationship between architecture and individual action in posthuman/new materialism thinking actualizes yet another important principle in (development) research:

> Although policy-makers, architects, designers, school leaders, teachers and, in some cases, students create spatial designs, the dynamism of these spaces are coproduced through the complex affective flows of human bodies, acoustics, airflow, textures, lightning, furniture and non-human creatures. (Charteris et al., 2017, p. 819)

Even if this is the case (whatever is 'flowing' and how), as researchers, in order to conduct analysis, we have to delimit what we include and exclude[2] in order to establish systematicity decisive to scientific knowledge building, and this requires

---

[2] We may remind ourselves that the etymology of "analysis" is "breaking up" (Barnhart, 2004); hence, analysis presumes making distinctions.

reduction. It is important in research not to mistake or conflate claims about the world (ontology) with how we learn, research, build knowledge about it (epistemology). Research always implies a reduction. This fact appears to be unrecognized in new materialism reasoning.

11.7.1 Implications of Posthumanism/New Materialism for ECEC

In the preceding section, I have engaged in a critical dialogue with posthumanism/new materialism[3] from primarily a Vygotskian perspective on how to understand children's development and play as a particularly important activity in this process. In this section, I will instead shift to ECEC and discuss what the differences in perspectives imply for such institutional activities. Hence, if, for the sake of argument, one were to take a posthuman/new materialism perspective, what would then be the implications for the activities of ECEC and the participants (children and preschool teachers, and other personnel) in these?

In Sweden, even a well-circulated document published by the Swedish National Agency for Education (Swe. *Skolverket*)—surprisingly—builds on this perspective. This text is used in the education of preschool teacher students. Since the text has clear implications for organizing ECEC in being used in educating preschool teachers, I will here use it to give a few examples of posthumanism thinking and discuss its implications for promoting children's development in ECEC. In the document, this perspective is presented as "an alternative way of thinking where one cannot distinguish between *who is learning* something from *what is learned*, or from *the physical environment* where learning happens" (Skolverket, 2012, p. 27, italics in original, my translation). This claim actualizes several questions important to ECEC. First, if it is impossible to distinguish between the learner, the content of learning and the environment, how can we then understand educational activity, including teaching, which per definition points beyond here-and-now, that is, that the learner appropriates something from one situation that is useful also in another? To give a concrete example: language learning. Many researchers, not least Basil Bernstein (1964), has clarified how the use of a deictic (local) language functional here-and-now only means that some children are not introduced to and are supported in appropriating a more expansive (a-contextual) language that is functional beyond the specific situation where it is learned, and consequently have difficulties in appropriating the knowledge of schooling and the kind of capabilities (not least literate ones) that it builds upon and promotes, and as critical to participation in society more generally. Thus,

---

[3] There are many other features of posthumanism/new matierialism that warrant critical scrutiny and debate; however, the purpose of this chapter is not to provide an extensive critique of this strand of philosophizing, but merely to critically discuss some key issues of children's development, play and ECEC, where Piaget and Vygotsky have much to offer in problematizing posthuman/new materialist thinking and, I argue, take us further than this latter day philosophizing.

abiding from distinguishing between what is learned (and taught, in my example: language) from the situation in which it is (taught and) learned means—however, unintentionally this is—to consolidate differences between children from different family (socioeconomical) backgrounds. Hence, the compensatory mission of ECEC (preschool) is countered.

Another consequence of informing ECEC by a posthuman/new materialism perspective concerns its anti-pedagogical stance. By displacing education to the physical environment, the professionals of ECEC (such as preschool teachers) are reduced to "adults" (the denomination usually used in such literature), who have no educational role other than arranging the physical environment for the child to interact (cf. "intra-active," Lenz Taguchi, 2011) with. To put it succinctly, posthumanism/new materialism reduces ECEC professionals (preschool teachers) to what, in keeping with the metaphorics of ECEC as grounded(!) in kindergarten, could be formulated as *kindergarten architects* (i.e., "child-garden architects"). As such, they would have no role to fill in creating other—such as language mediated—learning and development opportunities and support and thus would neglect the key task of working toward achieving the compensatory mission of preschool, central to its democratic and socio-political task, as I have already mentioned.

Considering the fact that ECEC typically is understood as a combined care and education institution—often captured by the name, "educare"—there are also ethical implications of a posthuman/new materialism perspective that needs to be critically illuminated. By not separating out humans from their environment (see above), posthuman/new materialism thinking take away human responsibility and accountability. To give a fictive example: imagine someone physically disciplining someone with a cane, as a common occurrence in school, if perhaps not in preschool, historically (even if forbidden today, if still not in all countries). If, as in posthumanism/new materialism thinking not being able to separate the individual from the physical environment, the teacher hitting the child could not be held accountable; in fact, according to this reasoning it would not even be the teacher doing the hitting. The physical discipline would simply be due to the 'flow of the force' (cf. above) and the teacher would be no more responsible than the cane. As absurd as this appears, this follows from the claim that it is not possible to separate an individual from the environment and ascribing also objects agency. It is self-evident that such a stance toward issues of care and ethics does not provide a stable ground for fostering a caring upbringing. It is difficult to see how such processes could do away with the unique features of mutual respect and acknowledgment of person-to-person interaction (e.g., Alcock, 2016; Tappan, 1998).

Displacing intentional action from children and preschool teachers to the objects as such (the so-called agency of matter, cf. above), implies a determinism, where children's development are "directed" by the environment. In this regards, it may be worth reminding oneself that one of the key functions of ECEC (as with school) is that what knowledge and abilities the child develop should not be determined by its primary environment (what its primary caregivers know and can) but allowing him or her to come in contact with and appropriate a much wider repertoire, implying a detachment for the here-and-now of one's environment. Displacing the education (teaching) from preschool teachers' actions to the material environment also implies a banalization of learning with the educational implication that the objects (the environment as such) "does" the teaching, which, consequently, as I have already argued, will further accentuate the differences in children's experiences and learning support, contrary to the ambition of ECEC to diminish inequality among (groups of) children.

11.8 Conclusions

To briefly conclude, through this critical debate, it has been clarified that posthumanism/new materialism:

- Repeatedly states *that*—for example, that matter matters, that everything is assembled, that environment and individual cannot be separated…—without showing through systematic analysis of empirical data *how* that is. Without the latter, such claims are void.

- Presents some things as if they were new, while they in fact are evident already in Vygotsky's writing; but ignore other parts that are decisive for understanding children's learning and development (e.g., Vygotsky on an important feature of the child's development as being able to resist the "pull of the environment" (i.e., detach oneself from it) and through remediating the environment); and Piaget on a foundational part of development as separating out oneself from initial unity with the primary caregiver and world, and thus appear as an individual).

- Has problematic implications for ECEC in terms of ethics in care of children.

- Restricts the role(s) of the professionals of ECEC to be "child-garden [*kindergarten*] architects," which is very much at odds both with guidelines (such as the Swedish national curriculum for preschool, as well as in many other countries' guidelines) and with the state of the art of research in ECEC (Fleer & van Oers, 2018), which emphasizes quality caregiver-child interaction as decisive for the developmental and learning support children receive in ECEC.[4]

In contrast to the latter point, the role of the preschool teachers (ECEC professionals) if taking a Piagetian perspective, would also be to organize the environment; however, it would not be restricted to this and it would have principles for guiding that design. Piaget himself was, of course, famously indifferent to the matter of the possible "acceleration of (natural) development," as it were, which he tended to refer to as "the American question" (Bryant, 1984) and his stance can be referred

---

[4] In addition, posthumanism/new materialism lacks concepts of the key phenomena of education (including education): learning, development, and teaching. However, I have not discussed these matters here.

to as "anti-pedagogical." Despite this stance, his theoretical work has had enormous importance to the design of educational practices (Säljö & Bergqvist, 1997). Alas, regardless of his own stance, his work has important implications also for thinking about education. Regarding the latter, it would be important to design an environment[5] where the child could encounter phenomena that she could assimilate as well as accommodate. However, the teacher's role would not merely consist of designing an environment; it would also be to initiate interaction among children, and among children and the teacher where she attends to the child's perspective and provokes cognitive conflict in order to support the child's accommodation process. If instead taking a Vygotskian perspective, the role of the teacher could be formulated as that of a more experienced participant interacting with children with the aim of introducing them to and supporting them in appropriating important cultural tools and practices. Contributing to establishing mutually engaging and meaningful activities where cultural tools and practices are necessary to the continuation and development of the activity—not least, the play—would be decisive to her role as a preschool teacher (ECEC professional).

In this text, through anachronistically letting theoretical principles and contributions of Jean Piaget and Lev Vygotsky (two twentieth-century scholars) come to life, as it were, in critical debate with contemporary (twenty-first century) philosophizing in and about ECEC, I have illuminated how this clarifies inherent problems with the latter, and I discussed what important implications these different theoretical and philosophical premises and reasoning have for children's lives in ECEC. On a meta-level, the reasoning implies the continuing actualization and relevance of Piaget and Vygotsky, two theorists for whom matter matters to human development.

References

Alcock, S. J. (2016). *Young children playing: Relational approaches to emotional learning in early childhood settings* (International perspectives on early childhood education and development, 12). Springer.

Barad, K. (2003). Posthumanist performativity: Toward and understanding of how matter comes to matter. *Signs: Journal of Women in Culture and Society, 28*(3), 801–831.

Barnhart, R. K. (Ed.). (2004). *Chambers dictionary of etymology*. Chambers.

Bernstein, B. (1964). Elaborated and restricted codes: Their social origins and some consequences. *American Anthropologist, 66*(6), 55–69.

Björk-Willén, P. (2022). Preschool children's pretend play viewed from a Vygotskian and a Piagetian perspective. In N. Veraksa & I. Pramling Samuelsson (Eds.), *Piaget and Vygotsky in XXI century: Dialogue on education* (pp. 109–127). Springer.

Bruner, J. S. (1990). *Acts of meaning*. Harvard University Press.

Bruner, J. S. (1997). Celebrating divergence: Piaget and Vygotsky. *Human Development, 40*, 63–73.

Bryant, P. E. (1984). Piaget, teachers and psychologists. *Oxford Review of Education, 10*(3), 251–259.

---

[5] When I write "design," I do not intend to imply that the natural world (e.g., an adjoining forest would not be considered relevant; on the contrary, it would be an important environment).

Charteris, J., Smardon, D., & Nelson, E. (2017). Innovative learning environments and new materialism: A conjectural analysis of pedagogic spaces. *Educational Philosophy and Theory, 49*(8), 808–821.

Cole, M. (1996). *Cultural psychology: A once and future discipline*. The Belknap Press.

Docherty, T. (1993a). Postmodernism: An introduction. In T. Docherty (Ed.), *Postmodernism: A reader* (pp. 1–31). Columbia University Press.

Docherty, T. (Ed.). (1993b). *Postmodernism: A reader*. Columbia University Press.

Fleer, M. (2010). *Early learning and development: A cultural-historical view of concepts in play*. Cambridge University Press.

Fleer, M. (2011). 'Conceptual play': Foregrounding imagination and cognition during concept formation in early years education. *Contemporary Issues in Early Childhood, 12*(3), 224–240.

Fleer, M., & van Oers, B. (Eds.). (2018). *International handbook of early childhood education* (Vols. I and II). Springer.

Hassan, I. (1993). Toward a concept of postmodernism. In T. Docherty (Ed.), *Postmodernism: A reader* (pp. 146–156). Columbia University Press.

Lakoff, G., & Johnson, M. (1980). *Metaphors we live by*. University of Chicago Press.

Lenz Taguchi, H. (2011). Investigating leaning, participation and becoming in early childhood practices with a relational materialist approach. *Global Studies of Childhood, 1*(1), 36–50.

Luria, A. R. (1976). *Cognitive development: Its cultural and social foundations* (M. Lopez-Morillas & L. Solotaroff, Trans.). Harvard University Press.

Marton, F., & Säljö, R. (1976). On qualitative differences in learning: I–outcome and process. *British Journal of Educational Psychology, 46*(1), 4–11.

Olson, D. R. (1994). *The world on paper: The conceptual and cognitive implications of writing and reading*. Cambridge University Press.

Olson, D. R. (2003). *Psychological theory and educational reform: How school remakes mind and society*. Cambridge University Press.

Piaget, J. (1951). *The child's conception of the world* (J. Tomlinson & A. Tomlinson, Trans.). Littlefield Adams (Original work published 1926).

Piaget, J. (1962). *Play, dreams and imitation in childhood* (C. Gattegno & F. M. Hodgson, Trans.). W. W. Norton (Original work published 1951)

Pramling, N. (2006). 'The clouds are alive because they fly in the air as if they were birds': A reanalysis of what children say and mean in clinical interviews in the work of Jean Piaget. *European Journal of Psychology of Education, 21*(4), 453–466.

Pramling, N., & Säljö, R. (2015). The clinical interview: The child as a partner in conversation versus the child as an object of research. In S. Robinson & S. Flannery Quinn (Eds.), *The Routledge international handbook of young children's thinking and understanding* (pp. 87–95). Routledge.

Säljö, R. (2009). Learning, theories of learning, and units of analysis in research. *Educational Psychologist, 44*(3), 202–208.

Säljö, R., & Bergqvist, K. (1997). Seeing the light: Discourse and practice in the optics lab. In L. B. Resnick, R. Säljö, C. Pontecorvo, & B. Burge (Eds.), *Discourse, tools, and reasoning: Essays on situated cognition* (pp. 385–405). Springer.

Säljö, R., & Mäkitalo, Å. (2022). Learning and development in a designed world. In N. Veraksa & I. Pramling Samuelsson (Eds.), *Piaget and Vygotsky in XXI century: Dialogue on education* (pp. 27–39). Springer.

Singer, E. (2022). Piaget and Vygotsky: Powerful inspirators for today's students in early education and developmental psychology. In N. Veraksa & I. Pramling Samuelsson (Eds.), *Piaget and Vygotsky in XXI century: Dialogue on education* (pp. 129–143). Springer.

Skolverket. (2012). *Uppföljning, utvärdering och utveckling i förskolan – pedagogisk dokumentation* [Follow up, evaluating and developing in preschool: Pedagogical documentation]. Fritzes.

Tappan, M. B. (1998). Sociocultural psychology and caring pedagogy: Exploring Vygotsky's "hidden curriculum." *Educational Psychologist, 33*(1), 23–33.

Tomasello, M. (1999). *The cultural origins of human cognition*. Harvard University Press.

Tryphon, A., & Vonèche, J. (Eds.). (1996). *Piaget-Vygotsky: The social genesis of thought.* Psychology Press.

Valsiner, J. (Ed.). (2005). *Heinz Werner and developmental science.* Kluwer Academic.

van Oers, B. (2022). Social representations of play: Piaget, Vygotsky and beyond. In N. Veraksa & I. Pramling Samuelsson (Eds.), *Piaget and Vygotsky in XXI century: Dialogue on education* (pp. 65–85). Springer.

van Oers, B., & Duijkers, D. (2013). Teaching in a play-based curriculum: Theory, practice and evidence of developmental education for young children. *Journal of Curriculum Studies, 45*(4), 511–534.

Veraksa, N. (2022). Vygotsky's theory: Culture as a prerequisite for education. In N. Veraksa & I. Pramling Samuelsson (Eds.), *Piaget and Vygotsky in XXI century: Dialogue on education* (pp. 7–26). Springer.

Veraksa, N., Colliver, Y., & Sukhikh, V. (2022). Piaget and Vygotsky's play theories: The profile of twenty-first-century evidence. In N. Veraksa & I. Pramling Samuelsson (Eds.), *Piaget and Vygotsky in XXI century: Dialogue on education* (pp. 165–190). Springer.

Veraksa, N., & Pramling Samuelsson, I. (Eds.). (2022). *Piaget and Vygotsky in XXI century: Dialogue on education.* Springer.

Vygotsky, L. S. (1966). Play and its role in the mental development of the child. *Voprosy psikhologii, 12*(6), 62–76 (Original work published 1933).

Wertsch, J. V. (1998). *Mind as action.* Oxford University Press.

Wertsch, J. V. (2007). Mediation. In H. Daniels, M. Cole, & J. V. Wertsch (Eds.), *The Cambridge companion to Vygotsky* (pp. 178–192). Cambridge University Press.